APPLYING
PSYCHOLOGY

Susan Sefton

to Crime

APPLYING PSYCHOLOGY

to crime

JULIE HARROWER

Series Editor: **ROB McILVEEN**

Hodder Arnold

A MEMBER OF THE HODDER HEADLINE GROUP

Order queries: please contact Bookpoint Ltd, 130 Milton Park, Abingdon, Oxon OX14 4SB. Telephone:
(44) 01235 827720. Fax: (44) 01235 400454. Lines are open from 9 am - 5 pm Monday to Saturday, with a
24-hour message answering service.
You can also order through our website www.hoddereducation.co.uk

British Library Cataloguing in Publication Data
A catalogue record for this title is available from the British Library

ISBN: 978 0 340 70556 8

First Published 1998
Impression number   16 15 14 13 12 11
Year   2010 2009 2008 2007

Typeset by Transfer Limited, Coventry, England.
Printed in India for Hodder Education, a member of the Hachette Livre UK Group,
338 Euston Road, London NW1 3BH by Replika Press Pvt. Ltd.

CONTENTS

Chapter Nine: Responding to Crime 188

Introduction: what are the consequences of becoming a victim of crime? crime prevention; zero tolerance; risk assessment; the future of criminological psychology

PREFACE

We are all interested in criminal behaviour, the deeds of those who for a variety of reasons go beyond convention. They act out impulses which we may all at some time secretly harbour, yet they also strike fear into us because they threaten the very stability which holds society together. It is this ambivalence, this fascination and repulsion which ensures that books, plays, television programmes and films with a criminal theme are always popular. Just take a look at the sales of books by Patricia Cornwell, James Patterson, Jonathan Kellerman and Sarah Dunant, not to mention the classic novels of Agatha Christie and Sir Arthur Conan Doyle, or the ratings of television programmes such as *Morse*, *A Touch of Frost*, *Silent Witness*, *Touching Evil*, the *X-Files*, *Millenium* and *Halifax f.p.*, etc. and films such as *Manhunter*, *The Silence of the Lambs*, *Seven*, *Copycat* and *Natural Born Killers*. All of these provide a means of escape from the humdrum, but they also highlight a 'darker' side of human nature, the details of which seem to hold a bizarre fascination for many of us.

People also tend to be fascinated by psychology, the scientific study of human behaviour. We would all like to know more about why we think and act the way we do, what influences us and what explanations are possible for the sometimes inexplicable. Whilst we may hold intuitive, common-sense theories of behaviour, we want to be offered a systematic explanation based on empirical investigation. The explosive combination of crime and psychology in many ways cannot fail! Within criminological psychology an attempt is made to explain an aspect of human behaviour which has confounded the most intelligent minds for centuries. Moreover, criminological psychology goes beyond offering theoretical explanations and provides practical applications in an effort to improve the effectiveness of our response to crime.

This book demonstrates some of the issues within the field of criminological psychology which illustrate this combination of theoretical and applied approaches. The choice may seem eclectic to some and certainly does not cover the entire field of criminological psychology nor of all types of crime, but the aim is to provide comprehensive coverage of particular areas which will allow certain themes to emerge. Those themes are gender, violence and culture, all of which need to be addressed by psychologists if our understanding of criminal behaviour – its generation, maintenance and resistance to intervention – is going to advance. Additionally, there is an attempt to highlight hitherto 'hidden' or unreported crime, such as rape, domestic violence and child abuse.

It should not need restating, but gender is the clearest marker of criminal propensity. Men commit more offences, and more serious offences, than do women. A host of theories has been presented to explain this difference and not always along the lines of how awful men are. Women's crimes have also been analysed (albeit rather belatedly) and the common background of vulnerability, disadvantage, abuse and dependency for all offenders, male and female, has become clear. The traditional critique of criminology and all its offshoots, including criminological psychology, that theories of criminal behaviour have been presented as universal but in fact relate only to men, has begun to be addressed. Yet the possibility of attempting gendered analyses of criminal behaviour, rather than developing a separate and parallel study of female crime, still seems rather elusive, with some notable exceptions, including Messerschmidt (1993), Newburn and Stanko (1994) and Jefferson (1996).

Part of the backlash to feminism has been a view that with equal opportunities more women will become like men and enter a life of crime, particularly those offences involving violence. Media coverage of so-called 'epidemics' of violence by girls and moral malaise as a result of single women bringing up children without the discipline a father would normally provide, reflect growing anxiety about a society which seems to be out of control, and yet there is little evidence of either 'moral panic' being true.

The association between crime, violence and masculinity is undeniable and yet for too long those studying crime, including psychologists, have studied the actions of criminal men whilst avoiding any analysis of the fact that masculinity itself must play a large part in the generation of criminal behaviour. Instead of viewing crime as a biological inevitability, as pathology or as the unfortunate result of social disadvantage, it may be more fruitful to view it as an arena or a proving ground for masculine power. That so much violent crime is perpetrated against women and children should also stimulate further research into the links between masculinity, power and sexuality and current work on the psychodynamic aspects of masculinity look extremely promising. Cultural images of masculinity are invariably laden with assumptions about dominance, power, control and invulnerability, and the cultural transmission of these messages in advertisements, books, magazines, music lyrics, videos and films reinforces and legitimises a mythology which is not helpful as we move into the 21st century.

On a more positive note, criminological psychologists clearly have a part to play in shaping our society in the next century. In addition to the many applications of psychological theory, such as treatment programmes for offenders, assisting the police and the courts, helping victims, etc., there is the possibility of becoming much more proactive in terms of wider prevention. Continued research into the development of offending behaviour shows consistent patterns in early childhood which can be recognised so that appropriate intervention can prevent a negative outcome. Disadvantage, disruption, neglect and abuse are very obvious markers, but a lack of opportunity to form stable attachments, to learn self-control and to develop empathy in order for a fully social intelligence to evolve are equally important contributors to the onset of antisocial behaviour. Psychological research should inform parental training programmes and educational intervention for young children and adolescents, whilst the net could be cast even further with the targeted development of prosocial attitudes and behaviour in the wider society. Psychologists do not need to remain in their ivory towers – criminological psychologists have already established their specialism as one which is rooted in practice. Now is the time to consolidate that progress.

chapter one

CRIMINOLOGICAL PSYCHOLOGY

CHAPTER OVERVIEW

In this chapter the problematic nature of definitions of crime will be explored, together with the extent of criminal behaviour and the sources which can be used to estimate the prevalence of different types of crime. The potential contribution of different areas of psychology will be evaluated and an account of the development of criminological psychology provided within the context of a constructive overlap between different disciplines which can further our understanding of criminal behaviour.

INTRODUCTION

Criminology attempts to integrate the potential contributions of a wide range of disciplines in order to study criminal behaviour and legal issues. Psychology is one contributor to this study and not the main one in any sense, but it does have an important contribution to make, particularly from an empirical standpoint. The methodological approach of psychology enables rigorous investigation and analysis of collected data which can then be used to support the development of theory.

Traditionally, however, psychology has been viewed as a rather simplistic and conservative contributor to our understanding of crime, mainly because of its emphasis on individual pathology, its reliance on positivism and an apparent neglect of possible social factors in the construction of criminal careers. Contemporary psychology, however, has much to offer in a very practical sense: crime scene analysis and offender profiling to assist the police in crime detection; training police officers to interview witnesses to improve their recall; assessing the 'dangerousness' of convicted offenders in order to determine the possibility of release; and the development of treatment programmes for targeted groups of offenders.

There has often been a tension between sociological and psychological explanations of crime. Psychology has tended to concentrate on the individual, with an emphasis on physical, physiological and personality factors, all of which can lead to a 'pathologising' of crime, i.e. a view that it is the province of a sick or disordered few, somehow different from the rest of us. In contrast, sociological explanations of crime have emphasised environmental and cultural factors, e.g. poverty and deprivation, discriminatory police practices, etc. The end result is that the one (psychology) predicts too little crime, whilst the other (sociology) predicts too much. What can be forgotten in this debate is the potential interaction between a whole range of variables, which might go some way towards providing the answers to the following questions.

- Why don't all individuals from deprived backgrounds become offenders?
- Why do some individuals from advantaged backgrounds become serious criminals?
- Why do so many young men become involved in crime while their sisters do not?
- Why is corporate crime viewed differently to other types of crime?
- When police officers break the law, is their offending worse?
- At what age do children become capable of offending?
- Can some vulnerable individuals be targeted in such a way as to ensure that they do not turn to crime?

WHAT IS CRIME?

This may seem a question to which there are obvious answers and yes, there would probably be widespread agreement on some acts being seen very clearly as crimes. These might include violence to the person and theft. However, there might be disagreement about whether these offences are still seen as crimes if the rule of law is challenged, for instance in wartime. Whilst legal sanctions hold, there is reasonable understanding about what constitutes crime (if it is against the law, it must be a crime), but this understanding tends to alter according to historical, cultural and power dimensions which may designate different behaviours as criminal at different times. Examples might include attempted suicide which until 1961 was regarded as a criminal offence, homosexual acts between consenting adults which were a crime until 1967, and incest which until 1908 was not regarded as a crime. The act of female circumcision is seen in some cultures, e.g. Egypt and Sudan, as acceptable, whilst in Britain it has been prohibited under existing child protection legislation. In contrast, male circumcision has never been against the law and still occurs today on religious or health grounds. In both cases, however, genital mutilation occurs without the consent of the individuals concerned.

Criminal behaviour is also designated according to age and intention. Thus, the same behaviour can be seen as criminal in one case and not in another. The age of criminal responsibility varies from country to country: in Scotland it is 8, in England and Wales it is 10, in France it is 13 and in Sweden it is 15. Individuals are deemed to have committed a criminal offence only if they can be shown to have had the intention of doing so; thus, people suffering from some forms of psychiatric illness are considered incapable of this aspect of criminal behaviour.

Ignorance of the law is not usually accepted as a defence, but some laws are interpreted rather liberally by the police in terms of prosecution, and examples would include some acts of unlawful sexual intercourse and the private use of cannabis resin. In these examples, it is clear that decisions are being made outside the strict letter of the law as to what constitutes criminal behaviour, and whilst these decisions may be very sensitively handled in most instances, it is easy to see how this power could be abused in a much more serious way in a totalitarian state.

We can only judge what constitutes criminal behaviour by reference to those crimes which come to the notice of the authorities and it is the data relating to these offences and these offenders which form a substantial part of most research in the area of crime. Unfortunately, the data are not representative in any sense. The vast majority of offences are not reported; Hollin (1992) estimates that only 25% of all crimes appear in the official statistics, leaving a 'dark figure' of unreported crime which is also largely inaccessible to researchers.

How Much Crime is There?

There are a variety of sources which we can draw on to estimate how much crime occurs, some more accurate than others but none wholly accurate. Until the 1950s official data sources were assumed to give a true picture of crime but it was then recognised that reported crime probably accounted for only a very small proportion of actual crime. Why should this be so? Official crime statistics reflect the crimes which are recorded by the police and this sounds reasonably foolproof, but unfortunately statistics are never value-free. Crime statistics are compiled as a result of someone reporting a crime to the police (having decided a crime has occurred) and then a police officer deciding to record that offence in a particular way. What might happen prior to these decisions being made? A member of the public may decide not to report an offence to the police for a variety of reasons, including not recognising certain behaviour as an offence, not wanting to get involved, not perceiving a victim, not seeing the offence as serious enough or not feeling that the police will deal with the matter appropriately. Before recording an offence, a police officer may need to decide whether the offence is serious enough to warrant intervention, is it part of a domestic dispute, could it have been committed by a child and is it one or several offences?

Crime is measured by counting criminal events or offenders but the crime rate which results is the product of prevalence (the number of persons committing crimes at any one time) and incidence (the number of crimes committed per offender) (Farrington et al., 1986). Recorded crimes do not necessarily coincide with the number of individual offenders, since some offenders commit multiple offences and some offences are committed in groups. Variations in crime rates between groups, or over time, may reflect changes in prevalence, incidence or both but the contributing factors are not clear. Moreover, massive age and sex differences in offending patterns are often concealed within official crime statistics.

A recognition of the inadequacy of official crime statistics led researchers to look for other sources, including self-reports of offending, insurance company records, participant observation in criminal groups and victim surveys. Most of these sources reveal a much higher crime rate than the official figures would suggest. When Groth et al. (1982) asked convicted sex offenders how many similar offences they had committed without apprehension, the men admitted to an average of five such offences. Most self-report surveys carried out with non-offender samples reveal that the majority of young males engage in some criminal activity during adolescence, and when Furnham and Thompson (1991) asked undergraduates to report their offending history anonymously, they found a mean score of 12.46 out of a possible 50.

The most well-known victim survey is the British Crime Survey which is conducted every two years and involves interviews with about 16,000 adults during which they are asked about their experiences of crime during the previous year. The estimated crime rate which results from the British Crime Survey is much higher than the official crime statistics would indicate. An example is the year 1995–96 when official figures put the number of crimes as 5.1 million, whilst the British Crime Survey revealed an estimated 19.1 million crimes during the same period. Significantly the British Crime Survey also reveals attitudes to crime rates and 75% of those interviewed believed the crime rate increased during the period 1993–95 (when overall official rates actually decreased). Whilst the British Crime Survey provides an alternative set of data to official crime statistics, it is by no means comprehensive. Inevitably, as with all surveys there is participant response bias which may skew the results and not all crimes can possibly be included since not all crimes have responsive victims, for example vandalism, corporate crimes and tax fraud.

The 1996 crime figures (released in March 1997) showed a 1.3% fall in recorded crime in England and Wales, resulting in a total of 5,033,000 reported offences (see Table 1.1). This constituted the fourth consecutive reduction in overall crime rates and was hailed as a vindication for tougher penal policies, but masked several other factors, notably that the decreases in overall crime are minor, especially in contrast to the 42% increase between 1989 and 1992 (the largest increase since records began) and that violent crime, which is the focal point of most public concern, increased by 11%. Included in the increase in violent crime was a 14% rise in rape and a 17% increase in 'life-threatening offences'. The phenomenon of 'repeat victimisation' was also revealed, with 4% of victims suffering repeat crimes. This was especially true in relation to domestic violence and for those living in disadvantaged areas.

Table 1.1 Notifiable offences recorded by the police, England and Wales (000s)

Offence	1996	Percentage change
Violence against the person	239.1	12
Sexual offences	31.2	3
Robbery	74.0	9
Total violent crime	**344.3**	**11**
Burglary	1,164.4	-6
Theft/handling stolen goods	2,383.0	-3
(includes vehicle crime	1,292.7	-2)
Fraud and forgery	135.9	2
Criminal damage	950.7	4
Other notifiable offences	56.6	10

Although violent crime only accounts for 6% of all offences, this is the area which occupies most people in determining their attitude to crime generally and indeed, their behaviour. The 1996 British Crime Survey revealed that more than one in 10 women and one in 20 men said they never went out after dark and one-third of the women who stayed in cited fear of crime as the reason. The same survey reported a 242% increase in domestic violence incidents since 1981.

Whilst concern remains high about the extent of violent crime, there do seem to have been reductions in other groups of offences. The 1996 crime figures show a 6% drop in burglaries, a 3% drop in theft and a 2% drop in car crime. There may be a number of explanations for this, including different police recording practices in response to a need to meet nationally set performance targets, improved security leading to decreased opportunity for crime, economic recovery leading to a reduction of acquisitive crimes or a drop in the population most likely to contribute to crime figures, i.e. 10–18-year-old males.

Table 1.2 Percentage change in notifiable offences recorded by the police over the previous 12 months, England and Wales

1987	1%
1988	-5%
1989	4%
1990	17%
1991	16%
1992	6%
1993	-1%
1994	-5%
1995	-3%
1996	-1%

Table 1.3 International Crime Victimisation Survey (1997)

Crimes per 100 population, 1996

Netherlands	62
England and Wales	60
US	51
Canada	47
Sweden	45
Scotland	44
Switzerland	43
France	43
Austria	32
Finland	31
N.Ireland	27
Average	45

Victims of contact crime (robbery, assaults and sex attacks) – %age of total

England and Wales	3.6%
US	3.5%
Sweden	3.1%
Finland	2.9%
Canada	2.7%
Scotland	2.7%
Switzerland	2.3%
France	2.2%
Netherlands	1.9%
Austria	1.6%
N.Ireland	1.5%
Average	2.5%

Unfortunately these small reductions in the official crime figures (see Table 1.2), which have been greeted with delight by politicians, do not seem to reflect the true picture of crime in the UK in the 1990s. The figures from the International Crime Victimisation Survey in July 1997 reveal a shocking picture of escalating crime, especially by comparison with other countries (see Table 1.3). Traditionally, America has been viewed as the home of violent crime, with crime rates the UK would hope never to match. Yet this international survey of 11 countries, based on interviews with 20,000 people, reveals that more than a third of those living in England and Wales reported having been victims of crime in the previous year – a record worse than America and beaten only by The Netherlands. When serious crimes are analysed (robbery, assault, sexual violence) the rate for England and Wales actually tops the table. The fear of crime in England and Wales is so great that, according to this survey, people are more anxious about going out alone on the streets after dark than people in any other country.

These figures reveal an alarming comparative rate of crime and one about which no one can feel complacent. Whilst the optimists amongst us might remark that 96.4% of people in England and Wales are not the victims of violent crime, it is clear that the unusually high fear of crime has real consequences for people in terms of how they feel able to determine the quality of their lives.

How can Psychology Contribute to an Analysis of Crime?

The suggestion that there is any possibility of one single explanation of criminal behaviour has to be totally rejected because not only is behaviour complex, crime is a social construct which changes over time and across cultures. This said, psychology can and does make a contribution to our understanding of criminal behaviour and from a range of different perspectives. Many of the theories stem from classic psychological studies, though there is also evidence of more contemporary developments.

Developmental psychology

Developmental psychology is concerned with the influences which are brought to bear on the social and intellectual development of an individual throughout the lifespan and the findings of developmental psychologists can inform our understanding of the origins and maintenance of offending behaviour.

Research indicates that intellectual development can be impaired by a poor environment (including the foetal environment) and a lack of appropriate stimulation. Hence the success of preschool programmes such as Operation Headstart in giving disadvantaged children an opportunity to succeed by influencing parental styles (Bee, 1995).

It is now widely accepted that young children need the opportunity to become emotionally attached to one or more caregivers and to experience some continuity of care during childhood, as Bowlby (1944) suggested in relation to child war evacuees separated from their families. Without this opportunity, children tend to have poorer outcomes in terms of psychological health (Rutter, 1971b). Criticisms of single parent families in terms of poor discipline and immorality tend not to take into account the desperate sense of loss which children may experience as a result of separation, divorce or bereavement, in addition to obvious income reduction.

Children who display behavioural problems tend to come from families which have harsh and inconsistent discipline patterns (Eron et al., 1991). It may be these children who subsequently become involved in crime, not because they have been programmed to do so, but as a result of self-fulfilling prophecies.

Gender is an important factor in a child's experience of socialisation, from both a biological and a social perspective. Boys tend to be more vulnerable than girls from birth (there are more male infant deaths and male accidents, and men die on average five years before women), and they also tend to be assessed as suffering from more school-related problems, e.g. dyslexia, stammering and behavioural disorders. Whilst girls are socialised into being polite and conforming, boys are encouraged to be aggressive, controlling and independent. Inability to comply with these expectations and low self-esteem associated with educational referrals may produce a vulnerability in some male children which can perhaps explain a tendency to over-compensate and seek success in offending behaviour (see Siann, 1994).

Adolescence is a time when the frequency of offending behaviour increases and the work of Farrington (1991a) would suggest that there are several factors in the backgrounds of children which are consistently linked to an increased risk of delinquency in adolescence. These include poor parental supervision, harsh and inconsistent discipline, family conflict, low income, parental indifference and rejection, underachievement at school, living in disorganised and disadvantaged communities, mixing with antisocial peers, and early onset of involvement in crime.

Social psychology

Social psychology focuses on the interaction between individuals, and areas of importance to understanding offending behaviour include the study of attitudes, attributions, deindividuation, group processes and conformity.

Whilst there are concerns about claiming too close a link between attitudes and behaviour, it seems likely that the attitudes offenders hold about themselves, their peers and crime itself will play a large part in the decision-making process before offending behaviour occurs. The area of social cognition within psychology has examined the factors which play a part in decision-making and the formation of beliefs and this can usefully be applied to the study of offending behaviour as an active decision rather than as a passive response to conditions.

Similarly, attribution theory suggests that when ascribing meaning to behaviour (why did person A do that?), we tend to pay more attention to dispositional factors than to the context in which the behaviour occurs (Heider, 1958). This means we assume person A acted the way she did because that is the sort of person she is, rather than because she was in a particular situation. These findings have important consequences for risk assessment when decisions have to be made about the likelihood of a behaviour occurring in the future, e.g. whether a prisoner is likely to attempt suicide.

Groups exert a powerful influence on individuals, often in the direction of conformity to group norms, and whilst much of the work in this area within psychology has taken the form of laboratory-based experiments (Sherif, 1936; Asch, 1951) and can therefore be criticised for low ecological validity, it is clear that adolescents in particular are likely to depend on peer groups to inform their judgement in terms of attitudes and behaviour and that peer pressure is bound to be very difficult to resist.

FIGURE 1.1 'Deindividuation' (the absence of a sense of personal responsibility) is said to occur during collective violence, which might explain this brutal assault by the police on Rodney King.

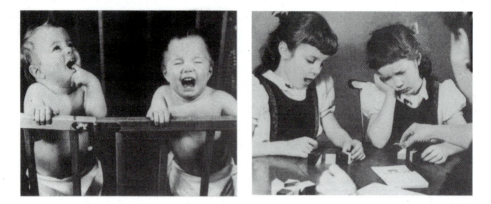

FIGURE 1.2 *The temperamental differences apparent at birth may continue throughout child-hood, even in identical twins, lending support to the view that there is a strong genetic component to personality*

Zimbardo (1970) described deindividuation as the process whereby individuals in a group situation can behave in ways in which they would not behave were they alone. Examples might include gang violence when personal thresholds of guilt, fear and inhibition converge towards a collective perception such that a gang member feels able to behave in a way which otherwise might produce strong internal prohibitions.

Biological psychology

Biological psychology is traditionally associated with a rather unhelpful deterministic view of behaviour which in the area of crime might suggest that biological deficits or genetic inheritance lead to offending behaviour. There are obvious dangers in an over-reliance on biology and genetics since there is considerable variation between individuals and a lack of clarity as to whether those biological differences which do exist are a cause or a consequence of behaviour. However, a more modern approach – 'biological interactionism' – acknowledges the influence of the environment in shaping and interacting with biological processes (Rowe and Osgood, 1984).

The work of Chess and Thomas (1984) illustrates that temperamental differences between individuals are present very soon after birth and that these can influence interactions with parents (making parent–child interaction very much a two-way process) and consequently affect later behaviour. They divide children into three categories: easy (a child who soon establishes regular eating and sleeping patterns, and adapts easily to new experiences); difficult (a child who tends to react rather slowly and negatively to new experiences, and whose daily routines are irregular); and slow-to-warm-up (a child who is somewhat negative in mood, does not adapt easily, and has a low activity level). Thus, a child who is difficult to soothe as an infant, and whose parents find this hard to accept, may subsequently display behavioural difficulties throughout childhood and adolescence as a result of this mismatch.

Genetic inheritance is seen to play a part in shaping future behaviour, though the influence of the environment is recognised. This is most apparent in studies which attempt to discover whether crime 'runs in families'. The answer is mostly yes, but with the important caveat that the relative contribution of heredity and the environment to this pattern is still unclear.

The influence of other psychological perspectives in furthering our understanding of offending behaviour, such as learning theory, individual differences and cognitive behavioural theory will be considered in the next chapter, but it is clear that psychology as a discipline has much to offer in terms of the analysis of crime.

WHAT IS CRIMINOLOGICAL PSYCHOLOGY?

Criminological psychology, or forensic psychology as it is also known, is a specific branch of psychology which attempts to apply psychological principles to an important real-life setting, the criminal justice system. It is very much rooted in empirical research and draws on a range of topics and perspectives within the field of psychology. One of its main areas of focus is the study of criminal behaviour and its management, but criminological psychologists are also concerned with crime prevention, risk assessment and court processes. Their contribution can be seen at a theoretical level but also at the applied level when practitioners such as clinical psychologists and prison psychologists are able to put some of the concepts and theoretical constructs into practice and evaluate their usefulness.

THE DEVELOPMENT OF CRIMINOLOGICAL PSYCHOLOGY

The study of crime – criminology – is a curious mix of disciplines, including law, sociology, anthropology, economics, psychology, geography, psychiatry, politics and statistics. Sellin (1938) described it as:

"... a bastard science grown out of the public preoccupation with a social plague." (in Bottomley, 1979, p.88)

whilst Garland (1994) says:

"As with most 'human sciences', criminology has a long past but a short history." (p.27)

Much the same can be said of criminological psychology. Discourse about the causes of crime and the link with human nature has existed for centuries, but it is only during the latter half of this century that the discipline of criminological psychology can be said to have emerged in its own right and indeed, only in the last 20 years that an established and acknowledged body of knowledge based on empirical research has been recognised.

At the turn of the century a debate ensued about the relevance of psychology to law. Psychologists were eager to demonstrate how their new research findings could be applied to the practice of law and in 1908 Hugo Münsterberg published *On the Witness Stand* in which he called upon lawyers to appreciate the relevance of experimental psychology to their profession. Münsterberg was particularly interested in improving the performance of witnesses in terms of recall. His pleas remained unheeded, however, and lawyers appeared to close ranks, dismissing the findings of psychologists as imprecise. A fallow period then occurred where work in the field of psychology as applied to law was rather irregular, though with some notable exceptions, e.g. Burt's (1925) *The Young Delinquent* and several psychoanalytic studies of young delinquents, e.g. Aichorn (1925). There was also the work of John Bowlby (1944) whose study of juvenile delinquents led to a theory of maternal deprivation as a key causal factor in offending behaviour.

In the 1960s, however, the picture changed and a new demand for applied psychology, particularly in the area of understanding criminal behaviour, emerged. Attempts to find the 'criminal personality' or the elusive 'criminal gene' were made. Chief amongst researchers in this area was Hans Eysenck (1964) who suggested that neurotic extraverts were more likely to become offenders because they are less conditionable, i.e. they do not learn well and will therefore be less likely to learn social control via the process of socialisation. Their personality characteristics of neuroticism and extraversion, as measured by Eysenck's scales, were held to be biologically determined. Eysenck's theories generated considerable interest and research, which is well documented by Bartol (1980), but the findings have not been wholly consistent and many writers have distanced themselves from their pessimistic determinism (Trasler, 1987).

Mounting concern about the apparent increase in crime rates, violent crime in particular, and a growing recognition of the need to provide rehabilitation programmes which actually reduce recidivism prompted the next wave of research. As a result, there was a dramatic increase in the application of psychological principles to criminological issues and the potentially positive role of psychologists within various systems was increasingly recognised, for example:

- in the legal system – assisting with trial strategy, juror selection, training and selection of police and magistrates, interviewing witnesses and offering expert testimony;
- in criminal detection – working with the police to develop offending patterns and constructing profiles of likely offenders;
- in the prison system – assessing offenders' needs, their likelihood of reoffending and devising treatment programmes;
- in the political system – offering advice on policy changes in relation to the treatment of offenders and victims.

A research unit was set up by the Home Office to explore these areas and the Division of Criminological and Legal Psychology was recognised by the British Psychological Society in 1977. A wide range of relevant journals specifically looking at these areas also began to appear. Examples include *Psychology, Crime and Law; Legal and Criminological Psychology; Forensic Update* and *Behavioural Sciences and the Law.*

WHAT DO CRIMINOLOGICAL PSYCHOLOGISTS DO?

Criminological psychologists can be found working within a wide range of contexts. Those with clinical or forensic training tend to work in psychiatric hospitals and special hospitals, whilst psychologists working for the Prison Psychological Service are situated in young offender institutions and prisons. These individuals will often be involved in risk assessment, establishing on the basis of a range of evidence what the degree of risk might be if certain offenders are to be considered for release. They will also be involved in devising treatment programmes for specific groups of offenders, for instance sex offenders or those who have a problem controlling their anger. A crucial part of this work involves research and evaluation in order to determine what constitutes successful treatment. Success may be evaluated in terms of a reduction in subsequent offending or in terms of personal growth and increased self-knowledge which may allow the offender more choice in the decision to reoffend.

There are many professionals working in both health and offender contexts who also have some psychological training, for example forensic nurses, prison officers, probation officers, social workers and police officers. They too may be involved in the processes of assessment and treatment. Criminological psychologists also work within an academic context, teaching on both undergraduate and postgraduate courses. All these professionals may offer consultative advice to a variety of agencies, including social services departments, probation and after-care departments and the police, and may also be asked to appear as expert witnesses in court cases. Criminological psychologists also engage in research activity and may be employed to do this by specific agencies such as the Home Office Research Unit or the police, or they may conduct independent research. The significant feature of research within criminological psychology is that it is almost exclusively of an applied nature. Thus, criminological psychologists may analyse official criminal statistics or conduct longitudinal studies of children in order to determine which of them become offenders or set up experimental studies whereby they can attempt, for instance, to discern the possible association between screen violence and aggressive behaviour. Whilst the potential range of issues to explore is enormous, there is a need to observe strict ethical guidelines when such sensitive matters are involved.

How Do You Become
a Criminological Psychologist?

If you would like to become a criminological psychologist you should first complete an undergraduate course in psychology which is acceptable to the British Psychological Society in terms of providing the Graduate Basis of Registration. You might want to combine your studies in psychology with other relevant subjects such as sociology or law. There are also an increasing number of courses which specifically link criminology with psychology, offering joint honours in these two subjects. If there is a dissertation requirement in your degree course you would be well advised to choose an empirical study in the area of criminology and psychology, e.g. attitudes to particular offences or the effectiveness of anti-bullying strategies in prison.

As a graduate, you must then complete a Masters degree in criminological psychology, investigative psychology or forensic psychology. It is often an entry requirement for these courses that you have relevant work experience and if you decide to join the Prison Psychological Service you will be sent on one of these courses as part of your professional training. Alternatively, you might decide you would like to follow the clinical psychology route and choose forensic psychology as your specialism within that context. You might then obtain a Diploma in Clinical Criminology. Again, you will need relevant work experience before you can join a clinical psychology course. The academic path can be joined by registering for a PhD in an area of criminological psychology which will sustain your interest for at least three years. Most teaching posts will require a doctorate in a relevant area and may also require some evidence of teaching experience.

chapter two

THEORIES OF CRIME

CHAPTER OVERVIEW

This chapter ambitiously tries to provide a summary of the various theories and explanations which have been offered to account for criminal behaviour. These include biological, psychoanalytic and social learning theories. Further account is taken of social factors and variables such as age, gender, ethnicity and mental state. Attempts to explain specific types of crime, rape and sexual offences against children are provided in Chapters 4 and 8 respectively.

INTRODUCTION

All the theories attempting to explain criminal behaviour which are included here represent part of the classic psychological nature versus nurture debate, i.e. is behaviour the result of heredity or the environment, and in relation to crime, is the criminal *born* bad or *made* bad? Do offenders rationally choose to commit crime or are they somehow programmed to do so? Genes are often said to set the limits on behaviour, whilst the environment shapes development within those limits. Thus, a child born with some potential to offend may, depending upon the familial environment in which he or she is reared, realise that potential or not. There are serious implications for intervention depending on which of the theories is accepted as the most convincing. As you will see, however, the divisions, overlaps and potential interaction between the variables described mean that it is almost impossible to settle definitively on any one group of theories, let alone a single theory, as a sufficient explanation for offending behaviour, and that there is an urgent need for interdisciplinary research which can take on board all these possible variables. Moreover, there may be a need to adopt a mode of analysis which rarely figures in criminology, namely trying also to understand the 'pleasures' of crime since clearly one of the major reasons offenders commit crime is because they enjoy it. Katz (1988) has spoken of the 'seductions' of crime whilst Hodge, McMurran & Hollin (1997) refer to criminal behaviour as an 'addiction'. Both perspectives recognise that the 'buzz' of risk, danger, fun, opportunism, status and financial gain as well as more unsavoury motivational factors merit serious examination. Joy riding is a good example of the type of crime which can benefit from this sort of analysis – it is dangerous, temporary and very risky yet extremely popular with young men. What do you think might be the attraction (see Kilpatrick, 1997)?

Before you read any further, look through a daily newspaper for accounts of particular crimes. What factors are stressed and what implicit or explicit suggestions are made as to why certain individuals have acted in the way they did? How convincing are some of the explanations and what real evidence is there to support them? Are there any moral judgements made in relation to particular types of crime? Are there differences in the way the same crime is reported in the tabloids and the broadsheets?

BIOLOGICAL THEORIES

These explanations are clearly in the nature camp of the nature versus nurture debate and are very popular at particular times because they remove any suggestion that crime might be the result of social inequalities. Criminal tendencies are seen as something which is in the nature of the individual criminal and not a result of the malfunctioning of society. There are several variations of biological theories of crime, some rather dated now though still enjoying limited currency, and they include constitutional and chromosomal theories, genetic transmission, family studies, twin studies, adoption studies and neurological factors.

Constitutional theories

If we believe that criminals are very different from the rest of us, it is not too big a step to assume that they will also look quite different from the rest of us. The theories of Sheldon focus specifically on physique or body shape. Do criminals share the same body shape and, if so, which is it? Sheldon (1942) described three basic body types (Figure 2.1) which he believed were correlated with particular types of personality. He developed his theories after studying a large sample of males in a rehabilitation institution, rating their body types and producing the following typology:

- thin and bony ectomorphs, who were introverted and restrained;
- large and heavy endomorphs, who were sociable and relaxed;
- broad and muscular mesomorphs, who were aggressive and adventurous.

Sheldon claimed that amongst this sample there were a large number of mesomorphs, some endomorphs and very few ectomorphs and that this

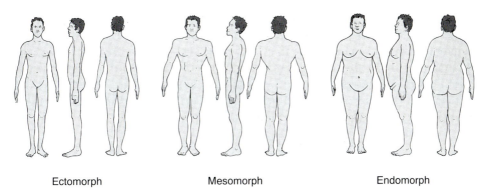

Ectomorph   Mesomorph   Endomorph

FIGURE 2.1 *Sheldon suggested that body shape was associated with personality type, and that mesomorphs were more likely to be criminally inclined*

pattern differed markedly from that in a control group. Although Sheldon's work was criticised on methodological and subjective grounds (because he rated his subjects' body types himself) his theories were supported in the area of criminal behaviour by Glueck and Glueck (1956) who found that in a sample of delinquents 60% were mesomorphs, whilst in a non-delinquent sample only 31% were, and by Cortés and Gatti (1972) who found in a sample of 100 delinquents that 57% were mesomorphic compared with 19% of controls.

Whilst these findings provide support for the view that delinquents are likely to be muscular and fit, it remains unclear what the exact association might be between mesomorphy and crime. It may well be that the influence of stereo-typing is at work, if the police and magistrates believe delinquents tend to be of a particular appearance then this may influence their decisions and could result in an over-representation of mesomorphs in convicted offender samples. Moreover, muscular types may be more likely to be invited by their peers to participate in daring and antisocial acts, may be more successful and therefore more likely to continue this behaviour and, if apprehended, begin to build up a criminal career.

We all tend to develop beliefs about what 'criminals' look like and this can determine our reactions to such people. There are several studies which would seem to bear this out. In 1939 Thornton showed 20 photographs of criminals to people who were asked to choose one of four crimes each of the criminals might have committed. He found that people could match faces to crimes more reliably than would have been predicted by chance. Forty-three years later Bull (1982) achieved similar results, this time using photographs of non-criminal individuals but still producing an association between some faces and some crimes which was stronger than could have been predicted by chance. How do such stereotypes develop? Media influence might play a part since villains always seem to come from the same stable in order to make them easily recognisable, but this hardly explains Thornton's results. Could it be that we are not very nice to people who we consider unattractive and that over time these individuals begin to lose faith in themselves and act to fit their stereotype? Masters and Greaves (1969) surveyed the incidence of facial deformities in 11,000 prisoners and concluded that 60% of them had facial deformities by comparison with 20% in a non-criminal population. This finding might raise the possibility that some of these individuals turned to crime because of the social consequences of their disability.

You will see already from the nature of this initial discussion how physical and social variables interact, not only in the development of behavioural patterns but also in the interpretation and selection of empirical evidence.

Chromosomes

The 1960s saw the emergence of a new explanation of violent crime in terms of an identifiable genetic abnormality – the XYY syndrome. We all have 46 chromosomes, in pairs, one of which determines our sex – XX for females and XY for males. There are a variety of chromosomal abnormalities, one of which involves the presence of an extra Y chromosome in males and it is usually linked to above-average height and low intelligence. The suggestion was made that prison and special hospital populations had more than their fair share of these individuals (Price et al., 1966; Jarvik et al., 1973) and that these XYY individuals or 'supermales' had a disproportionate inclination towards violent crime. The XYY defence was used in some criminal trials and suggestions were made that mass screening be carried out to detect these individuals at an early age, in order to take preventive action.

In 1966, when Richard Speck killed eight nurses in Chicago, it was claimed in the media that he had an extra Y chromosome which might have explained the excessive violence he used during his attack. However, subsequent examination revealed no chromosomal abnormality.

A comprehensive Danish study which screened 4591 men for the presence of XYY found only 12 cases (Witkin et al., 1976). Whilst these individuals were indeed more likely to be involved in crime than chance would have predicted (41.7% of them, by comparison with 9.3% of the XY individuals), it was not involvement in violent crime. Their conclusion was that the over-representation of XYY males in prisons and special hospitals was more likely to be the result of other characteristics – low intelligence and above-average height – and the social reaction that these characteristics may have produced.

Genetic transmission

These theories involve a search for the elusive 'criminal gene' and at their most extreme, they suggest that criminals are definitely born and not made. One of the founding fathers of criminology, Cesare Lombroso, held this view.

In 1876 he published *L'Uomo Delinquente* and argued that criminals were genetically different from non-criminals and this difference could literally be seen
in their faces (Figure 2.2). Lombroso suggested that criminals display a range
of physical characteristics which reveal clues that they are throwbacks to
more primitive times.

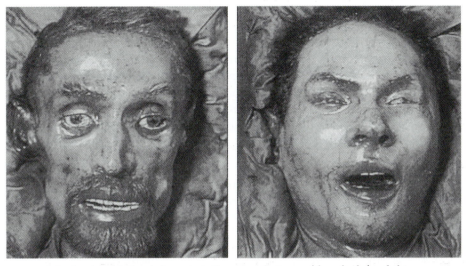

FIGURE 2.2 *Lombroso believed that criminals were evolutionary 'throwbacks' and this was
evident in their physical appearance*

"The criminal by nature has a feeble cranial capacity, a heavy and developed
jaw, projecting (eye) ridges, an abnormal and asymmetrical cranium ... projecting ears, frequently a crooked or flat nose. Criminals are subject to colour
blindness, left-handedness is common, their muscular force is feeble."

Lombroso went further and suggested that from the surveys he had carried
out in prison, he could detect physiological differences between different
types of criminal. Thus, murderers were said to have:

"cold, glassy, blood-shot eyes, curly, abundant hair, strong jaws, long
ears and thin lips"

whilst sex offenders have:

"glinting eyes, strong jaws, thick lips, lots of hair and projecting ears."

Lombroso's views received some indirect support from Goring, who in 1913
studied 3000 English convicts and found that although anatomical differences
were not as extreme as Lombroso had suggested, a common factor in his
subjects was low intelligence. At this time intelligence was regarded as
genetically determined and so criminal behaviour too was seen to be linked
to genetic inheritance. Within such a reductionist biological determinism,
characteristics such as intelligence and criminality are seen as fixed and

immutable. Any possibility of social factors influencing outcome is minimised. From this perspective it is a short step to compulsory sterilisation of those who are deemed 'immoral' or 'mentally deficient', a policy which not only existed in Nazi Germany, but in Sweden, Britain and the USA (see Rose et al., 1984).

It is easy now to criticise Lombroso's theories; for instance, his research methodology was not particularly rigorous (he did not use a proper control group, often relying on large groups of soldiers, and his criminal samples contained large numbers of the mentally disturbed) and his conclusions sound bizarre. Perhaps the most important criticism, however, is Lombroso's failure to recognise that correlation does not imply causality. Simply because his criminal subjects shared a significant number of physical anomalies does not mean that this made them criminal. It could be that poverty and deprivation produce physical defects, rather than the defects being the result of genetic transmission.

But in spite of the obvious criticism and lack of political correctness, could Lombroso have had something? Maybe we can rule out the possibility of genetic transmission, for as Rowe (1990) says:

> "No responsible geneticist would argue that a specific gene exists for crime, as specific genes may be identified for Huntington's disease or eye color." (p.122)

However, we are now much more aware of the power of the media and their role in perpetuating stereotypes and self-fulfilling prophecies, and if someone appears to fit our image of a 'criminal' do we assume the worst and thereby create a social reality?

Family studies

More recently researchers have searched for support for the genetic transmission of crime within criminal families. Their aim was to discover whether criminal tendencies can be inherited – does crime run in families? Earlier researchers had claimed this was so by looking at the family trees of criminals, e.g. Dugdale's (1910) study of the Jukes family and Goddard's (1914) study of the Kallikaks. These studies can be criticised because of their lack of methodological rigour and are now largely discredited as anecdotal, but many workers in welfare agencies would point out that a substantial number of their cases stem from a small number of families. Is this the result of prejudice, years of social deprivation or genetic transmission?

A consistent finding in current research is that criminal parents are indeed more likely to have criminal children, e.g. Osborn and West (1979) found that 40% of the sons of criminal fathers had criminal convictions, compared with a figure of 13% for the sons of non-criminal fathers, but it should be noted that 60% of the sons of criminal fathers did not turn to crime – why? What were the differences between these two groups of boys?

Once again, correlation does not imply causality and being born into a criminal family is not a necessary condition for criminal behaviour. Another variable which family members share, e.g. poverty or parenting styles, might account for the criminal behaviour. David Farrington and his colleagues (1991) carried out a 30-year longitudinal study of working-class boys to see which of them became delinquent and concluded that the important predictors are low income, a large family, parental criminality and poor child-rearing techniques (Table 2.1). They also noted, however, that 6% of families were responsible for 50% of all the crimes reported in their sample.

So crime does seem to run in families, but why? Established risk factors for antisocial behaviour (which may or may not result in criminal convictions) include parental criminality, ineffective and inconsistent discipline, family discord and a deviant peer group (Rutter, 1971a; Patterson, 1982) but the mix is so volatile that it is almost impossible to differentiate between the contribution of genetics and the environment. Nevertheless Farrington (1995) is quite clear about the areas which should be targeted to prevent the development of antisocial behaviour: improving school achievement (to avoid low intelligence and school failure); improving child rearing methods (to reduce erratic discipline and promote positive parent–child interaction); reducing impulsivity (teaching cognitive and interpersonal skills to combat egocentricity) and reducing poverty (providing increased economic resources for deprived families).

Twin studies

Psychologists have often studied twins, both identical (monozygotic or MZ) and fraternal (dizygotic or DZ), in an attempt to discover the relative importance of genetic transmission in areas such as intelligence, schizophrenia and criminal behaviour. MZ twins share the same genes whilst DZ twins, just like any other siblings, share about 50% of their genes. If twins share the same environment, then any major difference between them ought to be the result of genetic differences and would give strong support to the nature side of the nature versus nurture debate.

Researchers investigate the extent of difference by looking at 'concordance'. This is the degree to which twins display the same behaviour and is usually expressed as a percentage. So, a 50% concordance would indicate that in half of the total sample, both members of a twin pair displayed the same behaviour.

There have been several studies of twins and criminal behaviour and generally there is a higher concordance level for MZ twins than for DZ twins in the area of criminal behaviour (Table 2.2), indicating that genetic factors do play a role in the development of offending behaviour. However, this effect seems

Table 2.1 Summary of Farrington's findings (1991b)

- A longitudinal study of 411 boys born in the East End in 1953
- 20% had acquired convictions by 17 years
- 33% had acquired convictions by 25 years
- But 50% of the total convictions had been acquired by <6% of the sample, i.e. 23 boys
- Most of these chronic offenders shared common childhood characteristics:
  - rated troublesome/dishonest in primary school
  - came from poorer, larger families
  - more likely to have criminal parents
  - experienced harsh/erratic parental discipline and family conflict
- At age ten:
  - identified as hyperactive, impulsive, unpopular, low intelligence
- At age 14:
  - aggressive, with delinquent friends
- at age 18:
  - drank more, smoked more, gambled
  - had tattoos, bitten nails, a low pulse rate
  - associated with gangs
- At age 32:
  - poorer housing
  - marital break-up
  - psychiatric disorder
  - problems with own children

to be more marked in relation to adult crime than to juvenile delinquency (Goldsmith and Gottesman, 1995). Moreover, more modern twin studies suggest that high concordance rates for both MZ and DZ twins are more likely to be the result of a common environment than genetic factors (Lyons, 1996).

Table 2.2 Studies which have indicated concordance level for criminal behaviour in twins

	MZ	DZ
Lange (1931)	77	12
Kranz (1936)	65	53
Yoshimasu (1965)	50	0
Christiansen (1977)	60	30

The differences between these studies illustrates the problem in accepting their findings uncritically. All twin studies tend to suffer from the same potential difficulties, e.g.

- MZ twins look alike and may therefore generate more similar social responses than DZ twins. This means that in addition to sharing the same genes, they may also share an almost identical social environment.
- MZ twins often have a very close relationship and may therefore develop similar interests, which might include criminal behaviour.
- Possible misclassification of twin pairs, which is more likely to have affected earlier studies.
- Very small sample size in some studies, because of the inherent difficulties in obtaining access to criminal twins.
- Variable definitions of criminal behaviour.

In the absence of relevant data on twins reared apart, it is difficult to conclude anything other than a trend, though it is worth noting that recent studies looking at measures of personality and intelligence in relation to MZ twins reared apart have found some striking similarities (Bouchard et al., 1990).

Adoption studies

Researchers have also been interested in the criminal behaviour of adopted children because they can compare the influence of biological inheritance and that of the environment, i.e. the adoptive home. If the behaviour of adopted children is more similar to that of their biological parents than that of their adoptive parents, then strong support for the genetic argument will be provided.

In one of the early adoption studies looking at criminal behaviour, Crowe (1974) found that in a sample of 52 adopted children of imprisoned women, seven of them had at least one criminal conviction, by comparison with only one in a matched control group. Subsequent studies have supported these findings: e.g. Mednick et al. (1987) found that boys whose biological parent had a criminal record were more likely to have been convicted of a crime than were boys whose adoptive parent had been convicted. Thus, the biological parents' genetic contribution had a greater effect on behaviour than did the adoptive parents' rearing. When Walters (1992) carried out a meta-analysis of 13 adoption studies he found a moderate but significant association between heredity variables and crime, which led him to suggest that the individual genetic inheritance of criminal behaviour is 11–17%. However, the possible interaction effects between genes and the environment are highlighted by Bohman's (1995) findings (Table 2.3). The environment clearly seemed to have its most marked effect on those children who might have already been genetically predisposed towards criminal behaviour.

Adoption studies can be criticised on several grounds, e.g. adoptive families are often selected on the basis of their similarity to the original family, small sample sizes, contamination effects because the children have been adopted at

Table 2.3 Rates of criminal conviction in adopted children (Bohman, 1995)

	Adoptive parents had criminal record	Adoptive parents had no criminal record
Biological parents had criminal record	40%	12%
Biological parents had no criminal record	7%	3%

different ages (i.e. not necessarily at birth), etc. Nevertheless, the overall results of family studies, twin studies and adoption studies do suggest that heritable factors increase the likelihood of criminal behaviour. This is not to say that a life of crime is determined by heredity, but that an unfortunate mix of genetic and environmental factors may provide for some vulnerable individuals a higher probability of criminal behaviour.

Biochemistry

Some modern research points to a variety of biochemical factors which may be involved in criminal behaviour, such as allergies, environmental conditions (e.g. the presence of lead or radiation from artificial lighting) and diet (the use of food additives or deficiencies in vitamins or essential fatty acids). Hypoglycaemia (a state of low blood sugar) has also been suggested as a factor which may affect the functioning of the brain and contribute to antisocial behaviour (Virkkunen, 1986), as has low brain serotonin (Virkkunen et al., 1996). These attempts to explain crime are very difficult to put to the test because of methodological difficulties and are thus not without criticism (e.g. Gray, 1986). Moreover, it is difficult to see how they could possibly explain the diversity of criminal behaviour, nor its onset and cessation.

Neurology

One of the most controversial developments in the search for a biological basis for criminal behaviour is in the area of neuropsychology. When Charles Whitman killed 21 people during one day in 1966, shooting 16 of them from a Texas university tower, an autopsy subsequently revealed that he had a large brain tumour which might have been affecting the area of the brain responsible for controlling aggressive urges, the amygdala. Such conditions or serious brain injuries may cause dramatic personality and behavioural changes which can result in the acting out of violent impulses. In the 1970s, it was suggested that surgical intervention in such cases might be beneficial (Delgado, 1969) though ideological objections to such drastic and often irreversible action were legion. However, this did not prevent Mark and Ervin (1970) suggesting that brain dysfunction related to focal lesion was the cause of violence and should be treated by psychosurgery.

Another suggestion is that certain individuals, as a result of genetic predisposition or brain damage at birth, suffer from a cluster of symptoms which render them incapable of moral control and because of cortical underarousal, they are constantly seeking stimulation. The symptoms appear in early childhood and are subsumed in the term attention deficit hyperactivity disorder (ADHD). They include inappropriate degrees of inattention, impulsiveness, challenging behaviour and hyperactivity. The symptom cluster is also known as MBD or minimal brain dysfunction.

Moir and Jessel (1995) have suggested that this brain dysfunction can account for impulsive and seemingly irrational crimes, some of which involve violence. Moreover, they suggest that brain scans could identify the disorder in young children who are already showing behavioural problems and that treatment (Ritalin (a stimulant), biofeedback and parental training) could possibly prevent these children growing up to be seriously antisocial.

Another neurological disorder, developmental co-ordination disorder or dyspraxia, has also been seen as a possible contributor to antisocial behaviour. Sufferers will typically tend to be clumsy and accident prone, slow to reach milestones, unco-ordinated and unpopular because they do not fit in. If these symptoms are not recognised and addressed then the social consquences of ostracism may lead to seriously disruptive behaviour. When Madeline Portwood, an educational psychologist, assessed a group of young offenders she found that 61% of them were dyspraxic and yet none of them had been diagnosed as such (Portwood, 1996).

Whilst these theories may appear very attractive, a word of caution is needed. There are serious problems ahead if young children are to be labelled as potential criminals, and this kind of biological determinism often fails to take into account the complexity of criminal behaviour and how it is socially constructed.

PERSONALITY THEORIES

An interesting explanation of crime which attempts to combine biological and individual factors is that of Eysenck, developed over a period of 30 years (Eysenck, 1964; Eysenck and Gudjonsson, 1989). Whilst it is often presented as a general theory of crime, it actually attempts to explain why some people fail to follow rules and is probably more suited to explanations of psychopathic criminal behaviour.

Eysenck believed that certain personality types were inclined towards crime and these individuals could be described, within his own classification system, as neurotic extraverts who because of their genetic inheritance would be unlikely to learn the rules of social behaviour which most children acquire through the process of socialisation. These individuals would be outgoing sensation seekers, impulsively inclined towards the antisocial and undeterred by disapproval because of their resistance to social conditioning, but also characterised by high levels of anxiety and depression. At a later stage in the development of his theory, Eysenck introduced a third personality variable – psychoticism – which was marked by aggressive, cold and impersonal behaviour, and would also be associated with criminal tendencies.

Much research has been generated in attempts to verify Eysenck's prediction that criminals should achieve high scores in E (extraversion), N (neuroticism) and P (psychoticism). Whilst there has been some support for an association between P scores and criminal behaviour, there has been little support for the configuration of E, N and P scores. Moreover, there has been serious criticism of the authority with which this particular theory has been presented when there are misgivings about any evidence for its theoretical foundation (Trasler, 1987).

PSYCHOANALYTIC THEORIES

Freud himself had little to say about crime, but nonetheless his view of the small child as inherently asocial and motivated by pleasure-seeking and self-destructive impulses has been developed in order to explain adult criminal behaviour in terms of childhood legacy.

Normally children are socialised away from their instinctive impulses and in this process develop their superego or conscience. The success of this process does, however, depend on the relations between the child and its parents and if something goes awry the child may be left with a superego which does not function appropriately. A poorly developed superego will result in a lack of control over antisocial impulses, impulsiveness and a lack of guilt, leading to unacceptable behaviour. In contrast, an overdeveloped superego will produce a desire for punishment, unresolved guilt and a subsequent 'acting out' of behaviour which is likely to bring formal sanctions. Within these terms, juvenile crime is seen as a response to family dysfunction.

An alternative suggestion which remains within psychoanalytic theory is provided by the work of Bowlby who suggested that any disruption of the attachment bond between mother and child in the early years might lead to later deviance, mainly because of the consequent inability of the child to develop any meaningful relationships (Bowlby, 1944). This theory of 'maternal deprivation' led to serious concerns about the quality of mothering, especially in the case of 'latchkey' children in the 1950s. In spite of the potent critique provided by, amongst others, Rutter (1971a), it continued to hold currency in explanations of juvenile delinquency, though the focus did move more towards a failure to form attachments with caregivers because of inconsistencies in childcare, rather than the previously unhelpful emphasis on the role of the mother.

Whilst psychoanalytic explanations hold intuitive strength, their emphasis on all crime emanating from unconscious conflicts in childhood does not square with the idea that some criminal behaviour involves rational planning. Moreover, one of the essential assumptions of psychoanalytic theory is that females will have a less developed superego/conscience and will therefore commit more crime and this is simply not borne out by criminal statistics.

SOCIAL LEARNING THEORIES

Within a learning theory perspective, crime can be seen as a learned phenomenon in itself or as a failure of the socialisation process which endeavours to teach children how to behave. Children usually learn how to behave by acquiring an association of fear or anxiety with antisocial acts which prevents them from behaving similarly in the future. Trasler (1978) suggests that ineffective parental strategies or, in some individual cases, an inability to acquire conditioned fear responses may produce inadequately socialised children who then go on to offend. There are some similarities between this approach and that of Eysenck (1964) described earlier.

The view that criminal behaviour, in common with all other behaviour, is learned was most clearly expressed by Sutherland (1939) in his theory of 'differential association' which states that:

- criminal behaviour is learned;
- the learning is through association with other people;
- the main part of the learning takes place within close personal groups;
- the learning includes techniques to carry out certain crimes and also specific attitudes and motives conducive towards committing crime;
- the learning experiences – differential associations – will vary in frequency and importance for each individual;
- the process of learning criminal behaviour is no different from the learning of any other behaviour.

Sutherland was describing powerful social forces working on the individual, affecting skills, attitudes and beliefs, and within his theory there is not only a focus on the importance of socialisation in learning crime, but also on the importance of the value attached to that behaviour. Sutherland's theory was thus in many ways ahead of its time and represents a very definite move away from a view of criminals as in some way predisposed to a life of crime.

Sutherland also attempted an analysis of the gender differential in crime, arguing that boys are more likely to become delinquent than girls because they are less strictly controlled and are taught to be aggressive and active risk seekers, all characteristics likely to bring success in the criminal world and, indeed, in the world generally.

Subsequent developments of Sutherland's theory emphasise the role of rewards and punishments, whilst the acceptance of social learning theory allows for the consideration of learning by imitation or observation of others' behaviour and the importance of the social environment (Bandura and Walters, 1963). Peers who are held in high regard are very influential role models (Bandura, 1977), as are media stars, whilst rewards which might maintain certain behaviours take the form of status, self-esteem, financial incentives or just plain excitement. Akers (1990) goes even further, whilst sticking with Sutherland's original theory, and looks to the meanings of criminal behaviour for offenders, thereby adding a useful cognitive dimension. Thus offenders may take on beliefs about offences which allow them to maintain their behaviour. These beliefs may be positive, so car thieves might argue that joy riding is good fun and is the only way for them to access cars, whilst other beliefs allow the negative consequences of some offences to be 'neutralised'. Other offences are described as not having 'real' victims, e.g. shops, or as so trivial they don't really count.

SOCIAL FACTORS

It seems clear that social factors, such as family patterns, child-rearing strategies, school influences, peer pressure, poverty and unemployment, play an important part in the generation of criminal behaviour.

Family patterns

A range of studies has identified family patterns which may contribute to delinquency, and since a small number of families tend to account for a large proportion of offences (Farrington and West, 1990), it may be that the family has played a significant role. The identified patterns include:

- *family size* – if the family is large it may be that the children fail to receive individual attention and the poverty often associated with large families may result in parental stress, disorganisation and material deprivation (Farrington, 1991b). Exposure to delinquent siblings is another important factor and this is more likely in large families where there may be a 'contagion' effect, with children relying more on siblings than parents as models of appropriate behaviour (Offord, 1982);

- *family interaction* – parental conflict, indifference and low affection towards the children, poor communication and mistrust and a lack of shared leisure activities seem to be associated with the families of delinquents (Glueck and Glueck, 1956; Bandura and Walters, 1959; McCord, 1979);
- *family disruption* – the belief that 'broken homes' are associated with delinquency is borne out by several major studies, including McCord (1979), but the disruption may be the result of the quarrels and distress which may precede and follow divorce or separation rather than the event itself, since the loss of a parent through death does not seem to have the same effect (Rutter, 1971b).

Child-rearing strategies

Hoffman (1984) identifies three patterns of child rearing:

1 *power assertion* – which involves physical punishment, criticism and threats and material deprivation;
2 *love withdrawal* – which involves the withholding of affection as a sign of disapproval;
3 *induction* – which involves explaining to children what the consequences of their actions are for others.

The pattern most associated with the families of delinquents is that of power assertion (Bandura and Walters, 1959; McCord, 1979) where parents are observed to make frequent use of ridicule and physical punishment, which may lead to low self-esteem and higher aggression levels. Patterson (1982), however, points out that it is not necessarily the use of physical punishment *per se* which is damaging, but the use of severe and inconsistent punishment. He cites examples of parents who engage in prolonged and coercive exchanges with their children, making threats which are not then carried out, and he also describes families where parents work against each other in terms of discipline so that children are unsure of the likely response to their behaviour. It may be that families which are harsh but lax, extreme but erratic, contain the ingredients to engender antisocial behaviour both inside and outside the home.

School influences

It would seem that negative experiences at school are often linked with delinquency and that in many ways the school acts as a catalyst for pre-existing problems (Hirschi, 1969). Low academic achievement is a characteristic of many offenders but this is not to say that poor intellectual skills are the contributing factor. It may be that particular schools fail to engage with challenging pupils who then opt out of the school system, play truant and become involved in offending behaviour, failing to achieve the educational qualifications they may need to escape the spiral into a criminal career. Hargreaves (1980) identifies the features of a school which may contain high numbers of delinquent pupils and these include high staff turnover, low staff commitment, streaming, social disadvantage and a view of pupils as being of low ability.

It is clear from preschool enrichment programmes such as Operation Headstart in America that potential social and educational disadvantage can be tackled at an early age, but a recent study indicates that the particular type of preschool programme provided can reduce the chances of criminality developing (Schweinhart and Weikart, 1997). This study traced the progress of 68 children from poor backgrounds who were randomly placed in different preschool programmes at the age of four years. The conclusions of this study were that children from economically deprived backgrounds who are educated using traditional teaching methods are four times more likely to have a criminal record at age 23 than those who are given greater autonomy and are allowed to participate in the planning and review of their own learning activities. Interestingly, the children who were taught in a more structured learning setting initially demonstrated higher IQ scores than the children in the other programmes, but were not encouraged to develop problem-solving, decision-making or interpersonal skills. They subsequently developed more severe behavioural problems than their peers.

Peer pressure

The influence of peers is acknowledged as pivotal in the onset and maintenance of juvenile delinquency and reflects the shift of influence from parents to peers which naturally occurs during adolescence. Several studies show that delinquent acts are typically carried out in groups and co-offenders tend to live close to each other (Farrington and West, 1990). If individuals have experienced rejection at school and find little comfort at home, it should not perhaps be surprising that a peer group which offers opportunity and excitement is difficult to resist. Here at last is a social group in which approval can be gained and new attitudes and skills learned, albeit criminal ones.

It would be a mistake, however, to assume that peer pressure alone can explain all juvenile crime. Some offences are committed alone and when Agnew (1990) asked 1400 adolescents what had led them to engage in specific offences, he found that pressure from peers was only one factor, the others being a rational choice to obtain money or kicks or a result of anger or provocation.

Economic factors

An explanation for the massive rise in crime during the 1980s which was universally rejected by politicians was long-term and youth unemployment. Ironically, in 1751 Henry Fielding had suggested that unemployment and 'idleness' were the principal causes of crime and yet this common-sense explanation has tended to find little favour. In 1994 Benyan, after reviewing a number of studies of offenders, concluded that:

> "Youth unemployment leads to boredom, lack of status, alienation, different sub-cultural values, and, of course, lack of money ... Unemployment ... is one of the principal causes of the increased social disintegration, crime and disorder in Britain."

A year later Wells (1995) challenged Home Office research which disputed the link between unemployment and crime, pointing out that mass unemployment and the growth of single parenthood have resulted in poverty on a scale without precedent since the Second World War. A society 'with such large numbers of children in poverty runs the risk of massive delinquency'.

Farrington and West's (1990) longitudinal study also finds an association between crime and poverty, with their most persistent 32-year-old offenders having the least satisfactory employment record. The exact nature of the association between these factors and crime, however, is still not clear. If persistent offenders are often without a job it may simply be that they are less

FIGURE 2.3 *Is there a relationship between male educational under-achievement, unemployment and crime?*

employable because of fewer job-related skills. Supporters of sociological theories of crime, including those which focus on strain and anomie, suggest that groups who are economically disadvantaged will experience frustration and alienation from mainstream values and will therefore not feel obliged to abide by the rules of a society which does not appear to value them. Once again, this explanation of criminal behaviour has intuitive power, but the distribution of offences across all classes suggests that not all crime can be explained in these terms. Moreover, Campbell (1993), in her analysis of the 1991 U.K. riots, challenges the presumption that unemployment, because it is so threatening to male identity, leads to a crisis in masculinity, a moral decline and therefore more involvement in crime, and argues instead that forced unemployment can lead to a positive albeit criminalized reassertion of masculinity.

AGE, GENDER, ETHNICITY, AND MENTAL STATE

It will have become apparent from the previous accounts of crime theories that some factors tend to be taken for granted, or they are ignored or are assumed to relate only to specific types of offence, and yet explanations of crime cannot be complete without some consideration of these factors.

Age

Traditionally, concerns are expressed about the amount of juvenile crime, and research certainly confirms high rates of offending among adolescents. Delinquency appears to reach a peak at about 16–17 years and then seems to decline in the early 20s (Farrington, 1991b). Whilst the estimated rate of crime amongst adolescents is high – about 80% – the majority of these offences are minor, though violent crime tends to peak rather later than property offences. Concern about 'youth crime', however, can produce extreme reactions in politicians so, for example, we have Jack Straw (Home Secretary) announcing new strategies to increase parental responsibility for their children's criminal behaviour by imposing fines on the parents and also to introduce evening curfews designed to keep children off the streets (September 1997).

Attempts to account for the prevalence of juvenile crime point to biological and social factors such as increasing strength and independence, together with the emotional ambivalence of adolescence and a tendency towards experimentation in the search for identity. However, serious crimes committed by juveniles, such as murder, tend to generate explanations using concepts such as 'evil' as if children are in some ways naturally innocent and exempt from the destructive impulses which we all feel at some time. Clearly, when these rare offences occur they are extremely disturbing but the evidence would suggest that juveniles who do commit serious crimes tend to be damaged individuals who have unusual family backgrounds characterised by violence and mental illness, a history of abuse and a range of neuropsychological vulnerabilities (Bailey, 1996).

Gender

Probably the most significant feature of both recorded and self-reported crime is that more males than females commit offences, particularly violent crimes, in spite of claims that women are becoming more violent in the 1990s (Kirsta, 1994) or that, because of their inherent deviousness, they have always been more criminal but have simply been able to conceal it (Pollak, 1950). There have also been suggestions that the criminal justice system is more 'chivalrous' towards females and thus the gender difference is not as large as would appear from relying on official figures (Hedderman and Hough, 1994), but self-report studies bear out the differential (Hindelang, 1979).

Most explanations of the gender gap draw on accepted differences between males and females, such as dominance, aggression, physique and nurturance, whilst others point to female socialisation which tends to be characterised by greater parental supervision, more stress on conformity and therefore fewer opportunities for crime. Those females who do deviate are often viewed as having not only rejected society's rules but the traditional female role too and are described as showing 'double deviance' and risking 'double jeopardy' (Heidensohn, 1985). In fact, Lombroso and Ferrero (1895) suggested that criminal women were rare but those who had not been 'neutralised by maternity' were likely to become even worse criminals than men:

"... as a double exception the criminal woman is consequently a monster".

Criminology has notoriously ignored the fact of gender, preferring to offer universal theories of crime based on empirical work which has relied only on male subjects. As Cain (1989) points out:

"Men as males have not been the objects of the criminological gaze. Yet the most consistent and dramatic findings from Lombroso to post-modern criminology is not that most criminals are working-class ... but that most criminals are, and always have been, men." (p.4)

It was not until the 1970s that feminist criminologists such as Heidensohn (1968) and Smart (1977) pointed out this gross oversight. Since then, there have been significant developments in the area, with calls to 'feminise' socialisation in an attempt to reduce crime and to ascertain why females tend to conform rather than searching for why males offend (Heidensohn, 1995);

challenges to criminology to resist feminism at the cost of embracing conservatism (Smart, 1990); and suggestions that 'masculinity' itself should be examined more closely in order to understand why so many young men commit offences and are also the victims of crime (Messerschmidt, 1993; Newburn and Stanko, 1994; Walklate, 1995).

Rather than simply examining female crime as if it were somehow different and in so doing accepting a marginalised status within criminology which allows the discipline's gender blindness to be condoned and continued, it is suggested that a gendered analysis of crime is the only way forward. Messerschmidt (1993) provides an astute analysis of gender and crime, highlighting the particular aspects of masculinity, for example the collective processes of male youth groups and the 'public' arena in which masculine rituals are played out, as the major contributory factors to the predominance of male crime. As Oakley (1972) said 21 years earlier:

> "Criminality and masculinity are linked because the sort of acts associated with each have much in common. The demonstration of physical strength, a certain kind of aggressiveness, visible and external proof of achievement, whether legal or illegal – these are facets of the ideal male personality and also much of criminal behaviour... Thus, the dividing line between what is masculine and what is criminal may at times be a thin one." (p.72)

The potential for 'gendered' analyses of specific crimes is also demonstrated in, for instance, an examination of the murder of two-year-old James Bulger in 1993 where the motives of the killers are analysed within the context of a socially constructed masculinity (Jackson,1995). This presents as a contrast to the more traditional analysis provided by, for example, Smith (1995) where the troubled childhood backgrounds of the two juvenile killers are explored.

Ethnicity

There is often an assumption that black people, particularly young black men, are disproportionately involved in crime and this is often revealed in media coverage of crime. Official data and self-report studies would bear this out, in addition to the disproportionate likelihood of black people also being the victims of crime. However, as Feldman (1993) points out, the picture is not as clearcut as the official data suggest, so in relation to some crime the actual number of offences committed by blacks and whites is quite similar. The major difference is that significantly more blacks are likely to commit at least one offence, possibly casual, whereas individual whites are more likely to be 'high-rate offenders'. Additionally, more blacks are likely to be arrested and if convicted, sent to prison, though these findings relate to Afro-Caribbeans and not to Asians. Why should this be so and why should it lead to such a distorted view of black crime overall?

In Britain and America a higher proportion of people of Afro-Caribbean and black African origin are in prison than other ethnic groups. Is this because different ethnic groups are treated unequally in the criminal justice system or are rates of crime higher amongst certain ethnic minority groups? The research evidence suggests that black people are indeed treated unequally by criminal justice processes, but the differential in imprisonment rates is actually the result of higher crime rates among black people (Wilbanks, 1987). Reiner (1993) argues that methodological flaws beset any attempt to provide rational explanations of the differences in crime rates and imprisonment rates and that it is still possible to argue that black crime is the result of white racism.

Whilst some have suggested that blacks are more likely to be involved in crime because of genetic inferiority (Rushton, 1990), it is clear that a more likely explanation lies in the subculture of violence and social disadvantage which many black people share and the discriminatory aspects of the criminal justice system from which they suffer. Ethnic minorities represent 10.3% of the English prison population, compared with 6.93% of the population aged 16–24 years, and 5.5% of the total population (Home Office, 1991), and police stop-and-search powers have been shown to be used disproportionately against young black males (NACRO, 1997). Racial discrimination undoubtedly limits the educational and occupational opportunities available to ethnic minorities and there are biases operating in the legal processing of offenders which work against black people and which appear to be remarkably resistant to intervention.

Mental state

Not all offenders are mentally disordered and not all those who suffer mental disorder commit crimes, but there is a group of offenders who display mental disorder at the time of their offending or subsequently during a sentence of imprisonment and this group, though small, tends to attract considerable attention. This may reflect the unease and fear which people feel when dealing with those suffering from mental illness or learning disabilities and produces a debate over whether offenders in this category are 'mad, bad or merely sad' (Prins, 1994).

Criminal behaviour in psychiatric populations tends to be higher than in the general population (Prins, 1986), especially in relation to more serious offences, but this finding may reflect a high rate of offending by a small number of offenders within the inpatient psychiatric population which in itself is not necessarily representative. Similarly, many imprisoned offenders display evidence of mental disorder (e.g. Taylor, 1986), with depression and personality disorder being the most common. However, this may be the result of more mentally disordered offenders being apprehended because of easier detection or, more significantly, as a consequence of imprisonment rather than a cause. Prisons are not particularly healthy institutions and numerous studies have demonstrated their contribution to mental illness (Heather, 1977; Taylor, 1986).

The types of mental disorder most often associated with crime are schizophrenia, depression, psychopathy and mental handicap or learning disabilities. It would seem that the incidence of schizophrenia in the prison population is not dissimilar to that in the general population except in the case of violent offences where the incidence is higher (Taylor, 1986). This may be the result of the paranoid ideation associated with some types of schizophrenia but may also be partly attributable to environmental factors also associated with schizophrenia – homelessness, for example, or failure to take medication. Depression has also been associated with specific offences, including the murder of relatives (Lawson, 1984), though the exact nature of the association is as yet unclear.

Mental handicap or learning disability is generally taken to indicate an IQ in the region of 70 or below and the percentage of learning-disabled prisoners tends to be between 2% and 2.5%, close to the incidence of learning disability in the general population (Denkowski and Denkowski, 1985). In view of the greater likelihood of learning-disabled individuals being apprehended, it is perhaps surprising that they do not appear in higher proportions amongst offender groups.

Psychopathic disorder is not considered amenable to conventional psychiatric treatment and individuals assessed as suffering from psychopathy and who have offended are likely to be sent to prison rather than hospital if they are convicted. These individuals are persistent and serious offenders who present particular problems in terms of management within the prison system and are very likely to continue offending on release. Psychopaths are distinguished by a lack of remorse for their offences, egocentricity, impulsivity, an inability to form close relationships and a failure to learn from experience (Cleckley, 1976). Paradoxically, they can also be superficially charming and some are able for short periods to lead an apparently 'normal' life, though this may involve considerable deception of others. This, together with their lack of response to intervention, means that they can be very dangerous.

Offenders who suffer from mental disorder pose special problems for the criminal justice system and also for psychologists working within this system (Howells and Hollin, 1994). As was mentioned in Chapter 1, an offender must be considered capable of criminal intent before prosecution can occur and just how capable can mentally disordered individuals be? This dilemma was recognised in the 1959 Mental Health Act (amended in 1983) which allowed for mentally disordered offenders to be treated in hospitals rather than being sent to prison. But the decision about whether a mental disorder exists can still be fiercely argued in court, as was evident in the trial of Peter Sutcliffe (the 'Yorkshire Ripper') when the debate over whether he was 'mad', 'bad' or simply 'male' ensued (Smith, 1989). Sutcliffe was initially sent to prison, but three years later was transferred to a Special Hospital for psychiatric treatment.

CONCLUSION

So, after consideration of all these theories, are we any wiser about the causes of crime? There are many types of crime and many types of offender. Some experiences are shared, whilst others are very individual. Clearly, we all have a genetic inheritance or genetic potential, but in order for that potential to be released there have to be some environmental triggers. It also seems clear that the roots of antisocial behaviour lie in early childhood and that certain events in childhood can increase an individual's psychological vulnerability. These would include:

- insecure attachment;
- a weak sense of self;
- a dysfunctional family;
- coercive or indifferent parenting;
- physical, sexual or emotional abuse or neglect;
- the death of a parent;
- low family income;
- an acrimonious separation or divorce;
- low academic achievement.

However, these events can occur and be subsequently handled with enough sensitivity to ensure that children are not damaged by them, so in addition there is also a matching element between the child and its family environment, with a mismatch increasing the child's vulnerability. Moreover, the dramatic rise in offending behaviour at adolescence and its subsequent decline in early adulthood suggests that social factors must be operating too.

Plomin (1990,1994) has convincingly argued that genetics alone cannot explain adult behaviour and focuses much more on the way genes interact with the environment. He further suggests that the environment cannot be taken as a constant and that the 'non-shared environment' is a crucial factor in determining adult outcomes for children in the same family, i.e. what most affects children are the things they do not share with their siblings, their own unique individual experiences. Parents tend to think they raise their children in the same way but families alter over time, sometimes quite significantly, e.g. chronic illness, unemployment, high mobility, divorce, etc., and children's experiences vary too, e.g. having an influential teacher, developing a new interest, losing a friend, etc. Plomin suggests that it is these differences and the way they interact with genetic make-up which produce personality differences.

It seems that a complex combination of biological, psychological and social factors needs to be taken into account when trying to understand criminal behaviour, but as Wilson and Herrnstein (1985) point out:

> "Crime is an activity disproportionately carried out by young men living in large cities. There are old criminals, and female ones, and rural and small town ones, but to a much greater degree than would be expected by chance, criminals are young urban males." (p.26)

The fact that 81% of all offenders are male (Home Office, 1994) and that this pattern is repeated internationally inevitably begs the question that many criminologists have hitherto avoided asking – what is it about the cultural history and social construction of *masculinity* which ensures that so many young males become involved in crime? One of the most useful analyses of masculinity in relation to crime has come from theorists using the concepts of psychoanalysis and object relations theory in an attempt to place psychic processes within a social context. Thus, Jefferson (1996) analyses the life story of Mike Tyson, who came from a traditionally deprived background, became phenomenally successful as a boxer, was convicted as a rapist, served a sentence of imprisonment and managed to return to boxing success only to ruin his reputation by an horrific assault on his opponent in the ring, during which he almost severed the man's ear. Jefferson suggests that Tyson's need to adopt a 'tough guy' discourse to match his appearance in order to succeed involved learning to enjoy being 'bad' and that the subsequent psychological confusion led to inevitable problems which were impossible to contain. By extension, he argues that if boys learn how 'good' it can be to be 'bad' and how displacing fears of inadequacy about achieving an impossible masculinity onto more vulnerable others can not only reduce the fears but gain them status, male involvement in crime begins to become more understandable.

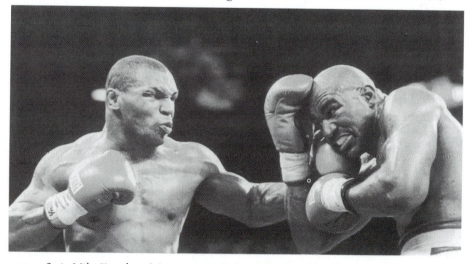

FIGURE 2.4 *Mike Tyson's inability to control his aggression has caused serious problems, but does not appear to have reduced his popularity*

chapter three

SERIAL MURDER

CHAPTER OVERVIEW

This chapter examines one of the most serious types of violent crime and one which has attracted considerable attention from the media – serial murder. The prevalence of this crime and attempts to explain it will be discussed, alongside the development of offender typologies and the concept of profiling. A historical account of serial murder is provided, with case studies to illustrate the distinguishing features which have allowed theoretical analyses to be developed.

INTRODUCTION

Murder is the intentional killing of another person and is not a common crime. Most murders occur in large cities but there are wide variations between countries, with the highest rates being found in Central America. The USA has the highest rate among industrialised nations, but that rate varies considerably between states. Thus, whilst in 1984 Colombia had a murder rate of 37.4 per 100,000 population, the USA had 8.5, Australia had 1.9 and England and Wales had 0.7. The US rate translates into about 20,000 murders per annum (with almost 2000 of those murders occurring in New York in 1993, though there have been decreases in subsequent years), whilst in England and Wales there were 729 murders during the period 1994–95, 61 more than during 1993–94.

One of the earliest analyses of murder was carried out by Wolfgang (1958) who studied 588 murders committed in Philadelphia between 1948 and 1952. He found that in 87% of these cases the offender and victim knew each other and in 37% of the cases, the killing followed a relatively trivial event such as a threat, an insult or an argument. The majority of murderers were male (82%), as were victims (76%), one or both of whom had been drinking (66%), and stabbing was the most common means of death. The typical scenario was that of acquaintances who had argued after drinking and a social psychological explanation seemed possible, which involved misattribution, loss of face, threats, refusal to comply, the encouragement of onlookers and brief but fatal violence (Luckenbill, 1977).

There are other types of killer, though, whose behaviour merits a different analysis altogether. The mass murderer and the serial killer seem to be involved in a quite different enterprise. The mass murderer kills several victims within a few moments or hours, often using a weapon in a public place, usually harbouring some kind of grudge and with little apparent concern about capture. Whilst his behaviour may not appear rational to the observer, the actions of the mass murderer may provide a brief moment of control in a life which is otherwise marked by failure, rejection and frustration. Hickey (1991) suggests that:

> "... for many (of these) killers the best way to lash out against a cold, forbidding society is to destroy its children. Gunning down children on a schoolyard not only provides the needed sense of power and control but is also a way of wreaking vengeance where it hurts the community the most." (p.5)

The most memorable incident of this nature was the Dunblane massacre of 16 primary school children and their teacher by Thomas Hamilton in March 1996. Hamilton was a misfit with inappropriate interests in young boys and also in guns. His attempts to run a range of youth clubs were continuously thwarted by parents who were disturbed by the nature of his activities and alerted the authorities. When Hamilton's paranoia could no longer be contained he walked into the local primary school shortly after morning registration and within a matter of minutes, he had killed 17 people and then himself.

In contrast, the serial killer will typically make strenuous efforts to avoid capture in order to continue his murderous behaviour. Usually male, he kills over a period of time, with an element of planning, and his victims are typically tortured or sexually assaulted before being murdered. The serial killer will have more than three victims, usually strangers, and there will be some commonality between his victims in terms of status, gender or location and also the mode of their death.

These two types of killer tend to be viewed rather differently. The mass murderer is often seen as suffering from mental illness and an explanation of his behaviour is couched in terms of temporary insanity. He is seen as very different from the rest of us. When Levin and Fox (1985) reviewed the literature relating to mass murderers they noted the high prevalence of childhood trauma, such as sexual abuse, brutal beatings and abandonment, in the backgrounds of such individuals. The serial killer, however, produces considerably more discomfort because accounts of serial killers tend to reveal the possibility that some personalities are able to lead quite 'normal' lives yet at the same time indulge in the most horrendous crimes. Examples would include the good-looking and charming Ted Bundy who, whilst working for the Seattle

Crime Commission, wrote a leaflet for women on rape prevention, and yet in 1989 was executed for the murder of at least 20 young women or the building contractor esteemed in the local community for his charity work, John Wayne Gacy, who in his spare time tortured and killed 29 young men and buried them under his home. When we read about people like this who are not considered to be insane but who seem to regard harming others as 'recreation', then a dreadful fear is generated about the very notions of community, safety, trust and decency.

HISTORICAL ACCOUNTS

Serial murder may appear to be a phenomenon of the late 20th century but there are notable examples of similar events in previous centuries, including:

- Gilles de Rais (born in 1404), at one time an extremely wealthy Frenchman, who is then said to have made a pact with the Devil which resulted in him killing several hundred young children, drinking their blood and engaging in necrophilia;
- Peter Stubb (born in 16th-century Germany), who ate his own son and murdered 13 young children and two pregnant women, engaging in sexual torture and cannibalism;
- Jack the Ripper who, in 1888, killed and disembowelled five London prostitutes and was never caught.

During the early part of the 20th century several other horrific multiple murders came to light, including Karl Denke, a German who was arrested in 1924 and admitted having eaten nothing but human flesh for the previous three years. It was not until the late 1940s, however, that the concept of murder committed without any motive became more apparent, alongside the notion of murderers perhaps killing to obtain some sense of meaning and status within a society containing more and more alienated individuals (Wilson and Seaman, 1990).

PREVALENCE

There are varying estimates of the extent of serial murder, but a report by the United States Department of Justice (1983) suggested that during the 1970s and early 1980s there were about 35 serial killers active in the USA, whilst Holmes and DeBurger (1988) suggest that as many as 3500–5000 people are killed by serial murderers each year in the USA. This said, the fear of becoming a victim of a serial killer is undoubtedly out of all proportion to the actual risk, which Hickey (1991) estimates as very low on the basis of existing data which indicates that the serial murder rate is 0.2 per 100,000 population.

The rapid increase in this type of crime in the USA, however, is notable. Between 1950 and 1970 in America there were only two cases in which an individual was responsible for ten or more murders over a period of time, whereas since 1970 there have been over 40 similar cases (Jenkins, 1988).

The picture in the UK is rather different. Gresswell and Hollin (1994) estimate that there are probably up to four serial killers active at any one time, and that between 1982 and 1991 there were 196 victims of multiple murder in England and Wales. Whilst there does not appear to have been an increase in this type of crime to parallel the US experience, Jenkins (1988) notes that serial murder accounted for 1.7% of all English murders during the period 1940–85, with a significantly higher proportion of 3.2% in the period 1973–83 (though this may be accounted for by the activities of two particular killers, Peter Sutcliffe who murdered 13 women and Dennis Nilsen who was responsible for 15 deaths). Significantly, however, in 1997 a Serious Crime Bureau was set up by the police in order to ascertain whether there are any links between some 200 unsolved murders of women in the past ten years. An earlier analysis of these crimes, Operation Enigma, suggested that some of the murders were connected and could be the work of British serial killers. The Serious Crime Bureau will work under the auspices of the National Crime Faculty and will involve police officers and civilians in a well-funded operation to collect data, analyse common features of offences and work closely with all forces investigating these crimes.

SERIAL MURDER TYPOLOGIES

Whilst serial murder constitutes only 1–2% of all homicides, researchers have developed typologies to categorise these offenders on the basis of the motives reported to have influenced their behaviour. These motivational taxonomies can help us to understand why certain offenders kill and may help identify patterns in a particular offender's behaviour. Thus, Holmes and DeBurger (1988) identify four types of serial killer:

1 the *visionary* type – those who claim they kill in response to the commands of voices or visions and are often considered to be suffering from psychosis;
2 the *mission-oriented* type – those who fervently believe their mission in life is to remove certain groups of people from the community. These groups may be very broad and could include the elderly, children, a particular ethnic group or prostitutes;

3 the *hedonistic* type – those who clearly derive satisfaction from murder, which may include financial benefits stolen from the victims. A subcategory of this type is the 'lust murderer' whose motives are sexual and sadism is an integral part of the pattern of behaviour;

4 the *power/control-oriented* type – those whose behaviour may have a sexual component but whose primary motive is the complete control of another person to the point of death.

The Federal Bureau of Investigation has extensive access to serial killers apprehended in the USA and a well-known study conducted by three of its agents, Ressler, Burgess and Douglas (1988), identified two types of serial killer – 'organised' and 'disorganised'. This division was based on information gathered from the scenes of crime and an examination of the nature of the crime itself, as well as data from interviewing offenders, and it allowed FBI agents to construct profiles of offenders. Thus, an 'organised' murderer would be profiled as being socially competent and intelligent, someone who plans their murders and tends to target strangers, more likely to use restraints, have sex with the victim before death and use a vehicle; whereas the 'disorganised' offender would be viewed as a socially immature individual who may know his victims and who kills spontaneously with unexpected violence, leaving a haphazard crime scene (Table 3.1).

Hickey (1986) points to three types of serial killer on the basis of mobility:

1 travelling serial killers, who cross states murdering their victims and often elude capture in this way;

2 local serial killers, who choose their victims from their home state;

3 serial killers who kill in their homes or places of work.

He believes that the media portrayal of the travelling serial killer is misleading since his data suggest that the majority of serial killers operate locally, with only 32–35% of all victims being murdered by killers who travel extensively.

Each new typology offers extra information which can be used to explore the motivation and aetiology of serial murder and whilst there may be overlaps and some typologies are more useful for some purposes than others, it is clear that the more information which is generated and categorised, the nearer we may be to understanding the nature of these crimes.

THEORIES TO EXPLAIN SERIAL MURDER

There have been many attempts to explain the motivation of serial killers, often by looking at their childhood history. Burgess et al. (1986) and Liebert (1985) noted that the backgrounds of sexually motivated multiple murderers were marked by a failure of empathic bonding and attachment between the

Table 3.1 Organised and disorganised murderers (Ressler *et al.*, 1988)

Characteristics	Crime scene	Postoffence
Organised		
Good intelligence	Offence planned	May return to crime scene
Social competence	Victim a targeted stranger	Anticipates questioning
Skilled employment	Personalises victim	May move body
Sexually competent	Controlled conversation	
High birth order	Crime scene reflects control	
Father's work stable	Demands submissive victim	
Inconsistent childhood discipline	Uses restraints	
Controlled mood during crime	Aggressive acts prior to death	
Use of alcohol with crime	Body hidden	
Precipitative stress	Weapon or evidence absent	
Living with partner	Transports victim or body	
Mobility		
Follows crime in media		
Disorganised murderer		
Average intelligence	Spontaneous offence	No interest in media
Socially immature	Victim or location known	No change to lifestyle
Poor work history	Depersonalises victim	
Sexually inhibited	Minimal conversation	
Father's work unstable	Crime scene sloppy	
Harsh discipline in childhood	Sudden violence to victim	
Anxious mood during crime	Minimum use of restraints	
Minimal use of alcohol	Sexual acts after death	
Minimal situational stress	Body left in view	
Living alone	Evidence/weapon often present	
Lives/works near crime scene		

child and its carer which resulted in the child becoming emotionally detached (e.g. Jeffrey Dahmer), whilst McDonald (1963) identified early childhood experiences including enuresis, firesetting, and torturing animals in the backgrounds of sadistic multiple killers (e.g. Ian Brady). In contrast, Jenkins (1988) found that six of the 12 English serial killers he studied had seemingly normal and respectable childhoods. Certainly, it would seem that the background factors described by Burgess et al. (1986) and others are indicative of the likely development of antisocial behaviours, but in themselves are not a sufficient explanation of serial murder. Thus, although Stone (1994) found in his study of 42 serial murderers that their childhood backgrounds typically featured severe abuse and neglect, one-third of them had not suffered abuse as children. Whilst violent adults seem often to have suffered child abuse, only a small proportion of abused children go on to become violent offenders, leaving unanswered questions about motivation.

There has also been a tendency to assume that those who commit random serial murder must be suffering from some form of mental illness, though in fact most people who are mentally ill are more likely to harm themselves than others. Thus, when Henn et al. (1976) examined the psychiatric assessments of 2000 people arrested for homicide between 1964 and 1973, only 1% of them were considered to be psychotic.

One avenue for research relating mental illness to serial murder has been that of dissociative disorders, such as multiple personality disorder, where an individual responds to unbearable stressful experiences such as child abuse by 'splitting off' from their personality and adopting alternative personalities, some of whom can cope with everyday life. A disturbing example was that of Sybil, whose life is documented by Schreiber (1973). Whilst these cases are fascinating, they are extremely rare. However, a notorious serial killer, Kenneth Bianchi (also known as one of the Hillside Stranglers), claimed to be suffering from multiple personality disorder and wanted to use this as his defence. He was interviewed under hypnosis and revealed another personality, 'Steve Walker', who came across as a cold and vicious individual who was responsible for the callous murder of 12 young women. By contrast, Kenneth Bianchi presented himself as a kind, loving husband and father who had been abused by his mother. There were suspicions that Bianchi might be faking this disorder and so Dr Martin Orme was asked to interview him. At the start of the interview, Dr Orme mentioned casually to Bianchi that in genuine cases of multiple personality disorder there were always more than two personalities and within minutes of being hypnotised, a third personality emerged. Subsequent investigations revealed that 'Steve Walker' was in fact a student from whom Bianchi had stolen academic certificates which he had then used to set up a counselling practice, sharing office space with a psychologist. Bianchi subsequently dropped his defence of insanity and pleaded guilty.

The most frequent psychiatric label attached to serial killers tends to be that of psychopathy. Henderson (1939) describes psychopaths as:

> "... those ... who conform to a certain intellectual standard, sometimes high, sometimes approaching the realm of defect ... who throughout their lives ... have exhibited disorders of conduct of an antisocial or asocial nature ... who ... have proved difficult to influence by methods of social, penal, and medical care and treatment and for whom we have no adequate provision of a preventive or curative nature. The inadequacy or deviation or failure to adjust to ordinary social life is not a mere wilfulness or badness which can be threatened or thrashed out of the individual so involved, but constitutes a true illness for which we have no specific explanation." (p.19)

Whilst our understanding of psychopathy has become more sophisticated since 1939, especially as the result of the work of Cleckley (1976), Meloy

(1988) and Hare (1991), it is fair to say that the mysteries remain. Psychopaths are generally viewed as aggressive, irresponsible, charismatic, hedonistic individuals who experience no remorse for their actions and appear not to learn from experience. Outwardly there may appear to be nothing abnormal about them, which is what makes them so dangerous, but their major interest is in controlling others and if this control is challenged they may react violently. Attempts to discover a genetic or biological explanation for psychopathy in terms of physiological functioning affecting learning have unfortunately produced inconsistent findings (Blackburn, 1983; Raine, 1989). Recent psychological research has tried to determine aspects of the psychopathic personality and suggests that psychopaths are less responsive to facial cues of distress than control groups (Blair et al., 1997) and more likely to use deception, whatever the context (Seto et al.,1997).

It is easy to see why many serial killers would seem to fit the label of a psychopath, especially those whose murders have a component of sexual sadism. For these individuals killing is not enough, they need also to torture and mutilate their victims. Sexual torture becomes the method by which the offender can degrade, humiliate and subjugate his victim, eventually gaining ultimate control.

Sexual sadism is one of the paraphilias identified in the *Diagnostic and Statistical Manual IV* (American Psychiatric Association, 1995), the manual used by clinical practitioners to assess patients. It is described as:

> "acts in which psychological or physical suffering of the victim is sexually exciting, including domination or torture."

Paraphilias are recurrent and intense sexual urges combined with arousing fantasies which were characterised by 19th-century psychiatrists as underlying 'unnatural sexual acts' or 'perversions'. They include necrophilia (sex with corpses), zoophilia (sex with animals) and paedophilia (sex with children) and often exist in multiples. Where an offender displays behaviour typically associated with one paraphilia, there may well be evidence of other paraphilias too.

The sadistic murderer has been described by Brittain (1970) as narcissistic and egocentric, an individual who feels inferior, especially sexually, and finds it difficult to relate to women. A desire for power over others is the main feature and offending is likely to follow a blow to the individual's self-esteem. Fantasy and offence planning enable him to feel superior and he is likely to use excessive force, becoming aroused by the victim's fear. Whilst some psychoanalytic accounts link sexual sadism with fixation at psychosexual stages, so that, for instance, degradation of female victims implies reaction formation against incestuous desires and buggery would indicate anal fixation (Kline, 1987), more comprehensive explanations draw on early experience of sexual abuse followed by a cycle of dysfunctional coping (Burgess et al., 1986).

Psychoanalytic explanations of serial murder focus on the dysfunctional nature of a parent–child relationship which may leave the child fixated at an immature stage of development (Gallagher, 1987). One case which lends itself to this type of analysis is that of Ed Kemper who had a very difficult relationship with his domineering mother which left him with feelings of ambivalence and frustration. At the age of 15 he killed both his grandparents but after a few years of treatment he was released into his mother's care. He subsequently attended regular sessions with his parole officer and his psychiatrist, both of whom felt he was making progress, but at the same time he was murdering female hitchhikers, dismembering them and saving various body parts, some of which he cooked. He eventually killed and decapitated his mother and then had sex with her corpse. Kemper claimed that this act 'liberated' him so that he no longer felt compelled to kill others.

Abrahamsen (1973), another psychoanalytic theorist, emphasises the sexual nature of many childhood traumas, which can then surface in the form of murder which has violent sexual components, including torture. Sex is used as a vehicle to gain control over victims by inflicting pain and suffering, which may echo the killer's own childhood experience of being helpless but restore a sense of power. It is tempting to apply this type of analysis to the offences of Frederick West who, together with his wife Rosemary, killed at least 12 young women, including his first wife and two of his own daughters, over a period of 20 years. The manner of his victims' deaths was horrific,

FIGURE 3.1 *Frederick and Rosemary West who were responsible for the horrific torture and murder of at least twelve young women between 1967 and 1992. Frederick West committed suicide in 1995, and Rosemary West is unlikely ever to be released from prison*

involving sexual torture and sadism, and yet to the community in which he lived West was a crude yet apparently 'normal' family man (Wansell, 1996). Both West and his wife, Rosemary, are said to have suffered serious sexual and emotional abuse as children.

Interestingly, Ressler et al. (1988) distance themselves from a psychoanalytic analysis of serial murder, preferring to focus on cognitive processes, and yet they describe similar developments such as negative life experiences giving rise to aggressive and possibly sexualised fantasies which restore a sense of control. When they interviewed 36 convicted sex murderers held in American prisons, 25 of whom were serial killers, between 1979 and 1983, they found that:

- 42% said they had been sexually abused as children, 32% as adolescents;
- 70% said they felt 'sexually incompetent' and relied heavily on visual stimuli such as pornography.

Similarly, Hazelwood and Warren (1995) found that in their study of 41 serial rapists, 76% of them said they had been sexually abused as children.

The role of fantasy appears in several theories which attempt to explain serial murder. Prentky et al. (1989) compared 25 serial sexual murderers with 17 single sexual murderers and found that for 86% of the multiple killers, fantasy preceded their offending, compared to 23% of the single murderers. Prentky et al. (1989) also found that fantasy rehearsal in relation to the planning and execution of offences was correlated with the degree of organisation of the crime. Gresswell and Hollin (1997) describe fantasy as an addictive process adopted by serial murderers in their attempts to recreate 'peak' experiences, to recapture the original euphoria they experienced when they killed their victims. Additionally, they use fantasy to 'try out' new features in anticipation of future offences. This theory of multiple murder as an addictive pattern of behaviour, not dissimilar to other addictions, is based on an analysis of every case of multiple murder recorded in England between 1982 and 1991 and interviews with 20 imprisoned perpetrators. It represents an impressive step forward in terms of theoretical analysis.

Hickey (1991) suggests a trauma control model to explain serial murder which incorporates the role of fantasy as a facilitator. The primary event in the process of becoming a serial killer is a series of destabilising traumas, which might include parental death, divorce, corporal punishment or sexual abuse, associated with an inability to cope with the stress of those events and a subsequent feeling of rejection which may be exacerbated by failure at school and isolation. The individual then deals with these feelings of inadequacy and self-doubt within a destructive framework, which might involve damaging objects, animals or other people, but begins to disassociate himself from the feelings and the behaviour by constructing a mask of self-control in a desperate attempt to regain control.

At some point in this process, Hickey (1991) suggests that the individual begins to make use of facilitators, such as alcohol, drugs or pornography, in order to decrease his inhibitions and assist in the generation of fantasies. The development of increasingly violent fantasies is seen as pivotal in this analysis as the individual considers acting out his fantasy. Ressler et al. (1988) concluded that 'sexual murder is based on fantasy' but the reality can never quite match the fantasy and so the cycle continues with each new murder generating new fantasies. During the actual offence the individual may revisit the trauma which he has endeavoured to protect himself from, the victim becoming the target for revenge, and he may experience some sense of relief as he regains a sense of control. The element of control may actually be more important than the death of the victim. However, this relief is essentially temporary and once the killer begins to experience feelings of failure or rejection again, he may seek new victims. Hickey (1991) describes this cycle of behaviour in his trauma control model,

> "Fantasies, possibly fueled by pornography or alcohol, reinforced by 'routine' traumatisations of day-to-day living, keep the serial killer caught up in a self-perpetuating cycle of violence ... For the killer, the cycle becomes a never-ending pursuit of control over one's own life through the total domination and destruction of others' lives." (p.73)

LUST MURDER

It has been suggested that traditional mainstream explanations of serial murder focus on the individual rather than placing the crime in a social context, alongside an unhelpful emphasis on pathology (Cameron and Frazer, 1987). A feminist analysis of serial murder emphasises the notorious absence from most explanations of any acknowledgement of the fact that the vast majority of sexual killers are male and their victims female and that the very process of male socialisation may be seen as contributing to the development of sexual sadism and possibly murder. Cameron and Frazer (1987) offer 'transcendence' – the desire to achieve immortality through some extraordinary act – as the explanation for male predominance in sexual murder, because it is the very essence of masculinity. Within this perspective serial sex killers are seen as a product of masculine culture, albeit exaggerated and hopefully untypical examples:

> "To understand why a boy grows up seeing women as objects of hatred and conflating aggression and masculine sexuality, it is necessary to go beyond his immediate environment, concentrating on the meanings and concepts cherished by society which inevitably permeate all our lives." (Cameron and Frazer, 1987)

Smith (1989) suggests that the case of Peter Sutcliffe symbolised a sea-change in the analysis of serial murder. Although there were claims that Sutcliffe, who murdered 13 women in the north of England between 1975 and 1981, was suffering from paranoid schizophrenia, it was clear that he had been able to live an apparently normal life, working as a lorry driver, married and part of a local community which did not regard him as a psychiatric case. No longer could sex killers be regarded as obviously different – here was 'somebody's husband, somebody's son' (Burns, 1985). A feminist analysis of Sutcliffe's crimes identifies him as a product of the social order, an order which emphasises male violence and portrays women as victims. As Smith (1989) says:

> "One of the chief ironies of the whole Yorkshire Ripper case is that the police spent millions of pounds fruitlessly searching for an outsider, when the culprit was just an ordinary bloke, a local man who shared their background and attitudes to an extraordinary degree."

and:

> "The urge to characterise Sutcliffe as mad has powerful emotional origins; it has as much to do with how we see ourselves and the society in which we live as it has to do with our perception of him and his crimes."

Eerily, Ted Bundy, another notorious serial killer, had said:

> "We are your sons, and we are your husbands, and we grew up in regular families." (Lamar, 1984)

For Jane Caputi (1987) sexual murder is the ultimate expression of sexuality as a form of power and the 20th century is marked by this new form of what she regards as no less than genocide. The role of masculinity in these crimes is undeniable, for whilst some women are extremely violent, there is little evidence to suggest that they derive sexual gratification from their crimes, whereas one of the most disturbing hallmarks of 'lust murder' is the shocking nature of the injuries, mutilations and sexual torture which many female victims endure. As de River (1950) states:

> "The lust murderer usually, after killing his victim, tortures, cuts, maims, or slashes the victim in the regions on or about the genitalia, rectum and breast ... as usually these parts contain sexual significance to him and serve as sexual stimulus."

Whilst many theories of lust murder suggest that early experience of sexual abuse contributes to the development of this type of sexual sadism, as Finkelhor (1986) points out, such theories fail to explain why females, who are predominantly the victims of abuse, do not seem to exhibit sexual sadism if they turn to murder.

One of the areas on which most theories demonstrate agreement is the low likelihood of successful rehabilitation if a sexually sadistic offender is caught (e.g. Hazelwood et al., 1995). A notorious example of this was Lawrence Singleton who was jailed in 1978 for the savage rape of a 15-year-old girl. During the attack Singleton hacked off his victim's forearms with an axe and left her for dead, but miraculously she survived. As a consequence Singleton escaped a charge of murder, serving only eight years of imprisonment, and was then released on parole despite massive opposition which resulted in legislation which now prevents the early release of offenders whose offences have an element of torture. Singleton, however, was able to move into a community which knew nothing of his previous record and in 1997 he was interrupted by a workmate during the rape and murder of another victim.

CHILD MURDERERS

The sexual assault and murder of children is a particularly abhorrent crime which strikes fear into the heart of society. It is very difficult to estimate the true extent of serial murder of children because whilst thousands of children go missing each year, the vast majority of these are runaways or parental abductions rather than murder victims. Nevertheless, the FBI reported that in 1987, 2398 children had been murdered and 28% of these were under ten years old.

Hickey (1991) found that amongst 60 serial murderers of children, the primary motive reported by male and female killers was sexual gratification, followed closely by enjoyment. Children present prime targets for serial murderers because they are generally more trusting and naive and therefore more easily abducted and overpowered.

What is clear from all the studies of serial child killers is that they do not fit the stereotype of pathetic and retarded old men. They are often young, highly manipulative and will plan their offences methodically, targeting potential victims in public areas such as playgrounds or shopping centres. Fitting into the category of psychopaths, they are also predominantly paedophiles with an unnatural sexual arousal pattern to children which they combine with an urge to dominate, control and hurt. De Young (1982) noted that:

> "The sadist sees the child victim as a representation of everything he hates about himself as well as the dreaded memories of his own childhood." (p.125)

CHARACTERISTICS OF FEMALE SERIAL KILLERS

Women are seldom viewed by the public as killers and indeed, the female serial killer is a rarity, but there are notorious exceptions which include Myra Hindley and Rosemary West. Of the women who do fall into this category, many are 'quiet' killers working in a caring capacity, such as Beverley Allitt (who murdered four children in 1991 whilst working as a nurse and was said to be suffering from Munchausen by proxy syndrome), or they kill as part of a team, usually paired with a man.

Hickey's study (1991) of 34 female serial killers revealed that:

- their average number of victims ranged from eight to 14;
- their average age was 32;
- 32% were categorised as homemakers, 18% as nurses;
- 97% were white;
- 76% had children;
- 33% killed strangers only;
- 25% killed family members only;
- 52% used poison to murder their victims.

Hickey concluded that female serial killers differ quite markedly from their male counterparts. They tend to be slightly older, less mobile, are unlikely to be sexually involved with their victims and use less violent methods to kill their victims (unless they offend with a male partner). Their motivation also differs, with over 50% of offenders killing for money. The fact that 47% of the female serial killers in Hickey's sample also mentioned motives of enjoyment and revenge, however, supports some of the biographical data which suggest that experience of childhood trauma, together with an inability to deal constructively with their victimisation, may contribute to subsequent offending.

CHARACTERISTICS OF MALE SERIAL KILLERS

As a result of media coverage of a few notorious cases, there tends to be a stereotypical view of the serial killer as a highly educated and mobile charmer who uses extreme violence and is sexually motivated. However, this is not necessarily an accurate picture and often the individuals who have killed the most victims do not fit this pattern.

In order to determine the characteristics of male serial killers, Hickey (1991) conducted a meta-analysis of studies concerning 169 American offenders and found that the average age was 28.5 and 85% of these offenders were white. Half of the offenders were categorised as local serial killers and the majority of their victims were adult strangers, with young women ranking the highest in preference. Choice of victim seemed to be determined by vulnerability, powerlessness and opportunity. Thus, prime targets were hitchhikers, women living alone, prostitutes and young children. Twenty per cent of offenders killed only males and 5% killed only children.

Hickey (1991) found that the male serial killers in his study came from a wide variety of educational and occupational backgrounds but the majority were not highly educated and tended to be in unskilled jobs. When attempting to categorise their chosen murder method, it became clear that for serial killers murder is a process rather than a brief act and 61% of offenders used a combination of methods. Thus, torture and mutilation would typically occur before the victim was killed by strangulation or a gunshot.

With regard to motivation, only one-fifth of offenders indicated that sex was their sole reason for killing, though it figured to some extent in the motivational accounts of 58% of offenders. Obtaining financial rewards and enjoyment through exerting control seemed to be just as important. In relation to their backgrounds, almost 60% had a history of prior criminal activity and 60% had experienced rejection in their childhood and had been unable to deal with the consequent stresses.

CHARACTERISTICS OF TEAM KILLERS

Perhaps the best-known examples of team killers are, in England, Ian Brady and Myra Hindley (both convicted in 1966 for the murder of three children) and, more recently, Frederick and Rosemary West (Frederick committed suicide in prison in 1995 and Rosemary was convicted in 1996 of the murder of 12 young women); and in America, Kenneth Bianchi and Angelo Buono (convicted in 1984 for the murder of ten women and girls) and Charles Manson and his 'family' (responsible for the deaths of at least eight people, including the actress Sharon Tate, in 1969). In the instances of male/female teams, the 'leader' of the team has tended to be male and someone who has exerted 'psychological' control over his partner or partners in an almost charismatic way.

Hickey (1991) found that 37% of his sample of serial killers fell into the category of team killers and their victim total tended to be less than solo killers. Team killers preferred to target young females and, with some exceptions, were least likely to choose children as victims.

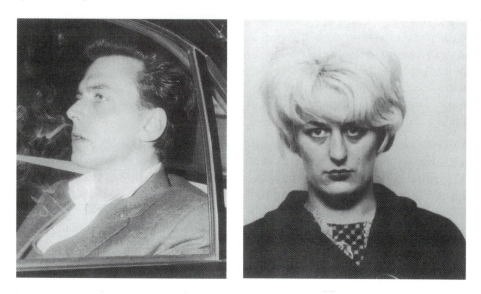

FIGURE 3.2 *Ian Brady and Myra Hindley who were found guilty of murdering three children in 1966. Although Brady is in a Special Hospital, and Hindley in prison, neither will ever be released*

CULTURAL VIEWS
OF SERIAL MURDER

Films about serial killers are very popular, and include *Manhunter* (1986), *The Helter Skelter Murders* (1988), *Henry: Portrait of a Serial Killer* (1989), *Sea of Love* (1989), *Blue Steel* (1990), *The Silence of the Lambs* (1991), *Kalifornia* (1995), *Seven* (1996), and *Copycat* (1996). There are also films about female serial killers, e.g. *Basic Instinct* (1992) and *Single White Female* (1992). Unlike the 'slasher' movies of the 1970s and 1980s, recent films about serial killers attempt a more serious analysis of the psyche of offenders, drawing on current research to inform their accounts. Thus, the serial killer on film is no longer simply the personification of evil; he or she is presented as a damaged individual with some native intelligence in that they have learned the 'rules' about serial murder, e.g. tricks for avoiding detection by, for instance, leaving no forensic clues.

Nevertheless, these films contain graphic scenes of violence, often with women as helpless victims, and it can be argued that the powerful imagery of these films, and indeed the books upon which they are based, make the serial killer doubly dangerous. We all, in some sense, become 'victims' because of the fear engendered by the (unlikely) possibility of becoming a victim, which may irrevocably alter everyone's behaviour. This is particularly true of women who may feel that the message of these films is that female sexuality is a powerful aphrodisiac for potential killers and that in their own interests, they should control any overt display. When women are only just beginning to claim responsibility and direction in relation to their own sexuality after years of repression, it would not seem particularly healthy, or indeed fair, for this to be discouraged.

It was *The Silence of the Lambs* (1991) which alerted film producers to the marketability of the serial killer, making these films almost a genre in themselves, though some 30 years earlier Hitchcock's *Psycho* (1960), which was based on the real-life serial killer, Ed Gein, had proved popular. The 'slasher' films which followed in the late 1970s and 1980s, however, lacked the indepth psychological analysis which had characterised *Psycho*. The hero of *Psycho*, Norman Bates (played by Anthony Perkins), was portrayed as a shy young man, damaged by a domineering mother to such an extent that he develops a disassociative disorder. By contrast, the 'heroes' of the slasher genre lack substance, show little character development and are often masked, perhaps not surprising when the main aim of these movies seems to be to hold the audience in suspense whilst a mountain of bodies steadily accumulates.

In contrast, *The Silence of the Lambs* has two serial killers in it but the real hero is a woman, Clarice Starling (Jodie Foster). She is a trainee at the FBI Behavioral Sciences Unit and is given the opportunity to interview a notorious serial killer in order to discover the identity of another killer who is still in the community. Although initially dependent upon both her male boss and Hannibal Lecter (Anthony Hopkins) for patronage, Clarice eventually pursues the investigation on her own terms and is successful.

There are television series too, such as *Twin Peaks* or *Millenium*, which draw on FBI research findings to authenticate the crime investigations they portray. Thus, the hero of *Millenium* has been involved in so many serious crime investigations that he is now able to 'see' what the serial killer saw at the crime scenes. This then informs his analysis, together with his wide knowledge of current research, such as 'disorganised' killers taking souvenirs from their victims or the 'organised' killer returning to the scene of the crime. Another series, *Profiler*, focuses on the work of a female offender profiler, a psychologist who helps police detectives to solve crimes. Whilst it is the area of offender profiling which most seems to have caught the imagination of the public as forming a bridge between psychology and crime, in the real world offender profilers rarely 'solve' crime. Instead, they assist the police in a variety of ways, including the development of interviewing strategies, crime prevention policies and the compilation of descriptions of likely suspects in serious crimes.

OFFENDER PROFILING

For Oleson (1996), offender profiling has become *the* sexy speciality of forensic psychology, with the offender profiler a new:

> "quintessential hero ... pitted against our new and modern monster, the serial killer." (p.11)

As might be detected by the tone, Oleson is concerned about the uncritical way offender profiling has been accepted as a viable contribution to the understanding of crime. Similarly, Campbell criticises the acceptance of profiling in the 1980s as a scientific technique, describing profiles as:

> "... romances of science that were irrelevant and overtouted." (cited in Jeffers, 1992)

So, whilst for some offender profiling offers a valuable detection tool which should cement the relationship between psychologists and police officers, for others it is a technique which has not yet been adequately tested, to some extent can be regarded as merely anecdotal and can only be validated *post hoc*, i.e. after the event, so its predictive value should not be overestimated.

What is offender profiling?

As Copson (1996) points out, there is no universally accepted definition of the term 'offender profiling'. He describes it as a 'term of convenience' used to cover techniques whereby the behaviour shown in a crime is used to draw inferences about the likely offender. For Turco (1993), psychological profiling of offenders involves:

> "the preparation of a biographical 'sketch' gathered from information taken at a crime scene, from the personal history and habits of a victim, and integrating this with known psychological theory." (p.147)

The resulting sketch can be used by police officers to reduce their list of suspects or to offer a new line of enquiry. Traditionally, the only clues noted at crime scenes tended to be hard evidence, such as bloodstains, saliva or semen, but with the advent of offender profiling there is a recognition that there may be less visible clues at the crime scene too, e.g. the choice of victim, the location, the nature of the assault, what is and is not said to the victim. All these clues define the offender and psychologists can assist the police in interpreting these clues.

The overall aim of profiling is to narrow the field of investigation, drawing inferences about the offender's motivation and personality from evidence left at the crime scene. Holmes (1989) suggests that profiling is most useful when the crime scene reflects psychopathology, such as sadistic assaults, and

90% of profiling attempts involve murder or rape. This said, profiling has also been used in cases of arson, burglary, robbery and obscene telephone calls.

Caution needs to be used in the application of profiling, however, and it should not be employed to specifically target a suspected offender or, indeed, to totally eliminate a suspect. Profiling is not intended to identify a specific individual so that they can simply be arrested. The profiler can assist the police in their collection of evidence by drawing up hypotheses about the offender and also the victim in such a way that all these items can build a composite picture.

History of offender profiling

Offender profiling as a process is not new, though the term was introduced by FBI agents during the early 1970s. In 1888, a police surgeon called Thomas Bond compiled a detailed description of Jack the Ripper. During the Second World War a psychiatrist, William Langer, was asked to compile a profile of Adolf Hitler by the Office of Strategic Services. Langer (1972) accurately diagnosed Hitler's psychiatric state and was able to predict his likely response to defeat, i.e. suicide.

Politicians became interested in the idea of psychological profiling to assist them in negotiating with foreign heads of State; so, for example, Wedge (1968) advised President Kennedy on how to interpret the behaviour of Kruschev at their next meeting. Not surprisingly, the potential of profiling as a means of identifying criminals and developing appropriate interviewing strategies for them soon became apparent.

There were successes and failures, though. In the mid-1950s James Brussel, a psychiatrist, was asked by the New York police to help them find the 'Mad Bomber of New York'. This person had carried out a series of bombings over several years and Brussel was able to build a picture of him by examining the crime scenes and the letters written by the bomber and provided such a detailed account of his likely personality, lifestyle, place of residence and even his dress sense that the police were able to arrest the bomber by a traditional process of elimination (Brussel, 1969). It is worth noting that the police were also assisted in this case by the clues left in one of the bomber's letters which indicated his previous place of employment. A less successful attempt at profiling concerned the 'Boston Strangler' who was initially profiled by a group of psychologists and psychiatrists as two male school teachers living alone, one of whom was probably homosexual. When Albert DeSalvo was finally arrested, he was revealed as a heterosexual construction worker living with his family (cited in Boon and Davies, 1992). It is true to say that if too much emphasis is placed on an inaccurate profile, considerable time and energy can be wasted in a criminal investigation.

Current approaches to offender profiling

Current offender profiling tends to follow one of two approaches, the first developed by the American Federal Bureau of Investigation primarily in response to serial murder (FBI 1985a, 1985b) and the second pioneered by David Canter (1994) and Paul Britton (1997) in the United Kingdom. It should be noted that although the bulk of the literature on profiling focuses on serious crimes, e.g. serial murder and rape, there is also valuable work being carried out using profiling in relation to other areas of crime, e.g. burglary and arson, in spite of the view of Ault and Reese (1980) that profiling is only suitable in crimes which demonstrate an element of psychopathology.

The American approach

In 1979 FBI investigators began to interview the growing number of incarcerated serial killers and sex murderers. They interviewed 36 sexual murderers and subsequently categorised them as either organised (n=24) or disorganised (n=12). As a result of their indepth interviews with criminals such as Charles Manson and Ted Bundy, amongst others, they began developing theoretical models which would allow the compilation of accurate profiles based on meticulous examination of crime scenes. Ressler (Ressler et al., 1988) was one of the interview team and he concluded that sex killers tended to be white, unmarried males who were either unemployed or in unskilled jobs. They tended to have previous psychiatric or alcohol histories, dysfunctional family backgrounds and had a sexual interest in voyeurism, fetishism and pornography. Their crime scenes provided information which could then be used to identify them as organised or disorganised killers. The FBI now train profilers worldwide, though their view is that profiles are not suitable in all crime investigations and are most useful in cases where there is some indication of psychopathology. The basis of their approach is that the crime scene and the offender's *modus operandi* will reveal indicators of individual pathology, which may fit into a pattern already observed from case studies of incarcerated offenders.

According to Holmes (1989), the aims of profiling within this framework are:

- to reduce the scope of an investigation by providing basic information in relation to the social and psychological core variables of the offender's personality, e.g. race, age range, employment status and type, educational background, marital status, etc.;
- to allow some prediction of future offences and their location;
- to provide a psychological evaluation of belongings found in the offender's possession, e.g. souvenirs or trophies from previous offences;
- to provide strategies for interviewing offenders which can take account of individual differences, but profit from experience with offenders who have displayed a common pattern of offending.

The major theoretical contribution made by the FBI team is their division of serial killers into two categories – organised and disorganised. An organised offender is identified if the crime scene reveals evidence of planning, the victim was targeted, and the element of control has been important. The offender might then be presumed to have the following characteristics: average intelligence, social and sexual competence and an intimate partner. In contrast, the disorganised offender is described as socially inadequate and someone who may know the crime scene and/or the victim and who lives alone. His crime scene will reveal evidence of an impulsive and unplanned attack using minimal restraint with no attempt to conceal the victim's body.

The British approach

In the United Kingdom offender profiling has been dominated by the work of David Canter, whose psychological expertise is wide but had not focused on crime until he was approached by the metropolitan police in 1985 to advise whether the behavioural science of psychology could contribute to criminal investigations. The following year he became centrally involved in what was initially a serial rape investigation and which subsequently became a notorious serial murder case. With his help, the police were able to arrest

Box 3.1   Profiling the 'Railway Rapist' (adapted from Canter, 1994)

During the period 1982–86, 24 sexual assaults occurred in North London near to railways. It was believed that one man was involved, though on some occasions he had had an accomplice. Between 1985 and 1986 three murders occurred, and forensic evidence together with certain aspects of the perpetrator's *modus operandi* suggested that there were links between the rapes and murders.

When Canter joined the detectives working on the case they compiled a table of all the offences with comprehensive details in an attempt to establish a pattern. A profile was subsequently drawn up, which included the following description:

- lives in the area circumscribed by the first three cases (1982–83);
- probably lives with wife/girlfriend, possibly without children;
- mid to late 20s, right-handed, 'A' secretor;
- semiskilled or skilled job, with weekend work;
- knowledge of the railway system;
- criminal record, involving violence.

When John Duffy was arrested in November 1986 he turned out to live in Kilburn, was separated from his wife, was in his late 20s, right-handed and an 'A' secretor, was a travelling carpenter for British Rail and was known to the police for having raped his wife at knifepoint. Duffy was initially 1505th in a list of 2000 suspects and the profile enabled prompt action to be taken. Canter compiled his profile by analysing the detail of the offences, e.g. what had been said, the nature of the sexual activity, knowledge of police procedures, etc.

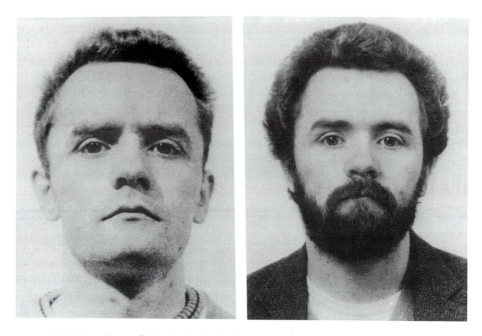

FIGURE 3.3 *Two photos of John Duffy, the 'Railway Rapist' issued by police after being found guilty of two murders and five rapes in 1988*

John Duffy, who was subsequently convicted in 1988 for two murders and five rapes, for which he received seven life sentences. The profile which Canter provided described Duffy and where he lived so accurately that the response of the police and the media was one of astonishment (see Box 3.1).

Canter's approach to profiling is much more rooted in psychological principles than is the approach of the FBI, and he describes profiling which is merely based on crime scene analysis as 'more of an art than a science' (1989, p.12). He believes that criminals, like all other people, act consistently, i.e. their actions have some coherence whatever the setting, and an analysis of their behaviour will reveal a pattern which can offer clues to their lifestyle during the non-offending part of their lives. Thus, he says:

> "What does a criminal reveal about himself by the way he commits a crime? ... as well as ... material traces he also leaves psychological traces, tell-tale patterns of behaviour that indicate the sort of person he is. Gleaned from the crime scene and reports from witnesses, these traces are more ambiguous and subtle than those examined by the biologist or physicist ... They are more like shadows (which) ... can indicate where investigators should look and what sort of person they should be looking for." (Canter, 1994, p.4)

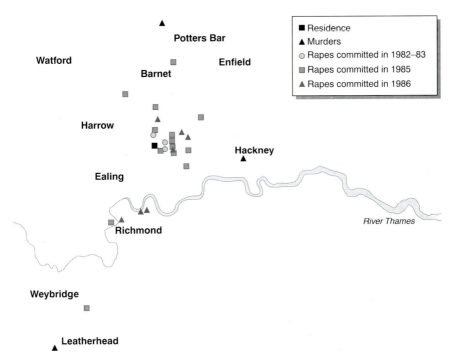

FIGURE 3.4 *The 'map' of Duffy's offences which enabled David Canter to compile an offender profile*

In addition, Canter suggests that we all operate within a social context, so there is an implicit *social* relationship between the offender and his or her victim which again will offer major clues to the pattern of the offender's life. Sensitive and detailed examination of the victim's testimony can reveal speech patterns, interests, obsessions and ways of behaving which will have also occurred outside the criminal act.

> "Criminals are performing actions that are direct reflections of the sorts of transactions they have with other people." (Canter, 1989, p.13)

For example, rapists may treat their victims in the way they treat most of the women in their lives. Thus, an offender who is hesitant and apologetic after the offence may be revealing their characteristic difficulty in relating to women in an appropriate way.

Canter (1994) has demonstrated that his approach to profiling is far removed from the processes described in the media. He suggests that interviews with serial killers who are known to be manipulative and disturbed sensation seekers are unlikely to be helpful and that his own approach to criminal investigation, which involves advising experienced police officers on the basis of correlations between banks of data (for instance, time and location of offences or choice of victim) and content analysis of speech, in an attempt to develop patterns and identify trends, is likely to be of more practical use. Interestingly, however, Gresswell and Hollin (1994) suggest that:

> "functional analyses of a large number of multiple murder perpetrators to facilitate the development of appropriate, testable, cognitive-behavioural models"

are the logical next step in British research. Their approach should not be seen as a repetition of the FBI indepth interviews of the 1980s, however, but as a challenging way to use profiling for clinical rehabilitation purposes.

Differences between the American and British approaches

Boon and Davies (1992) have borrowed terminology from cognitive psychology to draw out the differences between the American and British approaches to profiling. They suggest that the British approach is based on 'bottom-up' data processing, i.e. an analysis of existing evidence which aims to identify specific associations between offences and offender characteristics. In contrast, the American approach is described as more 'top-down' in its reliance on potentially subjective conclusions drawn from investigative experience of crimes and interviews with criminals. Boon and Davies (1992) suggest that in the American approach the concern is:

> "principally in what the serious offender does and when rather than in psychological questions as to why." (p.6)

However, the aim of both approaches is to predict when further offending is likely to occur and to identify the crucial details which will pinpoint the offender.

Critique

Offender profiling has undoubted potential if used properly by trained professionals. Geberth (1983), however, has described profiling as 'little better than information one could get from the neighbourhood bartender' and he was concerned to point out the danger of over-reliance on so-called 'expert' profiling without acknowledging the invaluable contribution of experienced police officers.

How successful is it? Holmes (1989) cites FBI data which reveal that in 192 cases of profile generation in 1981, arrests were made in 88, but in only 17% of these did the profile contribute to the arrest. Others (e.g. Oleson, 1996) point out that the seminal work of the FBI in establishing offender profiling may be methodologically flawed since no control groups were used to compare the evidence obtained from interviews with offenders and there is no mention of the statistical techniques used to analyse their data. Moreover, much of the evidence used by the FBI was simply information obtained in interviews with offenders and was accepted at face value.

In the UK, Copson and Holloway (1997) surveyed detectives who had worked on 184 cases in which offender profiling had been used and found that they believed profiling had led to the identification of an offender in only 2.7% of cases and had 'helped to solve' 16% of cases. They conclude:

> "Profiling can work very well, but certainly not in the way some practitioners, let alone dramatists, would have you believe. There is nothing in our findings to support the notion that complex offender characteristics can be predicted with any great accuracy. In fact, with some people you would be better off tossing a coin."

The potential of offender profiling is thus extremely challenging, but it needs to be thoroughly evaluated before it is hailed as the solution to criminal investigation. When Pinizzotto and Finkel (1990) attempted to discover whether professional profilers would be more accurate than informed laypersons, they asked groups of profilers, detectives, clinical psychologists and students to examine two closed police cases (a sex offence and a homicide) and to draw up profiles. What they found was that the profilers did indeed produce richer and more detailed profiles and in relation to the sex offence, they were more accurate than non-profilers, but the detectives were more accurate on the homicide case. Pinizzotto and Finkel concluded that the success of the profilers was the result of both confidence and experience rather than the use of an exclusive technique. The implications would therefore be that both training and practical experience are vital in developing profiling expertise and that productive liaison between the police and psychologists is the way forward in order to achieve both investigative and clinical objectives.

CONCLUSION

The phenomenon of serial murder and the development of theoretical analyses of their possible motivation which have led to offender profiling have clearly captured the imagination of the public and the increasing number of psychology students who want to become forensic psychologists. However, it would seem that a note of caution might be needed in order to ensure sufficiently rigorous analysis of the data available and to avoid psychologists joining a 'circus' of law enforcement in which their techniques are improperly used and their discipline denigrated. The potential for co-operation and collaboration between the law and psychology is one which must not be wasted as a result of opportunism.

chapter four

RAPE

CHAPTER OVERVIEW

This chapter explores the contribution psychologists have made to our understanding of rape and the myths surrounding this offence. It examines the different types of rape and attitudes to rape held by men, women, and society. Theories of rape are evaluated, as are typologies of rapists which seek to determine motivation. Finally, in an attempt to situate this offence within a wider, societal analysis, cultural depictions of rape will be examined.

INTRODUCTION

"Rape is a topic that abounds with myths and misconceptions. It is a complicated, emotionally charged, and highly misunderstood subject." (Groth, 1979, p.1)

As Groth points out, rape is an offence which, because it is such an intimate violation and one which often occurs in private and is consequently a matter of dispute between the parties concerned, produces abhorrence, disbelief and, ultimately, judgement. Its far-reaching consequences can affect individuals – victims, perpetrators, counsellors, friends and relatives – for a considerable period of time and in more global terms, it can be said to have become the arena for debate about the potentially gross miscommunication and mis-understandings between men and women.

Rape has been illegal in Britain since 1275 and the most recent legal amend-ment defined it as 'sexual intercourse with a person (whether vaginal or anal) who at the time of the intercourse does not consent to it' (Criminal Justice and Public Order Act, 1994). The significance of this amendment is the acknowledgement that rape can be committed against a man or a woman and that it can also occur within marriage.

Whilst a legal definition of rape might appear to present few problems, in the real world it is fraught with difficulties of interpretation, disagreement over evidence and the issue of consent, all made worse by a legal system which tends to hold the alleged perpetrator and victim equally responsible. Consider the real-life examples of rape in Box 4.1 and compare these to the traditional stereotype of rape, where the rapist is a stranger, motivated by sexual desire and his victim is a young, attractive female who may be considered to have provoked his advances.

Box 4.1 Examples of rape

In the early hours of Boxing Day 1996, a 53-year-old woman and her 9-year-old daughter were both raped in Northolt, London. The rapist was a well-dressed white male in his early 20s, who broke into their home.

In September 1996, an Austrian visitor to London, aged 33, was gang-raped and savagely beaten by eight youths, aged between 14 and 17. After the assault the victim was thrown into the Regent's Canal and left for dead. In court the attack was described as 'overtly racist in nature' with the victim being described by several gang members as 'the white bitch'.

In 1993 Austen Donellan was charged with rape. He had admired a fellow student for some time though she regarded him as simply a 'good friend'. She got drunk at a party and she and Mr Donellan ended up in bed together. He claimed they had consensual sex, whilst she described herself as so drunk she was 'a comatose vegetable' and only recalls waking up to find Mr Donellan having sex with her. Mr Donellan was subsequently cleared of the charge.

In 1995 a boy of 13 was raped and beaten while fishing in a village made famous as the home of the Brontë sisters. The boy was fishing after school when a man approached him and threatened him with a razor. After the rape, the boy hid in bushes until his whimpering attracted the attention of an elderly passer-by.

A nine-year old and four ten-year-old boys were arrested in West London in May 1997 for the alleged rape of a nine-year-old girl in the toilets of a primary school during a lunch break. They were subsequently acquitted in February 1998.

How many stereotypes associated with rape are challenged in these real-life examples?

PREVALENCE OF RAPE

Although there are official statistics relating to the incidence of rape, there are wide differences between the number of rapes which occur, those which are reported to rape crisis centres, those which are reported to the police and those which result in successful prosecutions. In the United Kingdom 5100 rapes were reported to the police in 1994, a rise of 11% on the1993 figures, but the conviction rate dropped from 24% in 1985 to less than 10% in 1993 (Temkin, 1995). In America there were 102,500 cases of reported rape in 1992, i.e. 85 reported rapes for every 100,000 women (FBI, 1993). However, rape is one of the most under-reported crimes and Koss et al. (1987) found that only one in five (21%) of stranger rapes had been reported, whilst only 2% of acquaintance rapes had been reported to the police.

Methodologically, it is therefore very difficult to detect the true extent of rape and this is well documented by Koss (1993) who, in an earlier study, found that in a sample of 6000 American students, 28% of women reported having been raped (Koss et al.,1987). In the same study, 7.7% of American college males reported having engaged in what they now considered to be rape or attempted rape and a further 7.2% admitted coercing a female into inter-course, primarily by continued verbal pressure or intentional intoxication. Koss (1993) concluded that the lifetime chance of a woman being raped is between 14% and 25%. The inaccuracy of the official statistics is also revealed by surveys of rapists – Groth (1979) found that convicted rapists admitted to an average of five undetected offences prior to conviction.

Notwithstanding the problems with official statistics, it is clear that there are wide differences between countries in relation to the reported incidence of rape. The rate in America is 13 times that of England and 20 times that of Japan (Smeal, 1991). Why should this be? Anthropologists such as Sanday (1981) suggest that cultural differences may make some societies more rape prone than others. Within these societies, men tend to have negative attitudes towards women, value violence and enjoy taking risks. Herman (1984) points out the match between this description and American society:

> "America's culture produces rapists when it encourages the socialisation of men to subscribe to values of control and dominance, callousness and competitiveness, and anger and aggression, and when it discour-ages the expression by men of vulnerability, sharing and co-operation."

Problems in interpreting rape research data

There are major difficulties in interpreting the research relating to rape. Often the data are hypothetical, e.g. asking participants about their attitudes to rape or measuring arousal to rape scenes. Alternatively, evidence is collected from rapists who have been convicted and imprisoned and it is then unwise to generalise in view of the massive amount of unreported or unconvicted occurrences of rape. Determining the extent of rape can only be attempted by comparing official crime statistics with self-reports.

Types of Rape

Most studies of rape illustrate that there are several different types of rape and whilst each produces traumatic consequences for the victim, each type may follow a specific pattern and each type of rapist may have a different motivation for his behaviour, all of which will impact on the victim and their chances of resistance and recovery.

Stranger rape

The type which is most familiar is stranger rape, where the victim is unknown to their attacker. It is these rapes which tend to figure largely in the media and are then sensationalised. A typical example would be the serial rapist, Peter Cook, who in 1975 carried out at least six rapes in Cambridge. Cook methodically planned these assaults, dressing as a woman, then donning a leather balaclava on which he had printed the word 'Rapist'. These offences produced a climate of fear and the newspapers printed lurid accounts of the deeds of the so-called 'Cambridge Rapist'.

It is more likely that weapons and violence will be used in stranger rape. Scully (1990) found that 62% of convicted rapists had used a weapon to subdue their victims and this weapon was most likely to be a knife.

Date or acquaintance rape

There is still considerable resistance to the notion of date rape or acquaintance rape, which is forced intercourse during a consensual encounter which may or may not have agreed romantic overtones. The term 'date rape' was first used in the early 1980s, but undoubtedly had occurred over many hundreds of years previously. Victims of date rape are less likely to define the incident as rape if there is evidence of previous romantic involvement or prior consenting sexual activity and courts often take a similar view. A study by Bostwick and Delucia (1992) showed that in a date rape scenario the victim is seen as more willing, and the assault as justifiable in the sense that the man may have been led to 'expect' intercourse.

The type of coercion used by the date rapist is rather different from that of the stranger rapist. Verbal 'manipulation' is more likely; thus Mosher and Anderson (1986) found that 44% of the date rapists in their sample had told their victim that not having sex would cause their relationship to deteriorate. Other tactics might include getting the victim drunk or simply ignoring her resistance (Muehlenhard, 1987). The traumatic effects of date rape, however, are no less serious than those experienced by survivors of stranger rape, particularly since there has been such a betrayal of trust and it is likely that the victim will question her own judgement (Katz, 1991).

Trying to estimate the prevalence of stranger rape in comparison to date rape is made difficult because victims are far less likely to report rape when it has been committed by someone they know. Thus, Katz and Mazur (1979) reviewed 18 different rape studies and reported percentages of stranger rape which varied from 27% to 91%. Russell's (1984) survey of victims, however, concluded that stranger rape accounted for only 17% of the total number of rapes, the rest having been committed by acquaintances, friends or relatives.

Roiphe (1993) has argued strongly that the prevalence of date rape has been overestimated and is part of feminist anti-male paranoia which unhelpfully places women in the role of perpetual victims. She acknowledges that rape by acquaintances does occur, but that this is more often to do with miscommunication and misunderstandings about courtship rituals and perhaps women need to be more assertive about what they do and do not want. A more sophisticated analysis of date rape places coercive sex within the context of assumptions about heterosexual sex which emphasise male activity and female passivity and the relative powerlessness of women in this situation, but also points to the dangers of thus placing women in the role of hapless victim out of touch with her own potential for sexual desire (Gavey, 1996).

FIGURE 4.1 *William Kennedy arriving at his attorney's office after being accused of date rape. He was subsequently acquitted when his account of events was believed rather than that of his female acquaintance*

The role of possible miscommunication and misperception in date rape has been put forward as partial explanation for inappropriate behaviour, but it can be perceived as drawing attention away from the intentions of the rapist and providing him with a means of avoiding responsibility. It is clear that there are misperceptions between men and women in relation to interpersonal encounters. Abbey (1991) cites her own research which shows that men may be socialised to view any form of friendly behaviour from a woman as an indication that she is interested in sex. When male and female participants took part in and also observed a recorded 'getting acquainted' conversation with each other and were then asked to describe their experiences, men consistently rated the behaviour of women as seductive and their own as flirtatious, whereas the women described their own behaviour and that of other women as merely friendly. When this type of misperception, together with a myth about male sexuality being an 'uncoiled spring' ready to be unleashed by female desire, becomes part of the dating script, it is not perhaps surprising that some victims of date rape may feel that they have unfairly provoked the men who have then raped them. Moreover, they may feel they should have known better and should have communicated their resistance more strongly, thus effectively taking away responsibility from the perpetrator.

Gang rape

Gang rape has often been viewed as a terrible but rare event, fitting into the category of stranger rape, but more recently it has been recognised that 'party rape' is a part of American campus culture, whereby vulnerable young women are gang-raped at a social event as part of some sort of initiation for a group of sexually inexperienced young men in the same fraternity group which affirms their masculinity (Sanday, 1990).

> "Cross cultural research demonstrates that whenever men build and give allegiance to a mystical, enduring all male social group, the disparagement of women is, invariably, an important ingredient of the mystical bond, and sexual aggression the means by which the bond is renewed. As long as exclusive male clubs exist in a society that privileges men as a social category, we must recognise that collective sexual aggression provides a ready stage on which some men represent their social privilege and introduce adolescent boys to their future place in the status hierarchy." (Sanday, 1990, p.21)

A particularly horrific gang rape occurred in America during 1989 when four 15–17-year-old African-Americans violently beat and repeatedly raped a white woman jogger in Central Park, New York. The victim was left for dead and many newspaper reports focused on the racial element of this crime. Messerschmidt (1993), however, provides a gendered analysis of the offence and emphasises the social and collective aspect of the event which allowed a very extreme display of violent male sexual conquest. He suggests that the behaviour of the boys, particularly their exuberance after the assault and their indifference to the suffering of the victim, can only be understood in the context of racial discrimination and disadvantage but that the major element was clearly related to masculinity:

> "Such group rape helps maintain and reinforce an alliance among the boys by humiliating and devaluating women, thereby strengthening the fiction of masculine power." (Messerschmidt, 1993, p.114)

Marital rape

Until the late 1970s, the concept of marital rape was not considered viable. Rape laws in most countries contained a 'marital exemption' dating back to the 17th century pronouncement by Matthew Hale, Chief Justice of England:

> "But the husband cannot be guilty of rape committed by himself upon his lawful wife, for by their mutual matrimonial consent and contract the wife hath given up herself in this kind unto the husband which she cannot retract." (Russell, 1990, pp. 129–130)

Thus, women were deemed to lose any rights in relation to unwanted sexual advances from their husband once they married.

In spite of the advances in women's rights, legislators seemed reluctant to change this ruling until 1991 in the United Kingdom, whilst in America by 1992 only two states had not ruled marital rape a criminal offence. A legal precedent was set in the UK in 1996 when a divorced woman obtained £14,000 in damages against her former husband for raping her in 1992. The damages were obtained in the civil courts after the police refused to prosecute, claiming that the man was most unlikely to commit a similar offence (reported in *The Guardian*, 10th September 1997, p.1).

The prevalence of marital rape appears to be extensive and often occurs within the context of existing domestic violence. Thus, in a random sample of American women Russell (1990) found that:

> "Approximately one in every seven women who has ever been married in our San Francisco sample was willing to disclose an experience of sexual assault by their husbands which met our quite conservative definition of rape." (p.57)

This finding was replicated in the UK by Painter (1991) and certainly calls into question the view of rapists as a separate group of psychologically disturbed individuals. Why would a man rape his wife? Finkelhor and Yllö (1985) found from their interviews with victims of marital rape that coercive sex and violence had been a pattern within their marriage and that rape often occurred once the woman had made it clear she was leaving the relationship. Certainly there seems to be a link between marital rape and marital violence.

Frieze (1983) found that in a study of 137 women who reported that they had been physically assaulted by their husbands, 34% reported having been raped by him too. When asked why, 78% said the cause was the husband's belief that the rape would prove his manhood, whilst 14% believed it was the result of their husband's drinking.

Male rape

Male rape is a phenomenon which is believed to occur mainly in prisons or between gays and until 1994 in the United Kingdom, it did not exist in law. Before 1994, a sexual assault on a man by another man could be categorised legally as buggery or indecent assault but not as rape and thus it was liable to attract lighter sentences. However, between 1984 and 1989 offences of buggery increased by 90% and of indecent assault by 24%. As this type of offence is most unlikely to be reported to the police, these figures must be considered an underestimate.

Men tend to be viewed stereotypically as controlling and initiating sexual activity, certainly not as potential victims of sexual assault. It is often assumed, therefore, that a man is:

"too strong to be overpowered and forced into sex." (Struckman and Johnson, 1992, p.86.)

There would appear to be several other myths surrounding male rape, as Struckman and Johnson (1992) found when surveying the views of American college students, the most prominent of which was the belief that male rape is confined to the homosexual community and that any victims of male rape must automatically be gay. Moreover, the view was expressed that male rape is not as serious a matter as the rape of females and that victims will not suffer as much distress. What research has been done in this area, however, indicates that the victims of male rape suffer depression, guilt, amnesia, loss of self-esteem and problems with future intimate relationships (Myers, 1989). One of the key areas of self-doubt seems to be in relation to sexual orientation, particularly if the victim has ejaculated whilst the offence is being committed. McMullen (1990) found that victims who had experienced this were less likely to have reported the offence because they confused the physiological experience of ejaculation with orgasm and felt their lack of consent would not be believed.

Mezey and King (1989) argue that homosexual and heterosexual men can be rapists or victims and that male rape is never provoked by an overwhelming sexual urge:

"Rape is a violent assault, an expression of explosive hatred. Penetration enables the assailant to subjugate and destroy the victim. The assailant is reassured of his masculinity in a perverted form; he can still penetrate, therefore he is still powerful." (p.36)

This element of power seems to be a major component in the male rape which occurs in prisons. Surveys in American prisons indicate that about 14% of male inmates report being raped and that often the motive is a demonstration of control to other prisoners, which can lead to the suicide of the victims. Male rape in prisons is seldom an isolated event and once it has occurred, is likely to be repeated and form part of a humiliating ritual from which the victim cannot escape (Wooden and Partner, 1982).

Juvenile rape

Boys between the ages of ten and 13 have only been liable to charges of rape since the Sexual Offences Act (1993). Before then cases were ranked as indecent assault and so it is difficult to obtain figures indicating the true extent of juvenile rape, though the delay in legislation indicates the prevailing belief that young boys are not capable of rape. There were ten charges of rape brought against boys aged between ten and 13 in 1994 and 11 in 1995, though only two of these charges in each year resulted in convictions (Home Office, 1996). Whilst these figures are comparatively low, considerable concern has been expressed about the extent of juvenile sexual violence and its possible link with experience of child sexual abuse, exposure to violent sexual imagery in the media and a reduction in the provision of sex education programmes in primary schools.

MYTHS ABOUT RAPE

We learn about rape from news stories and more often than not, these stories contain images of sex-crazed loners who impulsively assault young women not known to them but who have unwisely chosen to walk down some unlit street late at night. The fear which these accounts instil in women serves to constrain female behaviour but more significantly they perpetuate the myth that rapists are somehow unusual and odd, perhaps suffering from mental disorder, but are definitely recognisable as 'different' from other, normal men. Regrettably, this focus on 'differentness' and uncontrollable sexual impulses is simply not borne out by the evidence, as Table 4.1 indicates.

These myths were successfully used by Burt (1980) to explore individuals' likelihood or proclivity to rape. Burt argues that certain attitudes to women are widely accepted in Western culture but are particularly held by rapists and act as 'psychological releasers or neutralisers' to subsequent sexual violence (see Box 4.2). Subsequent data supports Burt; for example, Koss et al. (1987) found that male college students' levels of sexual aggression correlated with attitudes condoning violence against women and Scully and Marolla (1985) found that convicted rapists showed high acceptance of violence against women.

Table 4.1 Common myths about rape

Myth	Fact
Rapists are madmen/sick	Most rapists show no evidence of psychopathology
Rape is committed by strangers in dark alleys/parks	Most rapes occur indoors and most victims know their attackers
Rape is the result of a sudden sexual urge	Most rapes are planned and are not about uncontrollable libido, but rather humiliation, domination and degradation Rape is the sexual expression of power and anger
Some women ask for it by their provocative dress/behaviour	Rape can and does happen to any woman, in any situation
Women say no but mean yes – they just want to be persuaded	Women say no when they mean no
One man cannot rape a woman without there being signs of a violent struggle	The threat of violence is an effective weapon, but the police advise against a struggle which could provoke further violence
Some women are less 'innocent' than others, such as prostitutes	No woman is any more deserving of rape than another
Women like to be treated with force and fantasise about rape	Women have control over their own fantasies – they have no control in rape

Source: Donnelly, (1991), p.37

ATTITUDES TO RAPE

The attitude people hold towards rape will determine the way they view the offence, the victim and the perpetrator, and whilst groups of men may hold different views to those of groups of women, individuals within each of these groups can also hold a range of views about different aspects of rape. Thus, Barnett and Feild (1977) were able to show that people could believe that rapists are sexually motivated whilst also believing that a woman should be held responsible for preventing rape. They further found that 8% of women and 32% of men agreed that it would do some women good to be raped, whilst 4% of women and 17% of men agreed that most rape victims were 'asking for it'. Have attitudes changed much since then? Unfortunately not. In 1991, Holcomb et al. found that 32% of their respondents felt that

Box 4.2 Items from scales used to measure proclivity to rape (Burt, 1980)

Acceptance of Interpersonal Violence toward Women (AIV Scale)
1. Being roughed up is sexually stimulating to many women.
2. Many times a woman will pretend she doesn't want to have intercourse because she doesn't want to seem loose, but she's really hoping the man will force her.
3. A man is never justified in hitting his wife.

Scoring: Persons scoring high in acceptance of violence towards women agree with items 1 and 2 and disagree with item 3.

Rape Myth Acceptance (RMA Scale)
1. If a woman engages in necking or petting and she lets things get out of hand, it is her own fault if her partner forces sex on her.
2. Any female can get raped.
3. Many women have an unconscious wish to be raped and may then unconsciously set up a situation in which they are likely to be attacked.
4. In the majority of rapes, the victim is promiscuous or has a bad reputation.

Scoring: Persons scoring high in acceptance of rape myths agree with items 1, 3 and 4 and disagree with item 2.

some women ask to be raped and may enjoy it and 22% felt that any woman could prevent rape if she really wanted to.

Dietz et al. (1982) developed a scale to measure rape empathy, and when Layman and Labott (1992) applied it they found that, compared to women, men had more empathy for the rapist and rated victims more negatively. Although 'blaming the victim' has become a recognised phenomenon within crime studies generally (Lerner and Simmons, 1966) and is associated with a 'belief in a just world' (a reassuring assumption that crime does not occur randomly and is therefore only suffered by those who deserve this fate), it would seem that rape victims in particular are blamed for what happens to them (Baumgardner et al., 1988). This seems to be more marked when the victim is unattractive (Dietz et al., 1984) or resists the attack too much or too little (Branscombe and Weir, 1992). Thus, when Jones and Aronson (1973) asked participants to estimate the degree to which they thought the victim in a rape scenario might have been at fault but were told the victim was either married, divorced or a virgin, they assigned more blame to the virgin, as if she had in some way brought the assault upon herself. This was despite the fact that they believed the rapist in the scenarios who had raped a virgin deserved a longer prison sentence than in the other two cases. A belief in a just world requires us to believe that bad things can only occur to the disreputable, so a 'respectable' virgin to whom something bad has happened must have in some way provoked her fate.

Let me put it to you that the accused had **AMPLE** reason for believing you consented to the burglary.

Did you not place highly desirable commodities in **FULL** and **PROVOCATIVE** view of the window, precisely to **ENTICE** this innocent man to break and enter your home?

FIGURE 4.2   *In this Jacky Fleming cartoon the unacceptable notion that victims of rape in some way provoke their own victimisation is exposed*

In relation to date rape the assault was thought to be more justifiable if the victim went to the man's apartment, if she initiated the date and if the man paid for the date (Muehlenhard et al., 1985). Assumptions about date rape appear to start early too, so Koss et al. (1994) found that in a study of 1700 teenagers 25% of the boys said that it was acceptable for a man to force sex on a woman if he had spent money on her.

THEORIES OF RAPE

There have been many theories of rape, all attempting to explain the phenomenon. Early theories suggested chronic unemployment and difficulty in finding sex partners (Bonger, 1916) or inadequate socialisation (Guttmacher, 1951) or being brought up in a sexually violent subculture (Amir, 1971).

Many of these early theories based their findings on stranger rape, since the concept of date rape had yet to be 'discovered'. It is possible to group current explanations of rape into the disease model, biological theories, psychological theories and feminist theories.

The disease model

Traditionally rape has been viewed within a medical or disease model, i.e. the result of individual psychopathology. The men who commit rape are seen as suffering from an identifiable mental illness which makes them impulsive and not really responsible for their crimes. Alternatively, men who rape are seen as suffering from an uncontrollable sexual urge related to the normal male sex drive. Thus, early theories of rape describe rape as:

> "the explosive expression of a pent-up impulse" (Guttmacher and Weinhofen, 1952, p.116)

whilst Karpman (1951) states:

> "Sexual psychopaths are of course a social menace, but they are not conscious agents deliberating and viciously perpetrating these acts, rather they are the victims of a disease from which they may suffer more than their victims." (p.190)

This view of rape as somehow being the result of impulsive sexual frustration is countered by findings such as those of Amir (1971), who found that 71% of the 646 rapes he analysed were premeditated, and Scully (1990), who found that most rapists have sexual partners and an active sex life at the time of their offences.

Some psychoanalytical theorists focus on the victims of rape as having in some way provoked the offender. Victims are described as having an inner masochistic need to be raped (interestingly, the victims of burglary are rarely described as secretly having wished their houses would be broken into). If it is not the victim who is to blame, it is sometimes the mother or the wife:

> "There can be no doubt that the sexual frustration which the wives caused is one of the factors motivating the rape which might be tentatively described as a displaced attempt to force a seductive but rejecting mother into submission. The sex offender was not only exposed to his wife's masculine and competitive inclinations, but also in a certain sense was somehow seduced into committing the crime." (Abrahamson, 1960, p.165)

These views have been refuted by research evidence, for example Amir (1971), who showed that most rapes are planned, victims are often targeted, the majority of rapists do not suffer from any mental illness and most are married or involved in intimate relationships at the time of their offending.

If rape were the result of individual deficit then the occurrence of rape would be much the same across cultures, but there are in fact significant cross-cultural variations. Sanday (1981) surveyed 156 societies and found 47% to be rape free and 18% to be rape prone (the rest were in between). In 'rape-free' cultures women were treated respectfully, prestige was attached to female reproductive roles, the power of nature was revered and interpersonal violence of all kinds was low. By contrast, in the 'rape-prone' cultures the sexes were clearly separated, there was a general subscription to male dominance and male violence was sanctioned for solving personal problems.

Biological explanations

There are two forms of the biological explanation of rape – the sociobiological and the hormonal. Within the sociobiological perspective, rape is seen as a product of societal functioning rather than of individual pathology. Human sexual behaviour is seen to be driven by the need to maximise the potential for sexual reproduction, but there is an unavoidable difference between the needs of males and females which produces a tension. Females are vulnerable during pregnancy and need to choose a mate who will care for them and their offspring. Males, on the other hand, need not be so choosy and in order to maximise their genetic potential will aim to impregnate as many females as possible. Within this framework, rape is seen as a mating strategy used by unsuccessful males, i.e. those who have been unable to attract a female. In addition, rape can be seen as a result of a stronger sex drive in males and their greater physical strength, both of which characteristics are likely to have been favoured by natural selection, i.e. those males who can have sex with numerous females are more likely to have passed on their genes (McCammon et al., 1993).

Whilst this explanation can be viewed as simplistic and scientifically unproven, there is some evidence to support it. Thornhill and Thornhill (1983) point out that it is women around the peak age of reproduction who are most likely to be raped and that most rapists are poor and uneducated and therefore less likely to attract a mate. However, whilst it may be true that the majority of rape victims are of reproductive age, it is equally true that girls below the age of puberty, and women long past child-bearing age are also victims of rape, as are men. Moreover, many rapists do not ejaculate and may subject their victims to oral sex or buggery and in some cases gratuitous violence. These behaviours do not tie in with a compulsion to reproduce.

The hormonal version of the biological explanation of rape is perhaps less contentious. The possibility of hormonal imbalances, particularly sex steroids, leading some individuals to rape has gained some credence (Moyer, 1976), but can still only explain the behaviour of a small proportion of offenders.

Psychological explanations

Within the psychological approach there is a blend of theories combining a cognitive behavioural perspective and an emphasis on early childhood. The fact that many sex offenders report that they were themselves the victims of sexual abuse as children allows for the possibility of identification with the aggressor and the victim becoming an abuser in a 'cycle of abuse', but also the possibility of sexually abusive behaviour being learned, as is all behaviour. If children are exposed to sexually inappropriate behaviour at an early age they may develop dysfunctional sexual arousal and if this is combined with a belief system which justifies deviant behaviour, it may be very difficult to break this cycle.

Whilst this perspective certainly allows for innovative treatment strategies, it cannot explain why the vast majority of sex offences are committed by men, when the majority of victims of child sexual abuse are female. Clearly, exposure to abuse is not sufficient to explain subsequent offending. Moreover, there are some discrepancies in the reporting of child abuse by convicted rapists. Thus, Groth (1979) found that 90% of his offender sample said they had suffered childhood sexual abuse, though Scully (1990) found only 9% of her sample reported such abuse.

Another type of psychological explanation invokes social learning theory, suggesting that rapists learn to be sexually aggressive from exposure to rape scenes in the media which clearly associate sexuality with violence. Ellis (1989) suggests that many modern filmic images, including those in slasher and horror films but also music videos, provide a very graphic link between violence and sex. Viewers of these images may learn new behaviours but may also become desensitised to the pain and fear experienced by rape victims, leading to denial and self-justification (Malamuth, 1984; Zillman and Bryant, 1984). Rapists are also said to be susceptible to 'rape myths' (Burt, 1980), which will influence their belief systems and consequently their behaviour.

Feminist explanations

The feminist theory of rape was powerfully presented by Susan Brownmiller (1975) who argued that within patriarchal society men are encouraged to assert their dominance over women in a number of ways and that rape is simply one of them. Within the process of male socialisation, men are educated to think of women as property and as objects of sexual gratification. The legitimacy of these views is reinforced by media representation of male and female sexuality.

The significance of Brownmiller's thesis, however, is her extension of the idea that all males have the potential to rape to a view of rape as a strategy used by *all* men (not just rapists) to control women:

"Rape is a conscious process of intimidation by which **all** men keep **all** women in a state of fear." (pp.14–15)

Thus, the sexual motive of rape is effectively removed. Rape is seen as a 'pseudosexual act' and its motivation as power, anger, humiliation and dominance. Whilst Brownmiller's view is a theoretical one it is supported by clinical evidence, e.g. Groth (1979). Moreover, the rape of men seems to be rarely motivated by sexual desire, but more often by a wish to humiliate (McMullen, 1990).

The feminist view of overall male potential to rape is also supported by evidence, in spite of female and male protests about the radicalism of this view. Surveys have indicated not only that rape is relatively widespread in Western society (Koss et al., 1987) but also that 35% of male American college students would commit rape if they thought they would not get caught (Malamuth, 1981).

The suggested links between masculinity and misogyny, that negative attitudes to women and a valorisation of aggressive sexuality might make a contribution to the likelihood of rape, are compelling and could also go some way to explaining the prevalence of date rape, where anger at the rejection of sexual advances becomes the motivation for serious assault. If a sexual script is followed by only one of the actors then frustration may be an inevitable outcome.

Interviews with convicted rapists have shown that these men not only demonstrated a general distrust of women, but held quite repressive views on female sexuality (Scully, 1990). Their views upheld the double standard whereby male promiscuity is valorised whilst overt female involvement in sexual activity is seen as immoral. It would seem that these men's views were characterised by their adherence to a traditional acceptance of male superiority and a denigration of women who step outside the traditional female role.

Some feminist theorists argue that pornography causes men to rape women: 'Porn is the theory, rape is the practice' (Morgan, 1972). This theory is based on three assumptions: firstly, that images of women as objects of sexual exploitation tend to promote and legitimise male sexual violence; secondly, pornography is said to objectify women in that it eroticises certain body parts and dehumanises women, thereby making them objects and victims; and, thirdly, pornography models examples of sexual assault. Russell (1988) goes further to argue that pornography not only predisposes some males towards rape but it also undermines potential victims' ability to resist rape (Figure 4.3). Despite these claims there is little empirical evidence to support a causal link between pornography and rape and in fact, exposure to non-violent erotica actually reduces aggressiveness (Malamuth and Donnerstein, 1984).

The major weakness of some of the more radical feminist explanations of rape is the desire to explain all types of rape from one perspective alone, the

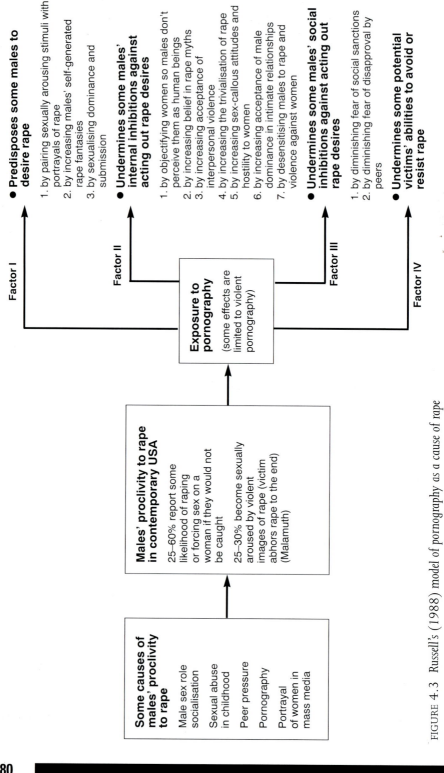

FIGURE 4.3 *Russell's (1988) model of pornography as a cause of rape*

Some causes of males' proclivity to rape

Male sex role socialisation

Sexual abuse in childhood

Peer pressure

Pornography

Portrayal of women in mass media

Males' proclivity to rape in contemporary USA

25–60% report some likelihood of raping or forcing sex on a woman if they would not be caught

25–30% become sexually aroused by violent images of rape (victim abhors rape to the end) (Malamuth)

Exposure to pornography

(some effects are limited to violent pornography)

Factor I

● **Predisposes some males to desire rape**

1. by pairing sexually arousing stimuli with portrayals of rape
2. by increasing males' self-generated rape fantasies
3. by sexualising dominance and submission

Factor II

● **Undermines some males' internal inhibitions against acting out rape desires**

1. by objectifying women so males don't perceive them as human beings
2. by increasing belief in rape myths
3. by increasing acceptance of interpersonal violence
4. by increasing the trivialisation of rape
5. by increasing sex-callous attitudes and hostility to women
6. by increasing acceptance of male dominance in intimate relationships
7. by desensitising males to rape and violence against women

Factor III

● **Undermines some males' social inhibitions against acting out rape desires**

1. by diminishing fear of social sanctions
2. by diminishing fear of disapproval by peers

Factor IV

● **Undermines some potential victims' abilities to avoid or resist rape** need for power, and to imply that 'all men are potential rapists.' Whilst all men may have the potential to rape, it is clear that not all do and there is thus a need to consider other variables which act on this potential. The value of feminist theories of rape is their emphasis on cultural and social aspects of sexual violence and their insistence that explanations in terms of individual psychopathology are no longer acceptable.

Integrated theories

There is the possibility of integration between the various theories of rape. Marshall and Barbaree (1990) suggest that males have a biological propensity for the pursuit of sexual fulfilment and a tendency to confuse sex and aggression. Male socialisation should ensure that these tendencies are appropriately controlled, but where individuals have suffered damage in early childhood they may become aggressive and non-empathic. They will probably suffer low self-esteem and may seek compensation through aggressive sex. These tendencies will be more extreme within an environment in which negative attitudes to women prevail.

Ellis (1989) has suggested that there may need to be different explanations for stranger rape and for date rape, but argues for a synthesis of previous theories. He proposes that the male sex drive is stronger than the female sex drive because of differential investment in reproduction and that men will tend to use force as a sexual tactic, having learned that this strategy can be effective, particularly in early courtship rituals. Ellis then argues that only those males with high testosterone levels and little empathy or sensitivity to punishment will go on to become rapists.

Lundberg-Love and Geffner (1989) provide a model for date rape which emphasises preconditions which, if occurring together, may explain the behaviour of both rapist and victim (Table 4.2).

RAPIST TAXONOMIES

How different are rapists from ordinary men? Feminist theorists would suggest not much, whilst other theorists disagree on the points of difference and point out the diversity of rapists.

There have been many studies carried out to determine the personality of the rapist. Some of these have been clinical (e.g. Groth, 1979), using convicted rapists as subjects, whilst others have used a variety of measures of rape proclivity, or high likelihood to rape, with ordinary participants in an attempt to correlate other variables with this tendency (e.g. Malamuth, 1986). The single best predictor of rape, at least amongst adolescents, seems to be that rapists have peers who condone and encourage sexual conquests (Ageton, 1983).

Table 4.2 Model for date rape (Lundberg-Love and Geffner, 1989)

Factors which enhance motivation to sexually abuse	Factors which reduce internal inhibitions	Factors which reduce external inhibitions	Factors which reduce victim resistance
Power and control needs	Attitudes:	Date location	Passivity
Miscommunication about sex	– traditional sex roles	Mode of transport	Poor self-defence strategies
Sexual arousal	– acceptance of violence	Date activity	History of sexual abuse
Emotional incongruence	– endorsement of rape myths	Alcohol or substance abuse	Traditional attitudes
Imbalance in power differential	– adversarial relationships		Poor sexual knowledge
	Prior abusive acts		

Studies with convicted rapists

Although the data from these studies must be treated with caution, it is clear that certain common themes do emerge. It was a study by Groth (1979) which first highlighted the possibility that a quest for sex might not be the primary motive of the rapist. Over a period of ten years Groth interviewed 500 convicted rapists and identified the motive of power and a need to dominate as the most common factors in rape.

> "Rape is always and foremost an aggressive act ... In every act of rape, both aggression and sexuality are involved, but it is clear that sexuality becomes the means of expressing the aggressive needs and feelings that operate in the offender ..." (Groth, 1979, pp. 12–13)

According to Groth (1979), in all cases of stranger rape there are elements of power, anger and sexuality, but one of these elements will predominate for any individual rapist.

The *power rapist* needs to assert control over his victims in order to compensate for feelings of inadequacy and he sees rape as a way of demonstrating his masculinity. He will use verbal threats, but his intention is not to cause physical harm, more a forceful seduction. He may even convince himself that his victim enjoyed the encounter, as one of the power rapists in Groth's (1979) study noted:

> "She wanted it; she was asking for it. She just said 'no' so I wouldn't think she was easy." (p.30)

The *anger rapist* is motivated by extreme rage against women, though the trigger which converts this anger to rape may be a dispute with a woman who is known to him. Unable to express his feelings, this rapist chooses a victim unknown to him in order to temporarily release his anger. He uses an unnecessary amount of force and will often force his victim to perform humiliating sexual acts. As one of the anger rapists in Groth's (1979) study said:

> "I wanted to knock the woman off her pedestal, and I felt that rape was the worst thing I could do to her." (p.14)

The *sadistic rapist* has eroticised sexuality and violence in a cruel and often fatal way. He plans his offending, enjoys tormenting his victim and it is her anguish and pain which bring sexual gratification. According to Hazelwood et al., (1995) this rapist, though rare, is highly dangerous and unlikely ever to respond to treatment.

This typology of rapists has been extended by Knight and Prentky (1987) and Hazelwood (1995) and has been crucial in developing offender profiles of serial rapists. At the heart of these theories, however, is the belief that rapists are suffering from some sort of psychological dysfunction and that the rape is an expression or symptom of this.

However, even a study of convicted serial rapists highlighted the heterogeneity of the sample and the possibility that many of them were not the stereotypical 'madman' many accounts of 'stranger rape' would have us believe. Hazelwood and Warren (1995) interviewed 41 men who had been convicted of more than ten rapes and found:

- the average age of the rapists at the time of their first attack was 21.8;
- 85% of the rapists were white;
- 54% had generally stable employment;
- 71% had been married;
- 78% were living with a partner at the time of the rapes;
- 87% scored average or above on IQ tests;
- 76% had been sexually abused as children;
- 54% had grown up in homes that were socioeconomically average or above;
- 51% had served in the armed forces.

Hazelwood and Warren (1995) also noted that descriptions of these men by their friends included 'average', 'friendly', 'a leader' and 'willing to help out a friend' and that the majority of the men themselves took a pride in their personal appearance and were well groomed.

Other studies of convicted rapists have concluded that rape is an almost inevitable outcome of a culture which accepts sexual violence against women as the norm. Scully and Marolla (1985) found that their sample of rapists did not tend to see their crimes as 'real' rapes – 25% of them described their victims as 'willing', and almost 50% of them claimed that their victims had 'enjoyed' the ordeal. These rapists spoke of their enjoyment of impersonal sex, and the feelings of power and conquest which accompanied it. Scully and Marolla concluded that 'Through rape men can experience power and avoid the emotions related to intimacy and tenderness'. In a subsequent study with convicted rapists, Scully (1990) found high acceptance of violence against women and 45% of the men she interviewed believed that women like to be hit because this means men care about them. Such beliefs clearly assist denial of responsibility and may even lead to a view that some women deserve to be raped if they step outside traditional female roles. Scully (1990) differs from Groth in her assertion that sexual motivation is a strong factor in rape and also in her view of the cultural influences which may make 'ordinary' men vulnerable to the possibility of rape because it is a 'low cost–high gain' crime.

Studies attempting correlations with 'rape proclivity'

There are several variables which appear to correlate with the likelihood of individuals to commit rape, or rape proclivity, as it is termed in the literature. These are negative attitudes to women, arousal to rape depictions, machiavellianism, hypermasculinity and affect intensity, all of which are explained below.

Studies using Burt's Rape Myth Acceptance Scale (1980) show that men with a high likelihood to rape also show high acceptance of rape myths and traditional beliefs about the role of women in society (Check and Malamuth, 1983). They also report more arousal to sexual violence and when plethysmography has been used to measure penile arousal, it is these participants who respond the most to rape scenes (Malamuth, 1986). Machiavellianism is a construct used to refer to individuals who are characteristically manipulative, deceitful, opportunistic and domineering (Christie and Geis, 1970). Hypermasculinity refers to a cluster of attitudes – callous sexual attitudes to women, a view of danger as exciting and violence as manly (Mosher and Sirkin, 1984). Affect intensity is the experiencing of emotions to a stronger degree than others (Larsen, 1984). Allison and Branscombe (1992) found that a combination of these three variables successfully discriminated between those who reported they would use force to obtain sex and those who did not.

CULTURAL DEPICTIONS OF RAPE

If rape is considered a metaphor for men's violent oppression of women, it should perhaps not be surprising that it appears so often in pornography, but its depiction in the media generally, particularly in film, must be considered more troubling in view of the messages about women and sexuality which are being transmitted to the audience.

Women are usually portrayed as victims, vulnerable and/or provocative, but their helplessness often also signals a likelihood of eventual sexual arousal. Examples of this genre include *Swept Away* (1975), *9½ Weeks* (1986); and *Tie Me Up, Tie Me Down* (1990). The classic film *Gone With the Wind* (1939) presents an extraordinary example of marital rape when Rhett Butler (Clark Gable) overpowers Scarlett O'Hara (Vivien Leigh) in spite of her protests, but the very next scene shows Scarlett waking the following morning and smiling contentedly. As Finkelhor and Yllö (1985) point out, these images present the idea:

> "that women secretly wish to be overpowered and raped, and that, in fact, rape may be a good way to reconcile a marriage." (p.14).

Even when films attempt to focus on the trauma of rape the perspective adopted is problematic. Thus, in *The Accused* (1988) the victim, played by Jodie Foster, is portrayed as a feckless, impulsive character who dances and dresses provocatively and is then gang-raped in a bar. Justice is eventually seen to be done, but not through a straightforward rape prosecution, rather via an unorthodox use of charges of criminal solicitation against the onlookers. The rape itself is never seen through the eyes of its victim, but only when a male character gives evidence in court. As Clover (1992) points out, 'Seldom has a set of male eyes been more privileged' (p.151). Interestingly, this film was based on a true story and several women's groups opposed its release because they felt that a mainstream entertainment film could not possibly deal with this topic with sufficient seriousness.

Whilst a clear causal link between violence in the media and violent behaviour has not been found, the research which shows that rapists and non-rapists alike are aroused by rape scenes in which the victim is seen to become sexually aroused (Malamuth and Donnerstein, 1982), and that exposure to aggressive erotica makes ordinary men more likely to have rape fantasies, to have less sensitivity to rape and to be more likely to accept rape myths and violence towards women (Donnerstein, 1984), should make us think seriously about the messages being transmitted via the media.

Interestingly, the theoretical move away from a view of rapists as necessarily psychopathic has also been mirrored in film. Thus, Clover (1992) draws our attention to a genre of 'rape revenge' films (e.g. *I Spit on Your Grave* (1977), *Lipstick* (1976), *Ms 45* (1981)) in which rape begins to be seen as a problem for women themselves to solve. Thus, the female victims of rape become almost 'masculinised' in order to exact a dreadful revenge, whilst the rapists are portrayed as increasingly 'normal', no longer rapist-as-psychopath more rapist-as-standard-guy.

CONCLUSION

There is no single type of rape, nor is there one type of rapist. Current theory suggests that traditional views of rape occurring as a result of certain troubled men being unable to control their sexual drive in the face of victim provocation are inadequate. Yet these stereotypical views have influenced attitudes to rape and the responsibility victims are supposed to bear for their suffering. The phenomenon of date rape in particular has highlighted the problematic nature of consent and how that is demonstrated.

Whilst public awareness of rape and the trauma suffered by rape victims has increased markedly during the 1990s, the incidence of rape continues to rise (by 14% between 1995 and 1996) and its escalation during periods of conflict should serve to reinforce its image as one of brutality, humiliation and dominance. Linking rape to sexuality has served the purpose of diminishing the offender's responsibility and placing blame on the victim. It has also conveniently diverted attention away from an examination of the links between male socialisation and the generation of attitudes which reinforce and make possible the crime of rape.

chapter five

MEDIA INFLUENCE ON CRIME

CHAPTER OVERVIEW

This chapter attempts to explore the possible association between the media and crime, notably television and filmic images of violence and violent behaviour, by examining the wide range of studies made in this area. There will also be an analysis of the alleged link between pornographic images in the media and sexual violence. Despite the massive amount of research on media violence, researchers still disagree quite vehemently on the conclusions that should be drawn. The role which could be played by the media in terms of crime prevention or promoting prosocial behaviour is by comparison largely under-researched.

INTRODUCTION

The part played by the media in our lives has grown immensely in recent years and yet its impact is still not fully understood. Technological advancements have ensured that we are bombarded with information designed both to educate and entertain. Whereas in 1989, 800,000 homes were linked to either satellite or cable TV, by 1994 this figure had risen to almost 4,000,000 (AGB, 1995). Our limited understanding of the impact of the media does not stem from a dearth of research, especially in the area of violence.

> "TV violence has received more attention in public and research debates than any other issue in the field of mass communications." (Cumberbatch,1992)

There is a massive interest in this area and considerable concern about the effects of media violence, especially on the young. This concern, however, is nothing new. In the *Edinburgh Review* of 1851 the melodramas at the local theatre were described as:

> "a powerful agent for depraving the boyish classes of our towns and cities."(cited in Conduit, 1993)

whilst music halls and 'penny dreadfuls' were blamed for inciting hooliganism, especially in the lower classes. Similar concerns were raised in the 1950s about the possible effects of horror comics and the popularity of films like *Rebel Without a Cause* and *The Blackboard Jungle* were seen by some to be directly connected to increased juvenile delinquency.

Common sense might indicate that there must be something in all this – why do advertisers spend thousands of pounds trying to persuade us to buy their products if the media has no influence? Parents are clearly worried about the effects of TV violence and a study by Ridley-Johnson et al. (1991) revealed that most of the parents they surveyed believed that TV violence did affect their adolescent children, inducing fear in girls and aggression in boys. So, what are the major concerns about media violence? As Cumberbatch (1992) indicates, the concerns seem to centre on three major areas – the extent of screen violence, the impact of new forms of media and, most important of all, the nature of the relationship between media violence and aggression.

Firstly, is there too much screen violence and is it increasing? Much is often made of the claims of an American psychiatrist, Frederick Wertham, who said that he had seen as patients adolescents who:

> "in comic books, movies and TV have seen more than 10,000 homicides" (Wertham, 1968)

but the claims of ever-increasing screen violence are problematic because of the need to accurately define screen violence and to ensure a consistent use of that definition. A recognised expert in the field, George Gerbner (1972), counted in his studies all acts of violence which included 'any overt expression of physical force'. Not surprisingly, the animal cartoon *Tom and Jerry* appeared to be one of the most violent TV programmes on air.

More recent figures show that the amount of violence shown on TV is perhaps not as high as critics fear. A recent survey revealed that violence accounted for only 1.39% of broadcast hours on ten terrestrial and satellite channels observed during a 28-day period in 1995–96 (Sheffield University Violence on TV in Britain Survey, 1996). This represented a small increase on the 1.08% recorded in 1994–95. However, an earlier content analysis of programmes shown over a four-week period revealed that 37% of programmes analysed contained violence and 71% of the violent acts recorded occurred on the satellite channels (Gunter and Harrison, 1995). Whilst the violence occupied only 1.07% of total programme running time, it emerged that a small number of programmes seemed to contain exceptionally large amounts of violence (1% of programmes contained 19% of all violent acts recorded). Most of the violence occurred in drama programmes, especially films. Similar results were reported in the US National Television Violence Study (1996) which involved a content analysis of drama and news programmes and found that 57% of 2693 drama programmes and 38% of the news programmes contained violence. The highest percentage of violent programmes were on cable channels, particularly those devoted to films.

Nevertheless, people are clearly concerned about the possible links between screen violence and aggressive behaviour. In the 1993 trial of two boys accused of murdering James Bulger, the judge said:

> "It is not for me to pass judgement on their upbringing but I suspect that exposure to violent video films may in part be an explanation."

In fact, the main evidence presented in court concerning the boys' media use was that one of them turned his head away whenever anything violent came on television, though it also became apparent that one of the boys' fathers had rented a video called *Child's Play 3* some weeks before the murder. Rather more substantial evidence was provided that both boys had long-term histories of maladaptive social behaviour and that they came from discordant family backgrounds. However, as a result of the press coverage of the trial, the video *Child's Play 3* was withdrawn, though the families and the police said there was no evidence that either of the boys had seen the video. The same video was also implicated in the murder of Suzanne Capper who had been tortured by a group of adolescents who were described as using the voice of Chucky, the doll character in *Child's Play 3*. Once again, there was no factual evidence to support such an assertion and yet the media was full of headlines urging a ban on violent videos.

Following the James Bulger case, the developmental psychologist Elizabeth Newson (1994) published a report purporting to represent the view of many child health professionals that the link between media violence and subsequent aggression was supported by research and suggesting that violent videos should be banned. However, as Cumberbatch (1994) and Barker and Petley (1997) point out, the report relies heavily on sensationalist news accounts and is highly selective in terms of evidence, resulting in a simplistic account of a particular moral view. Reading these different accounts gives a good flavour of the degree of disagreement between academics on this issue and the temptation to enter the arena of politics and policy making.

Certain films are still unavailable for viewing because of their association with violence. Stanley Kubrick withdrew his own film, *A Clockwork Orange*, when suggestions were made that copycat incidents of violence had occurred; *Natural Born Killers* was due for release on video but was withdrawn after the murders in Dunblane in March 1996; and there were moves to ban *Power Rangers* because of the killing of a Norwegian child in 1994 by a karate-style kick in the playground.

Are new forms of media entertainment potentially dangerous, e.g. video games, the Internet, virtual reality, etc.? There has always been concern about the impact of new media on the young, whether in the form of horror comics or 'video nasties'. Now we have consoles which allow children to take on the role of combatant in interactive computer games which show the audible and visual consequences of attacks involving chainsaws, bombs and machine guns, but even in 1982 the then US Surgeon General, C. Everett Koop, warned that video games were producing 'aberrations in childhood behaviour'. According to him, children were becoming addicted to the games 'body and soul', yet when asked to substantiate his comments, Koop admitted that he had no scientific evidence to support his views (cited in Selnow, 1984).

There are some important differences between TV and video/computer games in relation to depicted violence, though. For example:

- TV is passive, whilst video game playing is active;
- TV does not require constant attention, whereas video games do;
- TV can show real acts of violence (in news broadcasts), whilst video games show violence at a more abstract level.

Whilst concerns are expressed, this is still a significantly under-researched area. Studies so far indicate concerns about addiction to computer games amongst school children (Fisher, 1993), possibly linked to arousal and a particular personality type (Griffiths and Dancaster, 1995), and a subsequent concern about this preoccupation leading to isolation and possible desensitisation rather than it being viewed as a trigger to violence. Nevertheless it seems to be the violent 'beat-'em-up' games, e.g. *Doom*, *Mortal Kombat*, etc., which are the most popular and it is perhaps not insignificant that these games tend to be tailored towards boys – there are very few games on the market which are designed to appeal to girls. Toles (1985) found that in a sample of 100 video arcade games, 92% did not include any female roles and of the remaining 8%, 6% had females assuming 'damsel in distress' roles and only 2% in active roles. Zimbardo (cited in Dominick,1984) has commented:

> "Eat him, burn him, zap him is the message rather than bargaining and co-operation. Most games tend to feed into masculine fantasies of control, power and destruction."

There may be a need for additional concern about some of these games too, as Provenzo (1991) points out:

> "In addition to reflecting themes of violence and destruction, video games have a history of being sexist and racist. In the early 1980s the home video game *Custer's Revenge* had to be withdrawn from circulation as a result of consumer protests over its discriminatory treatment of women and native Americans. Players who were able to manoeuvre Custer through thorny cactus and a hail of arrows got to watch an officer sexually assault a helpless but smiling Indian woman tied to a stake."

Griffiths (1997), in his comprehensive account of the research so far into video games and aggression, concludes that whilst there is an indication that young children tend to play more aggressively after playing with aggressive video games, this effect may be short term and overall it seems likely that the differences in types of game and differential measures of aggression leave many questions about the link unanswered and the need for more systematic research very evident.

Is media violence harmful, especially to children? What is the nature of the connection between media violence and subsequent aggression? This is the major issue – does a connection between media violence and subsequent aggressive behaviour exist and how convincing are the empirical studies which have been carried out so far to investigate this possibility?

There is considerable research in this area, most of which concludes that media violence is an important factor which contributes to the level of aggression in society, but this is far from establishing a causal relationship between media violence and societal violence. When Michael Ryan randomly shot and killed 16 people in Hungerford in 1987, it was claimed that he had been inspired by the film *Rambo*, but there was no evidence to confirm this and there were clearly many other factors which contributed to his mental state. Similarly, the serial killer Jeffrey Dahmer's favourite film, and the one he watched before he went out cruising for victims, was *Return of the Jedi*, one of the most popular and uncontroversial films for children in the 1980s. On the darker side, however, there is evidence that the man who tried to assassinate President Reagan, John Hinckley, was inspired by his frequent viewing of *Taxi Driver*.

RESEARCH METHODS

There are three main research methods which have been used to explore the possibility of a link between media violence and aggression: natural variation, laboratory experiments and field studies. The results from these studies are not consistent, though laboratory experiments tend to show stronger effects.

Natural variation

This is the easiest method to employ because it involves no manipulation of variables, simply observation and measurement, though some of the longitudinal studies have taken many years and considerable effort to generate findings. It should be remembered, however, that these studies can only allow correlations to be established. The results they produce could therefore be due to other unmeasured or unobserved factors. Examples of these kinds of study include the following.

The work of Phillips (1983) seems to demonstrate that violent consequences sometimes follow real-life violence reported in the media. In the two months after the suicide of Marilyn Monroe in 1962 there were 300 more suicides than would normally have been expected during this period. Similarly, after televised events such as major heavyweight boxing matches the number of reported murders has been shown to increase by up to one-eighth. This increase peaks three days after the fight and is greatest for the most publicised ones.

Another famous study was the Rip Van Winkle Study begun in the 1960s, a longitudinal study investigating the viewing habits and aggression levels of children over a 20-year period. Eight hundred children aged eight who lived in a small semirural community in Judson River Valley, New York, were assessed. They were given an aggressiveness rating by their peers, their IQ score was obtained, their parents were interviewed and their three favourite TV programmes were noted. Ten years on, the same children were traced and interviewed and again some years later. Eron and Huesmann (1986) concluded that early exposure to TV violence was indeed related to later aggression, but only among males. As adults, the children who had watched the most TV violence were also aggressive drivers, they used more physical punishment towards their children and were more likely to have an arrest record (Lefkowitz et al., 1977).

These results were seen as impressive, but there were criticisms. For example, the study did not measure TV watching directly, but relied on information given by parents. The amount of TV viewing at age eight and subsequent aggression may have been due to some underlying common factor such as biological predisposition or lack of parental involvement; and during the intervening years 55% of the sample disappeared or at least failed to respond, so the group which was left may not have been representative.

It may be that the children who are already aggressive and interested in aggression are the ones who are not surprisingly going to show up as watching more violent TV, thus implying a causal link which is very misleading. A study by Singer and Singer (1981) did employ direct observation, with the researchers following groups of preschool children over a four-year period, observing their TV viewing and play behaviour for two-week periods several times each year. Singer and Singer did find a correlation between heavy viewing of TV violence and aggressive play, but the other factors which were also important were parental emphasis on force as a disciplinary tactic and the aggressive children having fewer hours of sleep.

Similarly, in another longitudinal study of 3200 school children and teenagers, Milavsky et al. (1982) found very small associations between levels of aggression and exposure to violent TV programmes and concluded that the influence of family background, social environment and school performance was more important and that the significance of TV viewing as an indicator of aggressiveness was very weak.

Other studies have attempted to investigate the effects of the introduction of television into communities which have hitherto been without it. Himmelweit et al. (1958) and Schramm et al. (1961) compared TV viewers and non-TV viewers but found very few differences in levels of aggression. In fact, Schramm et al. found that 11–12-year-olds in 'radiotown' were actually more aggressive than those in 'teletown'. Williams (1986), however, compared the behaviour of Canadian children in a community to which TV had only recently been introduced with children in communities where TV had been available for some time and found quite different results. The major finding was that aggressive behaviour in 6–11-year-olds increased over a two-year period following the introduction of TV while no such increase was found in the other communities.

Laboratory experiments

Two names dominate in this area, Albert Bandura and Leonard Berkowitz. Their work indisputably demonstrates that aggressive models on film increase aggressive behaviour amongst children and adults. However, their studies took place in the laboratory, a controlled setting which bears limited relevance to the real world, and the measures of aggression which they used were unavoidably artificial or contrived. Participants in experimental studies know they are taking part in an experiment so the normal barriers against antisocial behaviour may not operate in the same way. Nonetheless, the work of Bandura and Berkowitz remains significant in the area of media violence.

Bandura et al. (1963) carried out the famous Bobo Doll experiments which seem to show quite clearly that children do imitate aggressive acts which they have seen on screen – up to 88% imitated the aggression they had seen (Figure 5.1).

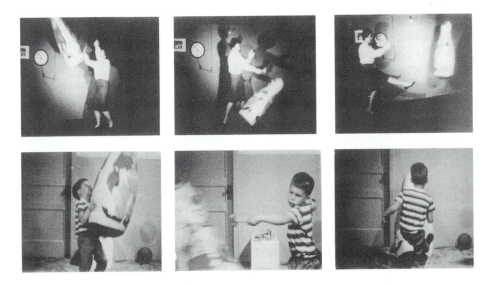

FIGURE 5.1 *Bandura's classic 'Bo-bo doll' studies demonstrated how children will imitate aggressive behaviour, especially if they see that behaviour rewarded*

However, whilst Bandura's studies convincingly show the power of imitation it should be remembered that the object of aggression in the film and subsequently attacked by the children was a plastic inflatable toy which was quite a novelty then and the children were deliberately frustrated before the free-play opportunity was presented.

Berkowitz (1965) wanted to investigate the Freudian concept of cartharsis. He was interested in whether watching TV violence might reduce aggression because aggressive drives would be vicariously discharged by the viewing itself. He devised an experimental situation in which subjects were either provoked or not (by having their intelligence insulted) and then they watched either a neutral film (on canal boats) or a clip of a boxing film (*Champion*, with Kirk Douglas). When they were shown the boxing film they were either told specifically that the violence in it was justified, or not. Berkowitz found that provocation produced more aggressive responses (measured by subjects rating the experimenter) and that justification of violence also produced more aggressive responses:

> "Media aggression depicted as being justified has the greatest probability of leading to aggression when the audience is already angry."

Interestingly, however, Berkowitz's subjects did not imitate the violence they had seen in *Champion*. They did not assault the experimenter (who was called Kirk!), they simply rated him as less likeable, but this was the measure of aggression used by Berkowitz in this particular study.

Field studies

These studies are often considered to be more acceptable because they are not as contrived as studies carried out in the laboratory and yet their results are still not consistent. The classic field study is the one carried out by Leyens et al. (1975) in a Belgian correctional home for boys. These boys were shown a diet of either aggressive films, e.g. *Bonnie and Clyde*, *The Dirty Dozen*, or neutral films, e.g. *Lily*, *La Belle Americaine*, every night for a week. Compared to pre-viewing baselines, the boys in the aggressive film condition increased their physical aggression in the week following exposure, whilst the boys in the neutral condition showed very little aggression. Leyens et al. (1975) commented:

> "It seems as if the films evoked among the spectators the kind of aggression they had been exposed to."

Once again, these look like impressive results but there have been criticisms on methodological grounds. For example, field studies by their nature cannot be as controlled as laboratory studies, the presence of observers might have influenced the outcome and the sample used could hardly be described as representative.

Another field study produced quite the opposite results. Feshback and Singer (1971) studied the residents of four boys' homes, subjecting some of them to a diet of 'violent' television and others to 'neutral' television over a period of six weeks, during which their behaviour was observed. They found that aggression in the 'violent' group was almost half that in the 'neutral' group and concluded that this was evidence for catharsis.

Recent studies

One of the most recent studies of the impact of media violence in the UK was carried out by Hagell and Newbury (1994). They compared the viewing habits of young offenders and a matched group of non-offenders and found that the offenders did not watch more violent TV and they had had less access to videos and computer games. They appeared to be more interested in the real world than in watching screens, but interviews with them about their early lives and their offending history revealed the following:

> "The overriding impression gained from interviewing the (offender) children was of lives that were full of change, chaos, and deprivation, in which the media were of less significance than was the case for non-offending peers."

Browne and Pennell (1997) have also examined the significance of the media for young offenders and conclude that for those individuals from violent backgrounds and who demonstrate low levels of empathy, it may be that violence in the media is 'read' rather differently. They attach more importance to the excitement of particular scenes and then want to 'relive' those scenes themselves. However, the results of their study, which involved interviewing young offenders before and after viewing violent films, show that it is vulnerable individuals who are likely to be most affected by the violence they see and that wholesale censorship would in no way address their problems effectively.

EVALUATING THE RESEARCH

What should we make of all the assertions and all the evidence? Some of the studies, especially those in a laboratory setting, seem to show a clear correlation between watching violent TV and subsequent aggressive behaviour. Many of the other studies, however, are flawed and the overall findings are inconsistent. A recent meta-analysis of 217 studies from 1957 to 1990 concluded that the research on media violence does indicate an effect upon subsequent aggressiveness among viewers (Paik and Comstock, 1994) but as Gauntlett (1995) points out, this statistical approach fails to take into account the methodological weaknesses of many of the studies included.

It may be that we have mistakenly viewed TV audiences and children as passive receivers of information and instead of TV moulding society, it could be the other way round – a particular society creates TV, reflecting and reinforcing a violent culture but hardly responsible for creating it. For example, Japan has very low levels of violence but very violent TV. The USA and Canada have similar TV but Canada's crime rate is much lower than the USA. The degree of violence in the USA is more likely to be connected to huge inequalities of wealth, racism, free access to guns and serious drug problems, rather than exposure to violent films.

A more helpful approach to the potential problem of media violence might be to steer the focus away from the contentious search for a clear link between screen violence and subsequent aggressive behaviour. Gunter and McAleer (1990) propose a model to explain how TV may affect behaviour without necessarily asserting that the link is direct and unavoidable.

- *Arousal* – the physiological response of excitement in viewers might be interpreted by them as anger. The arousal might also activate latent aggressive impulses.
- *Disinhibition* – watching violence on TV can lead viewers to believe that violence is socially acceptable and normal, especially when it appears so often as a way of solving problems.
- *Desensitisation* – if people become too accustomed to watching violence on TV they will be less shocked by it in real life.
- *Imitation* – people, especially children, will copy what they see if it looks like fun and is rewarded or at least not punished. Over time, people may discover that violence does solve some of their problems and are therefore more likely to repeat it.

In their overall evaluation of the evidence, Gunter and McAleer state:

"... the measurement of television's effects, and of factors that mediate those effects, is highly complex ... we are still a long way from knowing fully the extent and character of television's influence on children's aggressive behaviour."

According to Taylor et al. (1994):

"... media violence is not a sufficient condition to produce aggressive behaviour, nor is it a necessary one. Aggressive behaviour is multiply determined and media violence in and of itself is unlikely to provoke such behaviour ... However ... media violence can be a contributing factor to some aggressive acts in some individuals..."

Common sense would indicate that media violence, particularly if it is unnecessarily graphic or associated with rewards, can give the wrong messages to those who are vulnerable. It is likely that 5–10% of the population may be considered to fall into this category as a result of their background and the likelihood of their responding to frustration with violence. However, any legislation which is introduced to lessen this potential impact needs to address one of the fundamental dilemmas associated with crime in general, but exposure to media violence in particular. Boys and girls are exposed to violence on TV and yet it tends to be boys who are the most affected – why?

Violent films are immensely popular and if they are so harmful, why do so many people go to see these films, sometimes repeatedly? Hill (1997) chose to ask precisely this and discovered that viewers offered a variety of reasons, including setting themselves endurance tests and cathartically releasing anger and frustration aroused in real life.

One particular area of media violence which has prompted serious concerns and has generated prolific research is that of pornography and its possible association with sexual violence. As a preliminary to the discussion of this research, another topic – slasher films – will be described as an illustration of the less obvious but still troubling aspects of screen violence.

SLASHER FILMS

Whilst horror films have a respected history and not inconsiderable popularity (Jancovich,1994), concerns have been expressed about a genre of films known as 'slasher' or 'splatter' movies which appear to be particularly popular amongst adolescents. These films appeared in the late 1970s and 1980s and have acquired almost cult status. They include the *Halloween* series (1978, 1981, 1984), the *Nightmare on Elm Street* series (1984, 1985, 1987, 1989, 1995), the *Friday the 13th* series (1980, 1982, 1985, 1986, 1988,1989), *Texas Chainsaw Massacre* (1974, 1986, 1990), *Driller Killer* (1979) and *Evil Dead* (1983, 1987), amongst others.

The most worrying aspect of these films is their depiction of attitudes towards women. The 'hero' of slasher movies tends to be a serial killer who tracks down a group of teenagers, killing them off one by one in various grisly ways. The attacks are primarily directed against women, though some young men are also targeted. A distinguishing feature of these films is the use of the subjective camera shot from the killer's point of view – creating an identification between the audience and the killer, rather than with the victim. The young women who are killed have usually engaged in sexual activity just before their deaths and their death is presented almost as punishment for their overt sexuality. Wood (1986) argues that slasher films represent a conservative response to the women's movement in which:

> "The women who are terrorised and slaughtered are those who resist definition within the virgin/wife/mother framework."

Interestingly, however, whilst women may be the primary targets in these films, there is usually one female who finally manages to kill the killer. This female is often presented as unusual, intelligent and independent, but ultimately in control. She also tends to have an androgynous name, such as Laurie, and Clover (1992) has called these heroines 'final girls'. As Tudor (1989) has argued, however, masculinity rather than femininity may be the problem within these films. There is rarely any positive or effective male figure in the films and this could be seen as a reflection of a loss of faith in the male as hero, in film but also in society. Clover (1989) claims that slasher films actually challenge traditional associations between sex and gender. Women's roles are not presented as being determined by their biology and they are able to perform activities usually restricted to males. Masculinity *per se* is definitely not valorised, however. What becomes important is:

> "... masculinity in conjunction with a female body ... masculinity in conjunction with femininity."

Male authority remains the problem and the female who refuses her role as victim and rejects the positions of powerlessness associated with femininity eventually prevails. A more mainstream film about serial killers, *The Silence of the Lambs*, also contains this theme with an androgynous heroine, Clarice Starling (Jodie Foster), rescuing a female victim from Buffalo Bill, a feminised male who detests his penis and literally dons female skin to feel whole. Perhaps this is the way forward and slasher films can be seen as having transmitted a more positive message after all.

Maybe not. The release of *Scream* (1997) may herald the end of the slasher genre. Directed by Wes Craven (who also directed and appeared in the *Nightmare on Elm Street* series), this film is a self-consciously postmodern analysis not only of the genre but the debate on media violence itself. In *Scream* there are two serial killers, young men who appear to have been, so they claim, affected by maternal abandonment and peer pressure, but who exist within a teen culture addicted to slasher films and so familiar with their plots and dialogue that they eventually admit to having been malevolently affected by media violence. It is this which has challenged them to kill without real motive, though once again the links between sex and death are very apparent and there is, true to form, a final girl – Sydney (Neve Campbell).

PORNOGRAPHY

Pornography has become a symbol of all the concern expressed about increasing violence, particularly sexual violence, in our society. It is easy to identify as a possible cause because it is already associated with many features of society which are recognised as social problems and which seem to be

FIGURE 5.2 *Freddie Kruger in* A Nightmare on Elm Street (*directed by* Wes Craven *who also directed* Scream)

increasing, e.g. child sexual abuse, rape, etc. But what actually constitutes pornography? What would you find offensive to view or read and can you explain what it is which makes the material offend you? Would it depend on who was with you? And would you object to someone else making these decisions on your behalf?

In common with concerns about media violence generally, there is an under-lying assumption that we are 'empty vessels' waiting to be filled by media messages telling us how to behave. Since these messages can be bad, they should be regulated by censorship so that we are all protected from ourselves. The whole issue of pornography is, however, much more complex than either political lobbyists, radical feminists or psychological research would seem to indicate.

What is pornography?

The term arose in the 1860s and referred originally to the depiction of prostitution. Now it is considered to be material which is intended to cause sexual arousal, often for financial gain. No doubt about the definition then. What is problematic, though, is the notion of obscenity, because there are many different views on what constitutes obscenity. Legally, material which is 'likely to deprave or corrupt' is obscene and can be confiscated. We should be careful, though, about the assumptions we make about pornography, especially because it is such an emotive subject. Pornography is essentially representational and images are not the same as the events they appear to depict. If pornographic material involves children or unwilling participants, then this is not pornography but the photographic depiction of criminal offences and there are existing laws to deal with these horrific offences.

Are there different types of pornography?

Yes, there are magazines, videos, films, photographs, interactive material on the Internet and sex phone lines. Included within these can be erotica, educational material, soft porn, violent material (even 'snuff movies' where it is alleged that adults or children have actually been killed on screen), violent material which includes themes of degradation and also material which involves children or adults dressed as children, non-consenting adults and/or animals, etc. Some of these materials may be considered by some people to be artistic, educational or pornographic and some will definitely be obscene and therefore illegal.

What are the concerns about pornography?

One of the most memorable slogans from the women's movement in relation to pornography in the 1970s was 'pornography is the theory, rape is the practice' (Morgan, 1972). It seemed very clear to feminists at that time, and to many people today, that without a doubt pornography contributes to sexual violence and it should therefore be banned. However compelling an argument this might seem, there has been little consistent support for this view from the research conducted by psychologists over the last 30 years. Moreover, it seems to stem from an assumption that 'monkey sees, monkey does', a copycat model of behaviour which implies that we will all imitate behaviour unquestioningly, or an addiction model which assumes that some individuals are aroused by this material but require ever stronger doses to become aroused. The trouble with this approach is that it assumes that there are some individuals who are in some way deviant and different from the rest of us, but we all need protecting from pornography anyway.

However, let's look at the two sides of the debate, the pro-censorship lobby and the anti-censorship lobby, both of which cite psychological research as part of their argument. It is important, however, to distinguish between studies which focus on changes in attitude, sexual arousal (stated or measured) or behaviour, as a result of pornography (bearing in mind that subsequent aggression can only be hypothetical, i.e. not actual rape), and which type of pornography is used as the stimulus, i.e. violent or non-violent explicit material. Moreover, the traditional criticism of laboratory studies of sensitive issues such as pornography as lacking ecological validity is particularly pertinent in this debate.

The pro-censorship/anti-pornography side

Supporters of censorship call on:

- common sense;
- the testimony of abuse survivors;
- the testimony of sex offenders;
- civil rights;
- psychological research

in an attempt to prove a link between exposure to pornography and subsequent sexual violence and in so doing, form an unexpected alliance between feminism and the moral right.

Common sense suggests that pornography must affect its consumers in some way, otherwise they would not buy it. This moralistic view therefore assumes that it must be harmful, particularly if it is seen to undermine marriage, though there is little direct evidence to support this view. There are cultural differences, however, so, for instance, in Japan pornography is freely available and yet the rape rate is only one-sixteenth of the US rate. Research does suggest that in the laboratory men exposed to pornography will demonstrate more callous attitudes to rape victims (Malamuth and Check, 1983), so the effects of desensitisation may well merit further research.

Many survivors of child sexual abuse or rape claim their abusers used pornography to 'script' their offences, but pornography can only ever be one variable in the equation. Not all men (or women) exposed to pornography go on to commit offences and this would include all the pornography researchers themselves. It is not the pornography itself but an existing predilection to violence and dehumanising sex which is probably the main contributing factor in offending where pornography plays a part. Pornography does not *cause* deviant sexual orientation, though it clearly seems to be used to maintain deviant activity.

Before he was executed in 1989 for the murder of at least 20 women, Ted Bundy claimed in an interview that the cause of his crimes was exposure to pornography and violent films and this was seized on as evidence of the need to ban it. Bundy was a sociopath, however, desperate to project the blame onto anyone or anything rather than accept responsibility for his own actions. In fact, Bundy's favourite film was *The Collector* which was rated PG in America. There is also evidence to suggest that sex offenders have usually been exposed to less pornography than control groups of non-sex offenders (Kant and Goldstein, 1973).

Andrea Dworkin (1981), a feminist writer, and Catherine Mackinnon (1987), a feminist lawyer, have tried to make pornography a civil rights issue, arguing that pornography harms all women because of its misogynist imagery and it should therefore be removed from the public domain. In spite of some initial success, their aims to ban pornography have not been consolidated.

The work of psychologists is cited to support the alleged link between pornography and sexual violence. One line of research into the effects of sexually violent material on male viewers has examined the effects of depictions of rape. In a study which is typical of these investigations, Malamuth and Check (1983) found that when they showed subjects two versions of the same rape film, one of which had a 'positive outcome' in that the victim was shown as becoming sexually aroused, whilst the other had a 'negative outcome' where the victim reacted with fear and disgust throughout, all subjects showed some sexual arousal to the 'positive outcome' version. In other words, sexual violence may be a stimulant for a considerable proportion of the male population (Heilbrun and Seis,1988) and is reinforced throughout the media; hence, the belief in rape myths, e.g. all women secretly want to be raped or women mean 'yes' when they say 'no' (see Chapter 4). Malamuth additionally found that men who were more sexually aroused by depictions of non-consenting sex were also more likely to admit to beliefs which justified male domination over women.

Research which has focused on materials which contain some sexual elements but considerably more graphic violence against women, e.g. the slasher films on general public release, has shown that exposure results in callousness towards female victims of violence and that these effects are strongest for men who already possess certain negative attitudes or who are predisposed to sexual violence (Linz et al.,1987).

The anti-censorship side

Opponents of censorship may not approve of pornography but cite:

- the need to defend the right to free speech;
- the danger of pornography being just a scapegoat;
- the dubiousness of being seen to be in need of protection;
- the puritanism of the pro-censorship side;
- psychological research.

They include feminists who disagree with the anti-pornography stand adopted by, amongst others, Dworkin and Mackinnon (e.g. Rodgerson and Wilson, 1991; Segal, 1993; Williams, 1993).

The need to defend the right to free speech is seen as fundamental, particularly when the causal link between pornography and sexual violence against women has yet to be established. There is some sympathy with the notion that pornography 'harms' all women because of its view of them as less than human, but it is felt that this should be tackled by better education aimed at reducing sexism generally.

There is a danger that pornography will become a scapegoat because it is so easy to target, but it can hardly be held responsible for all the violence which has happened to women from time immemorial, i.e. before pornography became widely available. There are many other elements of patriarchy which have contributed to a view of women as objects, e.g. economic dependence, harassment, employment restrictions, etc.

Are we all so vulnerable that we need protecting? The view of media audiences as gullible is seen as rather patronising, as is the suggestion that we need protecting from ourselves – a rather Freudian view of us as a potentially seething mass of sexual urges only just under control. Moreover, the legalisation of pornography in Denmark, Sweden, Holland and Germany did not lead to any significant increase in sex crimes (Kutchinsky, 1973, 1991).

The puritanism of the pro-censorship side, which seems to valorise conventional 'vanilla sex' and outlaw any exploration of alternative expressions of sexuality, is also criticised. This is seen as particularly damaging for women who traditionally have been sexually repressed and who might therefore be considered as in need of some encouragement to explore their own sexuality (Vance, 1984).

Psychological research into pornography and its effect on *behaviour* is criticised for being laboratory based and artificial and therefore impossible to generalise from, but some of it is also cited as demonstrating that there are no proven links between pornography and sexual crimes and that in some studies exposure to non-violent pornography actually *reduces* aggression levels (Linz et al., 1987).

Commission findings

There have been several formal attempts to review the research relating to pornography, often as a result of public and political concerns. Unfortunately, their findings have not been consistent either. The first and largest enquiry was established in the US by President Johnson in 1968. Reporting in 1970 to President Nixon, the Commission on Obscenity and Pornography (often referred to as the Lockhart Commission) concluded:

> "In sum, empirical research designed to clarify the question on effects has found NO evidence that exposure to explicit sexual materials plays a significant role in the causation of delinquent or criminal behaviour among youth or adults. The Commission cannot conclude that exposure to erotic materials is a factor in the causation of sex crime."

The report was controversial and subjected to much criticism; some said it appeared to 'legitimise pornography'. President Nixon totally rejected the findings, describing them as 'morally bankrupt'.

Fifteen years later, a new enquiry was set up at the request of President Reagan and the Meese Commission reported in 1986.

> "We have reached the conclusion, unanimously and confidently, that the available evidence strongly supports the hypothesis that substantial exposure to sexually violent materials ... bears a causal relationship to antisocial acts of sexual violence."

The Meese Commission findings are unusual and almost totally unsupported; all other enquiries, including the 1979 Williams Report in Britain, the Frazer Committee in Canada in 1985 and the most recent British survey by Howitt and Cumberbatch in 1990, concluded that the research does not demonstrate a consistent trend. The Meese Commission findings were in fact criticised for relying too heavily on the work of psychologist Edward Donnerstein who always used violent pornography as opposed to erotica in his research. Significantly, Donnerstein himself said,

> "If you take out the sex and leave the violence, you get the increased violent behaviour in the laboratory setting ... if you take out the violence and leave the sex nothing happens."

The survey of all existing research on the effects of pornography carried out by Howitt and Cumberbatch (1990) concluded:

> "It would be a rather selective use of the evidence to make a strong case that pornography is so influential as a cause of sexual and other forms of violence against women and children that its elimination would result in a diminution of such attacks. One reason for this is that it is unlikely that pornography is the only determinant of sexual and other forms of violence and that pornography can be influential in the absence of other conducive factors...In many ways pornography seems to serve as a totem of society's ills and its convenience and tangibility as a focus makes it easier to identify as a cause of some unacceptable features of life."

PSYCHOLOGICAL RESEARCH ON PORNOGRAPHY

Psychologists have tended to study the effects of two types of pornography – violent, and non-violent – in terms of arousal, perceptions, mood states, attitudes and behaviour. These studies, however, have tended to take place in laboratory conditions, and as one of the leading researchers in this field states:

"One cannot, for obvious reasons, experimentally examine the relationship between pornography and actual sexual behaviour." (Donnerstein, 1984, p.53)

Consequently, there are many criticisms of these studies because of their lack of ecological validity, the use of college students as participants, ethical considerations, experimenter effect and the measures of behavioural effects used (Einsiedel, 1992).

The effects of violent sexually explicit materials

Most of the studies in this area have used three typical approaches in an effort to discover the consequences of exposure to violent pornography. The first involves measures of arousal (physiological and self-report), followed by questionnaires on the acceptance of rape myths, likelihood of rape, etc. (Malamuth and Check, 1983). The second exposes participants to different types of material (neutral, aggressive or sexually violent 'slasher'-type films) under the guise of a film evaluation study. Participants are then asked to take part in a mock rape trial and are subsequently questioned about rape empathy, attribution of responsibility and punitiveness (Linz et al., 1988). The third approach has been to expose participants to materials and then assess any subsequent effects by measuring their propensity to deliver 'electric shocks' (Donnerstein and Berkowitz, 1981).

The perceived reaction of the victims of sexual violence on film seems to have a significant impact on the arousal level of viewers. When Malamuth and Check (1980) showed their male and female participants different versions of a film depicting rape, the one showing the victim eventually becoming aroused and the other showing the victim's distress, arousal levels for male and female subjects were higher in the female-aroused condition.

Malamuth and Check (1980) also demonstrated that viewing sexually violent films produced greater acceptance of rape myths in male and female participants. Exposure to sexually violent material seems to result in aggressive behaviour towards females, though this has had to be measured in an ethically acceptable way, i.e. delivery of 'electric shocks'. Donnerstein and Berkowitz (1981) arranged for male participants to be either provoked or treated neutrally by a male or female confederate. They then viewed one of three films – a sexually explicit film, a film showing a rape or a neutral film. Subsequently they were able to deliver 'electric shocks' to the confederate. When the target of angered participants was male there was no difference in aggressive behaviour between the groups, but when the target was female, aggressive behaviour was higher in the rape film condition, regardless of provocation.

Linz et al. (1988) examined the desensitising effect of 'massive' exposure to violent pornography. Male college students were shown slasher films, e.g. *Texas Chainsaw Massacre*, *I Spit on Your Grave*, *Toolbox Murders*, etc., whilst other groups were shown sexually explicit but non-violent films (some more explicit than others). Participants viewed one film per day for five days and were then asked to witness a mock rape trial, after which they were asked questions about the defendant and the victim. Linz et al. (1988) found that:

- over time participants who were exposed to the slasher films showed fewer negative emotional reactions to the films and perceived them as less violent;
- this desensitisation spilled over into these participants' views of the 'victim' in the mock rape trial since they judged her to be less injured and less worthy than the other groups;
- these findings were particularly marked in those individuals who had been previously rated as high on psychoticism.

The effects of non-violent sexually explicit materials

Most of this research was carried out in the 1970s and concluded that non-violent pornography had few harmful effects on its consumers. In terms of behavioural effects, Baron and Bell (1973) found that exposure to 'mild' erotica inhibited aggression levels in males and females, whilst exposure to 'stronger' material had no effect on males' aggression and slightly increased that of females. Other studies found that exposure to erotica increased subsequent sexual behaviour temporarily but did not substantially change previous sexual patterns (Mosher, 1970; Byrne and Lamberth, 1970).

Other studies examined the effect of 'massive' exposure to sexually explicit material as opposed to short-term exposure in an attempt to discover any habituation or desensitisation effects. Zillman and Bryant (1984) assigned male and female participants to a six-week course in which they were exposed to explicit sex films. At various intervals they had measures of heart rate and blood pressure taken and were asked about their mood state. Over time, both male and female participants demonstrated habituation – their arousal levels diminished and they become bored with continued viewing.

Summary of findings from the psychological research on pornography

- Sexually explicit material, particularly commercial material which is intended to arouse, is effective in that it does produce arousal in offenders and non-offenders, male and female.
- Rapists appear to be aroused by both forced as well as consenting sex depictions whilst college males are less aroused by depictions of sexual violence. However, when the victim is portrayed as 'enjoying' her ordeal, arousal levels increase in the non-offender group too.

- Arousal to rape depictions seems to correlate with attitudes of acceptance of rape myths and to laboratory-observed aggressive behaviour.
- Whilst there appear to be few negative consequences of exposure to non-violent sexually explicit material, Check (1985) has suggested that non-violent material which is sexually explicit but also has themes of degradation may be more harmful in the long term.

The interpretation of these findings is very different depending on the ideological perspective adopted towards pornography and censorship. Russell (1993) concludes that exposure to all pornography (violent and non-violent) leads to habituation and desensitisation, an increased acceptance of rape myths and interpersonal violence against women. Moreover, she suggests that the slasher-type films which Linz et al. (1988) used are in fact more harmful to males than violent pornography so censorship should extend to this material too. In contrast, Segal (1993) points out that exposure to non-violent pornography does not lead to increased aggression or changes in attitude towards rape. Moreover, when Linz et al. (1990) showed participants a documentary on the negative consequences of rape and later these individuals viewed a violent erotic film and a video of a rape trial, the pre-film message seemed to have had a significant effect. Male participants indicated more depression after viewing the erotic film and were more sympathetic to the victim in the rape trial than were members of a control group. Thus, intervention and education can be effective. Exposure to violent pornography can produce arousal in some men and can negatively affect attitudes to women, but these effects are much more likely in those individuals who are already predisposed to consider using sexual violence against women.

CONCLUSION

As with the studies into screen violence, psychological research into the effects of pornography is inevitably limited in terms of its application to the real world because of its context. Experimental studies of pornography have tended to show an increase in non-sexual aggression in the laboratory, plus an increased acceptance of rape myths and more callous attitudes to rape victims. Whilst this can be seen as a possible contributor to attitudes and beliefs which might support sexual aggression, the exact nature of the relationship between pornography and sexual violence remains unclear. There is clearly a difference between the effects of non-violent pornography and violent pornography, with the element of violence and possibly degradation being crucial.

chapter six

FAMILY VIOLENCE

CHAPTER OVERVIEW

In this chapter the extent of violence which occurs within the family will be examined and also the late discovery of this particular aspect of family life. Resistance to the notion of spousal abuse, child abuse and elder abuse is still prevalent in spite of sustained efforts to raise public consciousness about family violence in an attempt to prevent further escalation. This seems particularly crucial in light of findings about the intergenerational transmission of violence which indicate that if violence occurs in childhood there is a legacy which is often carried through into the next generation. As Sartre said:

> "One is never finished with the family. It's like smallpox – it catches you in childhood and marks you for life."

Thus, whilst some aspects of family violence, such as emotional abuse or neglect, would not normally be considered as crimes in a traditional sense, they are included to highlight the potential consequences of such treatment in childhood, factors which have hitherto not been given sufficient prominence.

INTRODUCTION

Traditionally the family is viewed as a safe haven, the one place where we can be assured we will be cared for and protected from a sometimes hostile world. Unfortunately, the evidence would suggest that this is not always the case, nor has it ever been, despite the mythologies which have been built around the family and which to a large extent have protected it from scrutiny.

Family violence is not a new phenomenon. In the Bible one of the most notable incidents described at a very early stage is Cain killing his brother Abel. It was, however, the women's movement in the 1970s that caused the rapid increase in public awareness in relation to child abuse and spouse abuse, though in the history of Western society women and children have often been subjected to the utmost cruelty.

In ancient times children had no rights until the right to live was given to them by their father and if this right was withheld then the children were simply left to die. This was particularly likely if the children were deformed or sickly, if they were girls, twins or illegitimate. Children lucky enough to live were often seriously mistreated and it was not simply a question of this being hidden or ignored, it was considered to be the most appropriate form of child rearing. When the Pilgrim Fathers sailed to America they felt the need to 'beat the devil' out of their children and excessive physical discipline by modern standards was seen as the norm. Using physical punishment still seems to be the norm; in 1980 Straus et al. reported that over 90% of American parents use some form of physical punishment on their children. Whilst many would argue that this does not constitute abuse, it is clear that occasionally chastisement can escalate into a pattern of serious violence, which sometimes ends in the death of a child. In 1994 it was estimated that 1271 children died as a result of abuse and/or neglect in America (Weise and Daro, 1995).

A punitive approach was also adopted towards women and was based very much on the notion of possession. A Roman husband could chastise or even kill his wife if she did not obey him. In 1768, Blackstone's English common law asserted that husbands had the right to 'physically chastise' a disobedient wife, providing that the stick used was no thicker than the man's thumb, generating the phrase 'rule of thumb' to indicate normally accepted parameters or guidelines.

So, family violence may not be new but the academic discovery of it seems to be. The true extent of child abuse was acknowledged in the 1960s and that of spouse abuse in the 1970s, mostly as a result of the women's movement which encouraged survivors to speak out. There is now considerable research in the area of family violence, with whole journals devoted to its study, particularly the notion of intergenerational transmission of family violence. Two notable researchers in the field, Gelles and Cornell (1985), point out the unavoidable facts about family violence when they state:

> "... people are more likely to be killed, physically assaulted, hit, beaten up (and) slapped ... in their own homes by other family members than anywhere else, or by anyone else in our society." (p.12)

It is, however, difficult to estimate the true extent of family violence, especially since victims are often unwilling or unable to complain. Nevertheless, a fifth of all murders in the US and a third in the UK are family murders, with women more likely to be murdered in the home by someone they know (Blackburn, 1993). The extent of partner abuse, child abuse and elder abuse tends to be estimated separately though undoubtedly there are overlaps which may be considerable. Thus, Walker (1984) found that battered women reported that 80% of their batterers were also violent to their children and to their parents.

Since the family is the most important agent of socialisation, we should not perhaps be surprised that violence suffered or observed in childhood may be repeated in adulthood. Children who have been victims of family violence are, when compared to children who have not suffered victimisation, more likely to be violent adult offenders (Hotaling et al., 1990) and the greater the frequency and severity of victimisation, the greater the likelihood of future violent offending (Straus, 1994). Clearly, something has to be done, though we also need to recognise that not all children exposed to violence go on to become abusers and thus try to discover what the mediating factors are in this process.

Methodological problems studying family violence

Research in the area of family violence is beset by methodological and ethical problems. Traditionally aggression and violence have been investigated by psychologists in laboratory settings and these studies have quite rightly been criticised for their artificiality, but how do you study violence which occurs within the privacy of the family? Family life has always been considered sacrosanct; once the front door is closed it is nobody else's business what goes on inside. Moreover, the family has ironically been seen as a 'safe haven' for women and children, somewhere they can feel protected and secure. Any violence which occurs in families has been considered to occur in 'problem' families and as the result of individual psychopathology. The inherent con- servativism and privacy of the family has thus served to assist the denial of the true extent of violence which occurs within this 'safe haven'.

Research into family violence has tended to focus on separate areas, e.g. child abuse, spouse abuse, sibling abuse, elder abuse, etc., and although interest has been shown in the possibilities of the intergenerational transmission of violence (abused children growing up to abuse), the majority of the work tends to be done quite independently of the other parts.

Data on family violence tend to come from three major sources:

1 clinical samples (psychiatrists, psychologists, counsellors, medical records, etc.);
2 official reports (resulting from mandatory reporting, e.g. police data, divorce applications, NSPCC, etc.);
3 social surveys (large samples of respondents, using questionnaires, inter- views or telephone shots).

Longitudinal and experimental studies of family violence are, not surprisingly, rare. Each of the major data sources has its own validity problems, however. Clinical data cannot be used to generalise information because the samples are not representative, and it is often difficult to establish comparative control groups. Official records suffer from variations in definitions, different report- ing and recording practices, whilst self-report surveys may be contaminated by self-selection and distorted recall.

Spouse/Partner Abuse, Marital Violence and Domestic Violence

Men have controlled women within marriage for hundreds of years and yet it was not until the 1960s and 1970s that adequate recognition was given to the plight of women unable to escape a violent marriage. The first shelters for battered women were established in 1964 in California and in 1971 in Chiswick, England. As the number of shelters increased, so did organisations dedicated to the rights of battered women and gradually public awareness of the problem of domestic violence led to the introduction of legislation attempting to protect women and children.

Domestic violence, or spousal abuse, is a distressing reality in many households and one which affects men, women and children in a way which can have repercussions in all subsequent relationships. Grace (1995) defines domestic violence as:

> "... any form of physical, sexual or emotional abuse which takes place within the context of a close relationship."

Thus the term refers to physical and/or psychological violence by a man or a woman towards his or her intimate partner. It can occur within the context of marriage or cohabitation, heterosexual or homosexual partnerships or when couples are separated. Psychological violence is rather more difficult to define than physical violence, but may include threats of violence or suicide, causing damage or withholding rights.

Interviews with battered women indicate that abuse often occurs as a result of disputes over money, jealousy or domestic tasks and can escalate extemely quickly from quarrels to physical assault (Dobash and Dobash, 1988). The violence is usually followed by contrition and reconciliation but a pattern has been set which tends to recur and can culminate in extreme violence (see Case Study 6.1).

CASE STUDY 6.1
Marital Violence

O.J. Simpson was probably the most famous role model for black male children up until his trial for murder in 1995. He was a phenomenally successful sportsman who then became a media star, popularly known as the 'Juice'.

In 1992, after seven years of marriage, he and Nicole Brown divorced but they still saw each other and friends thought they might get back together again. However, in 1994 Nicole was found horribly murdered, with a friend, Ron

Goldman. Following a dramatic nationally televised car chase, O.J. was charged with both murders.

The reaction of the American public was one of shock. They could not believe that O.J. could have done such a thing and friends rallied round to support him. It soon became clear, however, that there was more to O.J. than met the eye. Reports began to appear which revealed O.J. had been violent to Nicole on several occasions and the police had been called out to their home at least nine times. He had been charged with spousal assault and convicted in 1989, yet

this side of him had never been made public. The 'spats' he had with his wife were seen as 'normal', in spite of photographs of a bruised and battered Nicole Brown and tape recordings of her desperate 911 calls for help.

O.J. Simpson was eventually acquitted of the murder charges, though in the subsequent civil case in 1997 he was ordered to pay $33.5 million to the relatives of Nicole Brown and Ron Goldman. What remains from the case, however, is the fact that O.J. Simpson was a wife beater, and yet his fans did not seem to care too much about this aspect of his character.

FIGURE 6.1 *O.J. (The Juice) Simpson (left) with his attorney, was famously acquitted of the murder of his wife in 1994*

What is the extent of domestic violence?

The true extent of spouse abuse is not fully known and has to be estimated from a number of sources. It is widely believed that there is serious under-reporting of domestic violence, not only on the part of victims but also by official agencies. What is accepted is that domestic violence is a big problem which affects the whole of society and one which has been ignored for too long. In America, Sherman (1991) estimates that three to four million women experience physical abuse by their partners. Dobash and Dobash (1979) found from their study of Scottish court and police records that whilst the largest category of interpersonal violence was between unrelated males, the second largest category was assault on wives (25.1%). Of the 1051 cases of violence within the home recorded by the police, wife beating represented 76.8%, child beating 10.5% and husband beating 1.2%.

Marital violence is often cited as the reason for divorce. Borkowski et al. (1983) looked at divorce petitions and reported that 32% of middle class and 40% of working class couples cited physical abuse as the major factor in divorce proceedings.

Surveys of women's refuges in the UK (Pahl, 1978; Binney et al., 1981) reveal that before leaving the matrimonial home women had experienced violence for seven years on average, and it was often only when children were also threatened that a decision to leave was made. In a large-scale survey on domestic violence in the UK Mooney (1993) found that 28% of the women surveyed had suffered physical injury from a partner, though only 22% of this group had reported it to the police, and 19% of the men surveyed admitted having hit their partner. One in ten of the women Mooney surveyed said they had experienced domestic violence within the previous 12 months.

The two American National Family Violence Surveys which have taken place to date (1975 and 1985) show that approximately 16% of American couples experienced at least one act of violence during the year prior to the survey and that this figure did not change markedly across the two time periods. The data from these surveys also indicate that wives hit husbands as frequently as husbands hit wives (Straus and Gelles, 1990).

Studies of homosexual relationships indicate that the incidence of domestic violence is similar to that in heterosexual relationships. For gay male couples, estimates of annual rates vary between 11% and 20% (Island and Letellier, 1991) whilst estimates for lesbian interpartner violence range from 17% to 26% (Renzetti, 1992).

Who are the victims?

Typically women are identified as the primary victims of domestic violence and this is borne out by the work of Dobash and Dobash (1979), whose survey of police records in Scotland showed that women were the victims in 94% of all reported domestic violence incidents. When Straus and Gelles (1990) analysed 500 reports of domestic assault, they found that women had experienced an average of 7.2 assaults per year from their husbands. Moreover, women are significantly more likely to be injured in violent disputes than are men (Brush, 1990).

This said, there are men who also suffer as the victims of domestic violence, as the work of Straus and Gelles (1990) shows. Indeed, some early studies found almost equal frequencies of both severe and non-severe violence by husbands and wives, although husbands repeated the violence more often and were more likely to inflict serious harm (Straus, 1980). Grace (1995) indicates that as many as 20% of victims of domestic violence may be men, though in a survey of sociology journal articles published between 1974 and 1994, there were 380 articles on battered wives and only three on battered husbands (Lucal, 1994), demonstrating the disproportionate coverage of this issue. Moreover, it is highly likely that in view of the possible stigma attached to men reporting their own victimisation, there may be serious under-reporting of this type of domestic violence (Stanko and Hobdell, 1993).

Whilst acknowledging the capability of women to act violently within an intimate relationship, it may be the case that in incidents of reported domestic violence women have actually acted in self-defence rather than initiating violence, which can then cloud the issue of allocating responsibility (Saunders, 1988). The debate about who is the victim in marital violence can have real consequences in terms of policy decisions since if the focus is moved from battered women to family violence in general then funding for women's shelters may be reduced and legislation to protect women may be halted.

Who is to blame?

When people are asked whose fault domestic violence is, their role as either victim or perpetrator significantly influences their response in a particular direction. Moreover, if people are asked to read a hypothetical account of domestic violence and are then asked to apportion blame, the factors which influence their response seem to be their own gender and the gender of the victim and perpetrator described in the account.

Thus, Overholser and Moll (1990) found that aggressors cite external causes, whilst victims either blame themselves or situational factors relating to the aggressor, e.g. 'It's only because he's been drinking'. When third parties were asked, Pierce and Harris (1993) found that women, compared to men, regarded accounts of domestic violence as more violent, felt more strongly that they would have called the police, and felt more strongly that the victim should leave the batterer. Harris and Cook (1994) found a similar gender difference when the victim was the husband, in that the female respondents showed a stronger reaction against the batterer than did the males. However, the overall results of Harris and Cook's study showed that a wife-battering incident is taken much more seriously than a comparable husband-battering.

A tendency to blame the victim of spousal abuse has been resisted strongly by feminists, who argue instead that unequal power relations and prescribed gender roles are more likely to be contributory factors. Dobash and Dobash (1988) similarly argue that wife beating is 'deeply embedded in the existing intentions of male aggressors' and that these intentions are moulded by a context of patriarchy. Using the word 'intentions' is deliberate in that it implies a rational choice, albeit in particular circumstances, rather than the behaviour being seen as somehow beyond the control of the individual.

Research on the characteristics of abusers suggests that the majority of them have experienced violence in childhood, either as victims or witnesses. Thus, Fitch and Papantonio (1983) report that 71% of their sample had witnessed parental violence. This finding squares with the 'cycle of violence' hypothesis whereby abuse is viewed as the result of similar behaviour having been observed and then learned via imitation. What may also be learned are traditional attitudes to women which, if challenged, may result in violence (Rosenbaum and O'Leary, 1981). It is further suggested that abusers may have low self-esteem and that their violence compensates for feelings of inadequacy, especially in the workplace (Johnson, 1988). However, none of these explanations is really adequate to explain why abuse occurs in the home and other theorists have focused instead on the dynamics of the intimate relationship between partners.

It has been suggested that female victims of spousal abuse may have been victims of childhood abuse which then renders them vulnerable to continuing victimisation. Their subsequent expectations of victimisation may lead to a developing dependency in relationships which reveals itself in a helpless compliance in the face of violence. This in itself may reinforce the abuser's behaviour (Walker, 1984).

Explaining domestic violence

Barnett et al. (1997) identify macrolevel explanations (cultural, social and structural) and microlevel explanations (socialisation, interpersonal and intrapersonal factors).

Cultural

In some cultures violence, including marital violence, is more acceptable than in others. Broude and Greene (1983) surveyed 71 societies and discovered wife beating in 57 of them. Cultural acceptance of marital violence may be overt but can also be covert so that whilst marital violence is condemned, legislation is never made sufficiently strong to combat it effectively. Thus, Briere (1987) found that 79% of a sample of college males said that they might hypothetically hit a woman in certain circumstances, Peltoniemi (1982) found that 44% of Finns did not support legal interference in family violence and Dibble and Straus (1980) found that 28% of Americans believe that hitting a spouse is sometimes necessary.

An acceptance of marital violence seems to be associated with the patriarchal view of legitimate male domination within marriage. Husbands who demonstrate patriarchal beliefs and attitudes tend to be more violent towards their wives (Smith, 1990). Whilst this accords with feminist explanations of marital violence, as Dutton (1994) points out this cannot explain why only some individuals choose to hit their wives when presumably patriarchy will have influenced all males in contemporary society. Moreover, studies of gay and lesbian partner abuse have not revealed significant gender power differentials.

Social and structural variables

Sociologists have tended to look for patterns in the data on marital violence which might indicate which structural characteristics (such as age, gender, socioeconomic status, race, etc.) are associated with this behaviour. Their findings indicate, however, that it is not always possible to predict violence.

Marital violence occurs most frequently between the ages of 18 and 30 (Straus et al., 1980). In spite of the findings of more female-to-male violence than was hitherto believed, men tend to instigate violence in the home and are more likely to be involved in repeat assaults and severe violence (Saunders, 1988). The National Family Violence Surveys indicate that marital violence is more prevalent in lower-class families, though it is accepted that this may reflect the 'invisibility' of violence in wealthier homes. In relation to race, whilst the findings indicate more violence in minority families (Stets, 1990), this may be indicative of differential arrest policies and other variables.

Socialisation

Studies consistently show that men who have suffered or witnessed parental violence are more likely to be violent towards their partner and that women who have suffered similarly are more likely to become victims of domestic violence (Kalmuss, 1984; Doumas et al., 1994). The suggestion is that inappropriate problem-solving strategies which have been learned in childhood are then carried into adult relationships.

Interpersonal and intrapersonal factors

The repeat patterning of domestic violence has prompted some to suggest that the interpersonal relationship between specific couples may be a crucial contributing factor to this pattern. This is a very different perspective from those theories which attribute blame to one party in the relationship. What is suggested is that previous agendas, unresolved problems and inadequate communication styles lead to high marital dissatisfaction which may subsequently be expressed by an escalating pattern of violence, reconciliation and further violence (Burman et al., 1993).

It is clear that in domestic violence some part is played by alcohol and drugs, though estimates vary between 20% and 80% (Leonard and Jacob,1988), and this may be because alcohol and some drug use increases the likelihood of aggressive behaviour or the use of alcohol and/or drugs may be symptomatic of stress.

Women who are involved in domestic violence

Traditionally battered women have often been blamed for their own victimisation, mainly because they are regarded as consenting adults and in a very different category from other vulnerable groups, such as children or the elderly. There have also been suggestions that women are inherently masochistic, as Freud suggested, and that they stay in abusive relationships because that is what they enjoy. As Sylvia Plath wrote:

> "Every woman adores a fascist
> The boot in the face, the brute
> Brute heart of a brute like you."
> (from *Daddy*,1962)

Not surprisingly, many feminists have taken issue with a view of women as naturally masochistic since it tends to legitimise unacceptable violence towards women and disregards the cultural conditioning which may ensure that some women appear to adapt to and accept an unsatisfactory life when they may in fact be committed to an abusive relationship because they have become so dependent on serving the needs of others that they have lost sight of their own needs (Caplan, 1986).

When Ewing and Aubrey (1987) asked people to read a scenario about a violent couple and then complete a questionnaire, they found that over 60% of the respondents felt that if a battered woman were really afraid she would simply leave. Unfortunately, the consequences of being beaten within an intimate relationship make this apparently rational decision very difficult to make. Women who have been abused tend to be characterised by excessive and recurrent fear of another beating and feelings of helplessness. These feelings have been described as 'learned helplessness' which Gerow (1989) defines as:

> "... a condition in which a subject does not attempt to escape from a painful or noxious situation after learning in a previous, similar situation that escape is not possible." (p.193)

Walker (1984) used the term to explain why women stay in abusive relationships, drawing on the work of Seligman (1975) with dogs given inescapable

FIGURE 6.2 *This 'Brookside' story-line raised awareness of the problem of domestic violence, when after years of abuse the 'battered' wife Mandy (pictured here with daughters Rachel and Beth, and friend Sinbad), chose the final solution of murdering her husband in order to protect her children*

electric shocks who subsequently seemed unable to learn ways of escaping. Walker suggested that women who are continually abused become passive, depressed and unable to intellectually consider solutions to their problems. She went on to describe a condition she called 'battered woman syndrome' which is characterised by symptoms not dissimilar to post-traumatic stress disorder and this was presented as a defence in trials where abused women had killed their husbands after long periods of abuse. The argument was that these women had no alternative, no escape route, and their only hope for survival against stronger opponents was to kill them whilst they were disarmed.

Quite apart from these psychological problems, there may be other reasons why abused women do not leave their abusers. Very often, abused women do not want to leave; rather, they want the violence to stop and they may quite rightly fear that leaving will make matters worse. There may also be very obvious economic reasons for staying in an abusive relationship. An abused woman may be faced with a very stark choice – having a home and financial security with an abusive partner or having no home and little income. A belief in making relationships work, a fear of loneliness and social isolation may also contribute to what to outsiders might seem an irrational decision to stay.

The cyclical nature of domestic violence – battering followed by contrition – can also be seen to mirror the schedule of intermittent reward and punishment which in animal learning studies has been shown to increase the strength of responses (Barnett and LaViolette, 1993). This might explain the development of long-term attachment to a partner who alternately assaults and rewards with love and attention, which makes it difficult to contemplate leaving (Dutton and Painter, 1993).

Men who beat their partners

The majority of men who are violent towards their partners deny or minimise their actions and may even believe their behaviour is appropriate. Not surprisingly, studies show that exposure to violence during childhood is associated with later male-to-female violence, though interestingly, observations of abuse seem to be a more powerful indicator than direct experience (Hotaling and Sugarman, 1986).

Male socialisation which leads men to expect their wives to treat them with due deference can also promote problems if women begin to demonstrate some independence (Birns et al., 1994). Other messages about masculinity encourage men to be tough and emotionally distant, which can reduce the quality of communication within a relationship (Cohen, 1990). Factors in relationships which seem to cause particular difficulty include jealousy, insecurity and emotional dependence, though ironically male commitment to the marriage is often high. Langhinrichsen-Rohling et al. (1994) found that batterers saw themselves as 'doing more and getting less' in the relationship, consistently underestimating the quality and number of caring gestures from their wives.

When compared to non-batterers, batterers tend to be poor problem solvers who do not cope well with stress, often resorting to violence very quickly (Allen et al., 1989).

Summary

Aggression between partners is widespread, despite increasing awareness of the problem as an integral part of intergenerational transmission of violence. Women tend to be the major victims of battering, though the existence of a comparable battered husband syndrome needs to be recognised. Marital violence occurs in all segments of society, although it seems to be more commonly associated with lower socioeconomic groups, so stress may be a major factor. Male socialisation clearly plays a critical role in teaching young boys to expect male dominance in relationships, but ineffective communication in interpersonal relationships seems to produce a tension which if left unchecked can spiral into a pattern of escalating violence.

CHILD ABUSE

Child abuse, like family violence generally, is not a new phenomenon but it has only relatively recently been recognised and investigated and even then, not always adequately. A French professor of forensic medicine, Auguste Tardieu, is credited with the first academic study of ill treatment of children in 1860, but public concern about physical cruelty to children was first raised in America. The first Society for the Prevention of Cruelty to Children was founded in New York in 1874, following the case of an eight-year-old girl called Mary Ellen who was being ill treated by her foster parents and could only be rescued by a prosecution brought under a law against cruelty to animals (Pleck, 1987). The publicity surrounding this case led to the formation of the society (SPCC), and a similar one in Britain was set up in Liverpool in 1882. Other cities soon followed suit in setting up societies and together they campaigned to make child abuse a criminal offence. This led to the Prevention of Cruelty to Children Act in 1889.

In spite of these efforts there was no systematic policy for recording or reporting cases of suspected abuse and public concern about the physical abuse of children did not really emerge until the 1960s when a paediatrician called Henry Kempe noticed numerous healed fractures on the X-rays of some of the children he examined and called this phenomenon the 'battered child syndrome', describing:

> "a clinical condition in young children who have received serious physical abuse, generally from a parent or foster parent" (Kempe et al., 1962).

Even then, there was considerable resistance on the part of the medical profession and indeed the public to the idea that children might be the deliberate target of quite vicious cruelty. Public alarm about individual cases of horrific abuse has tended to provide the impetus for urgent changes in legislation and services, e.g. the deaths of Maria Colwell, Tyra Henry and Jasmine Beckford.

Child sexual abuse seems like a recent development by comparison to concerns about physical abuse and neglect but in fact the issue was raised in Victorian England because of the number of young girls in brothels. At this time, the age of consent was 12 but as a result of public outrage this was raised to 16 in 1885. Incest, however, was not made illegal until 1908 and it was not until the 1970s that academic interest in child sexual abuse began to emerge as a result of the women's movement encouraging survivors to speak about their childhood experiences. The true extent of abuse began to be assessed and once again, policies began to be introduced which would alert professionals to the signs of abuse in order that prompt action could be taken.

There are several different kinds of child abuse, though some may overlap:

- physical abuse, which involves non-accidental injuries, such as bruising or fractures, but which can also include Munchausen by proxy syndrome, where children may be subjected by their carer to unnecessary and repeated medical or surgical intervention;
- sexual abuse;
- emotional abuse;
- neglect and 'failure to thrive', a condition whereby as a result of indifference or deliberate neglect a small child fails to achieve its developmental milestones.

It is very difficult to determine the true extent of these types of abuse because official statistics do not provide the full picture and yet academic studies tend to use different definitions of child abuse and so produce very varied results. NSPCC figures for 1994–95 show that in the UK, 35,000 children were placed on child protection registers, a 7% increase on the previous year's figures. 40 percent were registered on the grounds of physical injuries, 30% for neglect, 24% for sexual abuse and 6% for other reasons, including emotional abuse. More girls than boys tend to be registered, particularly for sexual abuse.

Certain family and social characteristics have been frequently noted in cases of child abuse. The parents' own childhood will often have been deprived and the couple may have married young with little preparation for parenthood. They are often socially isolated and mobile, antagonistic to authority figures and very sensitive to criticisms. Parental needs tend to come before children's needs and there is often marital discord. Children who suffer abuse also tend to share certain characteristics. They are often delicate babies requiring attention or may have been the result of an unwanted pregnancy. They are seen by their parents as a problem. Family circumstances very often do not help the situation, so environmental stresses such as poor housing and financial difficulties contribute to a general lack of coping.

Physical child abuse

"It's all so confusing, this brutal abusing.
They blacken your eyes and then apologize.
Be Daddy's little girl and don't tell Mommy a thing.
Be a good little boy and you'll get a new toy.
Tell Grandma you fell off the swing."
(Benatar et al., 1981)

These are the lyrics of *Hell is for Children*, recorded by Pat Benatar in 1980 and drawing attention to the plight of abused children, largely ignored until the 1960s. In this verse the child not only suffers physical abuse but is made complicit in a web of lies which will not only confuse them but ensure that they are unable to tell anyone the truth.

One of the problems associated with physical child abuse is an acceptable definition. When does parental discipline or frustration or ignorance cross the line into unacceptable violence? Initially definitions relied on some evidence of observable harm, such as cuts or bruises, though current opinion regards physical child abuse as physical injury caused by other than accidental means that results in a substantial risk of physical harm.

Indicators of non-accidental injury may include parental responses such as an unexplained delay in seeking treatment, inappropriate or vague explanations of the injury (even if supported by the child and other family members) and a history of previous injuries. Particular types of injury may give cause for concern too: bruising in or around the mouth (which may indicate force feeding), old and new bruising, fractures in very young children or inexplicable burn areas (for instance, a child is unlikely to burn its bottom and not its feet or hands).

FIGURE 6.3 *The NSPCC uses bold imagery to alert the public to the horrors of child abuse and to raise funds for their child protection work*

Whilst the most common form of physical child abuse contains an element of excessive chastisement, there are some unusual manifestations of physical child abuse which would indicate more complex motivation. These include deliberate and sadistic forms of punishment, such as poisoning, fatal pepper aspiration and intentional burns. Another manifestation is Munchausen syndrome by proxy which was first identified by Meadow (1977) and involves children being subjected by adults to unnecessary medical intrusion. In order to do this, the adult may deliberately cause symptoms in the child (e.g. administering excessive doses of laxative) or may intefere with laboratory specimens (e.g. adding blood or faeces) in order to give the impression of illness. The perpetrator is very often the child's mother and she may have, in addition to a history of psychiatric illness, extensive knowledge of health-related areas which enables her to abuse the system (see Case Study 6.2). Recent studies indicate that families in which this condition occurs may have a history of unexplained sibling death (Meadow,1990).

CASE STUDY 6.2
Munchausen syndrome by proxy

In 1996 a mother said to be suffering from Munchausen syndrome by proxy killed her four-year-old son by feeding him salt in his fizzy drinks for ten days. This resulted in the child suffering crippling fits of vomiting, diarrhoea and stomach cramps. He was taken to four different doctors by his stepfather but none of them diagnosed the child's condition.

The mother told police that having two small children 'had worn her down' and that giving the four-year-old salt 'made him sleep so that I could get some rest.' She was jailed for life in 1997, after psychiatrists said that her personality disorder was so severe that it would be untreatable in hospital. (reported in *The Guardian,* 18th June 1997, p.9)

The true extent of physical child abuse is difficult to estimate because there are often differences between official reporting rates and self-report rates and whilst there was a dramatic increase between 1976 and 1987 which may be explained by higher public awareness, there has subsequently been a levelling-out process which may reflect the introduction of prevention and treatment programmes. Nevertheless the American National Committee to Prevent Child Abuse estimates that in 1993, 715 children died as a result of physical abuse and 520 children died as a result of physical neglect (McCurdy and Daro, 1994).

Are some children more likely to be victims of physical abuse than others? The evidence seems to suggest so. Very young children and adolescents seem to be the most vulnerable, as are males and children from low income families, but there are additional factors which may put children at increased risk. These include having been born prematurely, suffering birth complications or some form of disability (physical, emotional and mental). It is suggested that these children produce excessive strain for already vulnerable parents who may be disappointed about their child's condition and unable to come to terms with their feelings. Additionally, some children may be perceived as unwanted, particularly by a step-parent for whom they may be a reminder of previous relationships, or they may become symbolic targets for unresolved problems within a relationship (see Case Study 6.3).

CASE STUDY 6.3
Physical child abuse

A three-year-old girl who was 'simply disliked' by her father died from a fractured skull after being beaten once too often. She was the child of an arranged marriage, and was brought up for considerable periods of time by her maternal grandmother. She used to cry when her father collected her, and during the last year of her life she was beaten regularly. When relatives complained about the child's cuts and bruises the father told them, 'She's my child – I can do what I like'. The parents had a second daughter who appeared to have no problems. The mother was described as 'either too timid, frightened, uncaring or scared of losing her other younger daughter to complain to the authorities'. (reported in *The Guardian*, 3rd June 1997, p.10)

Which adults are likely to physically abuse children? There tend to be slightly more physical abuse reports concerning female perpetrators than male (53%:47%) and perpetrators in the majority of cases (80%) tend to be parents. Studies which have compared non-abusive parents to physically abusive parents indicate that there are common characteristics shared by abusive parents. These include anger control problems, low frustration tolerance, depression, low self-esteem and deficits in empathy and rigidity (Lahey et al., 1984). Frude (1991) also points out that abusive individuals often have unrealistic expectations and negative perceptions of their children. They may regard their children as being deliberately difficult and yet their expectations make it impossible for the children to succeed. Such children may develop a 'frozen watchfulness', always waiting for the inevitable rebuke and accompanying slap or kick and forever trying to avoid being noticed.

Whilst at one time explanations of physical child abuse tended to centre on the pathology of the perpetrator, it is now accepted that physical child abuse is not a simple behaviour but a very complex set of interacting behaviours. Parent–child interaction is seen as a critical factor contributing to abuse. This is not to suggest in any way that particular children are responsible for their own victimisation but rather that difficult child behaviours may interact with specific parental behaviours to create an unholy mix (Wolfe, 1987). An example of this might be a parent who experienced childhood abuse themselves, thereby presumably having learned through experience that using violence is an acceptable method of raising children, and then being faced with a child who does not conform to expectations and is difficult to control. With appropriate intervention, this situation can be resolved but if additional stress factors occur it may be difficult to contain the potential for abuse.

Another perspective on physical child abuse focuses on the social context rather than individual factors, specifically the finding that a high proportion of abused children come from poor and socially disadvantaged families (Sedlak, 1991) and that a feature of these families may be social isolation, e.g. a lack of extended family or peer support (Gil, 1970). Physical abuse can also occur in more advantaged families, but may be easier to conceal from the authorities.

Sexual child abuse

Whilst most people would agree that the sexual abuse of children is abhorrent, it is fair to say that, there is not total agreement. Throughout history and in some cultures, sexual interaction between children and adults has been regarded as quite normal. Aristotle claimed that if adult males masturbated young boys this would hasten their manhood (DeMause, 1974) and the Sambia of Papua New Guinea still believe that young boys must swallow the semen of older boys and men in order to become men themselves (Herdt, 1987). Interestingly, this Sambian practice does not encourage homosexuality and there is a strict taboo regarding incestuous exchanges. There are also contemporary groups which propose that adult–child sexual relations are appropriate and healthy (Hechler, 1988).

As with attitudes to sexuality in general, it is often difficult to determine whether attitudes reflect behaviour and the area of child sexual abuse seems to be particularly fraught with ambivalence and secrecy. There is a popular myth that only perverted old men called paedophiles sexually abuse children and that these individuals are easily recognisable. However, it is now very clear that much sexual abuse occurs in the home, may have occurred across generations, have involved more than one child and have been maintained as the terrible secret of the family. Moreover, sexual attraction to children may not be so unusual. Thus, Briere and Runtz (1989) found that 21% of their male undergraduate students reported having experienced sexual attraction to children and an alarming 7% indicated some likelihood of having sex with a child if they could avoid detection and punishment.

This said, there is general agreement that adults who engage in sexual encounters with children are abusing their power in a way which will undoubtedly have negative consequences for the child. The element of coercion, whether explicit or implicit, is a crucial factor. There are, however, many definitions of child sexual abuse and this may explain why there are often wide variations in estimates of the prevalence of this type of abuse. Shechter and Roberge (1976) provide a working definition:

> "Sexual abuse is defined as the involvement of dependent, developmentally immature children and adolescents in sexual activities they do not truly comprehend, to which they are unable to give informed consent, or that violate the social taboos of family roles." (p.60)

What is the frequency of child sexual abuse? There are two main sources of information on which to estimate the prevalence of child sexual abuse – official data such as the numbers of children referred to agencies and self-report studies. The first source tends to produce lower figures than the second, but when Wild (1986) reviewed referrals of child sexual abuse to paediatricians in Leeds he found an increase from zero in 1979 to 161 in 1985. NSPCC figures show a similar pattern with a 90% increase in reported cases of child sexual abuse between 1984 and 1985, a period when this type of abuse began to be seriously recognised. In relation to self-report studies, Baker and Duncan (1985) found that of their 2019 respondents, 206 (10%) said they had been abused before the age of 16 and West (1985) found that 46% of the 600 women he surveyed reported being sexually abused as children. Finkelhor's (1994) review of 21 studies of child sexual abuse found rates ranging from 7% to 36% for women and from 3% to 29% for men, the abuse rates for women being generally 1.5–3 times the rate for men.

All surveys have shown that more girls than boys are victims of sexual abuse, though the potential under-reporting by boys is considerable in view of the particular pressures they may experience, e.g. fears of being considered homosexual and not wanting to appear helpless. Finkelhor (1986) reviews the evidence on risk factors for child sexual abuse, suggesting they include:

- living with a stepfather;
- having a mother who is employed outside the home, is disabled or ill;
- marital conflict;
- parental drug and/or alcohol problems;
- having a poor relationship with one or both parents.

The majority of perpetrators are male, though female perpetration may be more common than surveys suggest, particularly in daycare settings (Finkelhor et al., 1988).

Children rarely make up stories of sexual abuse by members of their own family, but professionals also need to be aware of presenting symptoms of sexual abuse which may appear independently of disclosure by the child. These may include sexually precocious behaviour, sexualised drawings and play, regressive behaviour (e.g. soiling or wetting), recurrent ill health (e.g. headaches, abdominal pain) and sudden poor performance at school with a reluctance to go home. Medical examinations may reveal more direct physical consequences of sexual abuse, particularly 'reflex anal dilatation' which is a recognised indicator of long-term sexual abuse and may leave the muscles of the anus slack. This technique was much criticised during the 1987 Cleveland child abuse crisis (see Chapter 7) and yet it is now accepted that anal penetration of very young children is far more common than genital penetration.

What explanations have been offered to account for child sexual abuse?

Blaming the victim

Early explanations tended to focus on the role of the victim and his or her responsibility for encouraging the sexual abuse to occur. As recently as 1993, a British judge, Ian Starforth-Hill, described the eight-year-old victim of attempted rape as 'not entirely an angel herself'. Whilst it has been observed by many authors that men who sexually abuse children will often rationalise their behaviour by describing their victims as 'seductive', and this fits with a view of male sexuality as uncontrollable, it is also true that in contemporary images of children there can be a thinly disguised sexual element which may be read as somehow legitimising a view of children as sexual beings. Thus, society has some responsibility for generating inappropriate cultural imagery which in its most extreme form is child pornography. Attributing blame to victims and describing them as colluding in their own abuse also significantly shifts responsibility away from the abuser. The role of psychoanalysis in perpetuating an image of the 'child as seductress' has not been at all helpful in treating the victims of sexual abuse.

Blaming the mother

Some accounts of child sexual abuse explicitly place responsibility for the abuse on mothers who are described as frigid and who, experiencing relief at the transfer of sexual attention, then passively collude with the abuse (e.g. Justice and Justice, 1979). Certainly having an absent or ill mother is an important predictor of the likelihood of sexual abuse, though it is more likely that the mother in an abusive family is as much a victim of abuse as her daughter(s) and to such an extent that she is unable to intervene. Once again, however, responsibility for the abuse is shifted from the abuser and so completely that many abused children will blame the mother for failing to protect them.

Male socialisation

There is some suggestion that the socialisation processes associated with masculinity may explain greater male involvement in child sexual abuse.

These processes would include men being socialised towards attraction to sexual partners who are younger, smaller and more vulnerable than themselves. Additionally, it is suggested that male sexuality is predicated on gratification as an end in itself, what Hollway (1984) has called the 'male sexual drive discourse'. If abusers describe their sexuality in similar terms, as somehow biologically driven and therefore uncontrollable, they can conveniently displace responsibility for their actions. When Glaser and Frosh (1988) suggested that:

> "... there are systematic features of masculine sexuality which contribute to sexual abuse." (p.25)

there was outrage expressed in the British tabloid press that all men were being branded as potential child abusers and that this would seriously impair men's attempts to become more involved in parenting. What Glaser and Frosh (1988) were emphasising, however, was the very damaging link between sex and power which is an integral part of the social construction of masculinity and which can result in fear, misogyny and violence.

Dysfunctional families

Families in which child sexual abuse occurs are clearly dysfunctional though the children in such families may be unaware of the inappropriateness of their parents' behaviour for a considerable time. Some sexually abusing families are totally disorganised and chaotic and within them, sexual attitudes are very poorly defined with almost any kind of sexual behaviour permitted. These are, however, in the minority and may be well known to the authorities. The majority of families in which sexual abuse occurs would seem quite normal to an outsider, but they are often rather isolated with roles and boundaries becoming confused and distorted. On the surface, however, these families are distinctly conventional with traditional sex role divisions and the powerful role of the father being paramount (Herman, 1981). There may be collusion between family members and sexual abuse becomes the family secret which, if revealed, might result in the disintegration of the family unit. It is this sort of pressure which may be brought to bear on the victim of abuse to ensure they do not tell. Family members are thus bound:

> "... into a collusive system in which the incest can continue for many years" (Furniss, 1984, p.310)

Daly and Wilson (1988) suggest that living in a particular kind of family, a stepfamily, is:

> "... the single most important risk factor for severe child maltreatment yet discovered".

When they studied data from Canada, America, England and Wales, they found that children under the age of two were 70 times more likely to be killed by step-parents than by genetic parents. Similarly, when the NSPCC carried out an analysis of the circumstances of 10,000 children on child protection registers in 1992, they found that those children living with a father substitute face a substantially increased risk of abuse. Stepfathers who had married into the family were more likely to sexually abuse than cohabitees and unmarried partners were more likely to be physically violent. Evolutionary psychologists would argue that this is easily explained by the lack of investment parents will make in their partner's children by comparison to their own. There is a natural tendency to invest in one's own children because they will continue the genetic chain. Opponents of this view would claim that living in a reconstituted family brings unique stresses and that some stepfathers may feel marginalised from their new partner by the demands of children to whom they have little natural affiliation and it is therefore not surprising that for vulnerable individuals, stepchildren may become the target for aggression or seduction.

The abuser

Most early explanations of abuse which focused on the abuser assumed that there must be some individual psychopathology which would explain such aberrant behaviour, but whilst there may be elements of antisocial tendencies such as impulsivity and disregard for others which are associated with child sexual abusers, the overall findings indicate that this group of offenders is not characterised by psychiatric disorder (Williams and Finkelhor, 1990). Childhood experience of abuse and the development of deviant patterns of sexual arousal are more likely to be associated with abusers (Laws and Marshall, 1990).

Finkelhor (1984) has presented a valuable model of abuser psychology which incorporates four different factors, or preconditions, which he feels must operate for child sexual abuse to occur.

- *Emotional congruence* – the abuser must find sexual contact with a child emotionally gratifying, possibly because of some social inadequacy, and the abuse can generate a sense of power.
- *Sexual arousal* – the abuser has to find children arousing and this can be accounted for by childhood victimisation which has created deviant sexual patterns and these might then be legitimised by pornography.
- *Blockage* – alternative avenues for sexual gratification are not available.
- *Disinhibition* – the usual constraints which operate in relation to child sexual abuse have to be broken down and this can happen as a result of alcohol or drugs which may lead to cognitive distortions, e.g. that the child welcomes sexual attention. Alternatively, it has been suggested that inhibitors can be built into natural father–child relations which may not be present when there is a stepfather involved in childcare. Thus, if a man has been involved on a regular basis with the natural intimacies of child rearing a sufficient taboo will have been established in relation to possible sexual contact. This taboo may not operate in the case of a stepfather and

Finkelhor (1984) has suggested that the presence of a stepfather is the highest predictor of the likelihood of child sexual abuse (see Case Study 6.4).

CASE STUDY 6.4
Sexual child abuse

A man was jailed for seven years in June 1997 after it was revealed that he had sexually abused his stepdaughter since she was 10, leading to her becoming pregnant and having a baby at the age of 11. The man had married the girl's mother five years previously and they had two children of their own. He said that he had first attempted to have sex with the girl during a trip to the seaside when he gave her a pint of beer and that they had then begun a 'relationship' which involved having sex at least once a week. (reported in *The Guardian*, 20th June 1997 p.4)

The 'false memory syndrome' controversy

During the late 1980s and 1990s it became apparent that in parallel with an increasing acceptance of the prevalence of child sexual abuse, there were cases emerging of adults in therapy remembering abuse in their childhood which had hitherto been undisclosed. There followed lawsuits claiming compensation and the possibility of 'delayed discovery' was accepted. Some critics, however, began to argue that it was possible that these 'recovered' memories were in fact false memories, planted by overzealous therapists jumping on the bandwagon of child sexual abuse.

Psychologists have appeared to defend both sides of this controversy. Thus, Loftus et al. (1994), on the basis of Loftus's respected studies into reconstructive memory (see Chapter 7), claim that memory is subject to distortion and suggestibility, especially in the vulnerable under the influence of an authority figure such as a therapist; whilst Briere and Conte (1993) argue that repression is a very plausible consequence of child abuse and that a signficant proportion (59%) of their clinical sample of abuse survivors did not have full recall of their trauma. An example of this is the case of Susan Lees, a 38-year-old English law student who began experiencing symptoms of post-traumatic stress disorder, including flashbacks of serious physical and sexual abuse in childhood. When she obtained Social Services files she discovered that her memories of abuse were corroborated by this documentation, though she had had no previous recollection of the events which had occurred before she was five years old (cited in *The Guardian*, 2nd March, 1997).

When the British Psychological Society was asked to examine the concept of false memory their Working Party on Recovered Memories (1995), chaired by Professor John Morton, concluded on the basis of a large-scale survey of clinical practitioners that whilst false memory syndrome is possible, it is unlikely and that most recovered memories are likely to be genuine, particularly within the context of competent and professional therapy. A clear distinction was drawn between clinical practice in America and in the UK, and whilst it was recognised that unscrupulous therapists could manipulate vulnerable individuals, this possibility was considered to be significantly reduced if rigorous professional safeguards are maintained.

EMOTIONAL ABUSE

Every act of abuse contains elements of emotional abuse and yet this category of abuse on its own is probably the least likely to result in intervention and is extremely difficult to prove. Whilst physical abuse produces clear evidence and allegations of sexual abuse are often supported by some evidence, emotional abuse produces scars that do not heal and which have a lifelong legacy. Emotional abuse has only been a separate category on NSPCC registers since 1981, using the definition:

> "... children under the age of 17 years whose behaviour and emotional development have been severely affected, where medical and social assessments find evidence of either severe neglect or rejection."

Garbarino et al. (1986) provide a more meaningful interpretation when they suggest it is:

> "... a concerted attack by an adult on a child's development of self and social competence, a pattern of psychically destructive behaviour" (p.8)

which can take five forms: rejecting, isolating, terrorising, ignoring or corrupting the child. It is now increasingly recognised that emotional abuse, or psychological maltreatment as it is known in America, may be the most destructive form of child abuse yet one which is often overlooked because its effects are rarely visible or immediate.

In some families one particular child may be singled out for this type of treatment and siblings encouraged to scapegoat their abused brother or sister. These children may become 'household drudges', carrying an inappropriate burden of domestic work and never receiving any positive attention. Alternatively, some parents may emotionally abuse their children by being so overprotective and possessive that they prevent any social contact, refusing to allow their children to attend school or mix with other children.

Emotionally abused children are likely to develop low self-esteem, be anxious, aggressive and withdrawn. They are likely to experience problems in personal relationships and are unlikely to achieve educational success. These problems are often carried into adult life and emotional abuse as a child is a more powerful predictor of adult depression than physical abuse (Briere and Runtz, 1990).

NEGLECT

As is the case with all forms of child abuse, child neglect is not new but it was not until the early part of the 20th century that it was recognised as a social problem. Even now, however, neglect is often seen as less compelling than other forms of abuse and less serious in its consequences, with some professionals unwilling to judge or blame parents suspected of neglect. This may be because of difficulties in agreeing the parameters of neglect, especially when taking cultural differences into account.

Most experts will agree, however, that child neglect concerns deficits in the provision of a child's basic needs. A child's growth and development may suffer when he or she receives insufficient food, love, warmth, care, praise or stimulation. A child suffering from neglect will often thrive when placed in a different environment such as a foster home, and for professionals to suspect neglect the child may be short in stature and underweight for his or her age, may look unkempt and dirty, be unresponsive or inappropriately attention seeking with adults.

Other forms of neglect may affect children before they are born, e.g. the abuse of alcohol or drugs by the mother-to-be, or in the very early years of a child's life when the neglect may result in a clinical condition known as 'failure to thrive'. The term was first applied to describe children raised in institutions at the turn of the century. These infants were often characterised by marked deficits in growth and a range of abnormal behaviours, such as head banging, rocking and withdrawal. These consequences were then recognised as a possibility in families where small children were neglected, that neglect producing both physical and psychological symptoms.

The majority of cases of child neglect occur in children below the age of five years and there appears to be no gender bias. Rates of neglect tend to be higher in socially disadvantaged families, as does severity of neglect (Claussen and Crittenden, 1991). The consequences of child neglect can be significant and long-lasting. The quality of attachment between neglecting parents and children can lead to serious social maladjustment, but there may also be intellectual deficits, emotional and behavioural problems.

ELDER ABUSE

Violence against the elderly is very much the 'Cinderella' of family violence and consequently there is limited research in the area. It has been suggested that our knowledge of elder abuse is similar to the extent of knowledge of child abuse some 20 years ago. It affects about 2–4% of the elderly, though reliable estimates are difficult to obtain because of disagreement over what constitutes abuse. Elder abuse also occurs against a backdrop of changing attitudes to the elderly and some confusion about responsibility and individual choice. Whereas at one time old people were cared for within their extended families and there was acceptance of this responsibility on the part of grown children, there is now far less agreement on whose responsibility it is to look after old relatives. This can place the elderly in a very vulnerable situation where their predicament may simply be ignored.

Mistreatment of the elderly can take several forms, though most experts distinguish between neglect and abuse, with two modes of intent – unintentional or intentional (Hudson, 1991). Two categories tend to receive minimal attention, though both can be very serious, and these are self-neglect and direct or indirect sexual abuse. The concept of self-neglect does not sit well within a framework of abuse which requires a victim and a perpetrator and there are difficulties with assessment and recognising the individual's right to self-determination. However, an elderly person who does not, for instance, follow medical advice or who fails to look after themselves properly and their relatives collude with this behaviour is placing themselves at serious risk of harm. Reluctance to acknowledge the possibility of sexual abuse of the elderly has prevented research in this area, but there are increasing reports of direct sexual abuse or indirect forms such as exhibitionism or forced viewing of pornography (Ramsey-Klawsnik, 1991).

Elder abuse has been described as a 'women's issue' because the elderly population is disproportionately female (Dunn, 1995), but it would seem to be a problem for men and women, especially as they become more frail. When Pillemer and Finkelhor (1988) carried out an extensive telephone survey into elder abuse they found that 52% of victims were in fact male and abusers were not always adult offspring (24%) but included spouses (58%), siblings and grandchildren (18%).

In trying to explain elder abuse, experts have drawn attention to the stressful situation in which it often occurs – long-term care which is costly and may bring few rewards. Looking after a dependent old person can produce considerable stress for the carer and their family, especially if the care is not shared evenly between siblings.

CONCLUSION

When considering the short-term and long-term costs of family violence, it is clear that action must be taken to address this problem and to help those caught in the cycle of violence to escape. All the research indicates that family violence is far more common than we realise and that it occurs in all strata of society, but that much of it remains hidden perhaps because of our unwillingness to confront the unimaginable. Whilst there are many different forms of abuse which occur within families, explanations of abuse tend to reveal a pattern of themes. These include environmental stress factors such as unemployment, poverty and lack of social support together with personality factors which may be the result of childhood experience of abuse, such as an acceptance of violence, low self-esteem and inadequate problem-solving skills. Placed within a context of gender relations defined by power, these factors seem to work together to increase the probability of violence occurring in the family. Whilst there is disagreement amongst the experts as to the chief contributory factor in explaining family violence, there is almost universal agreement that funding should be directed towards its prevention rather than reacting after the fact.

chapter seven

PSYCHOLOGY IN THE COURTROOM

CHAPTER OVERVIEW

In this chapter the potential contribution of psychology to the courtroom will be examined. The jury system is admired throughout the world as a means of securing reliable judgements in relation to criminal offences and psychologists have devoted considerable time to studying the decision-making processes which occur behind the door of the jury room. Part of the evidence which jurors consider may be the testimony of eyewitnesses and well-grounded research in the area of memory has been usefully expanded to examine the dangers of relying too heavily on this type of evidence. The status of child witnesses is also examined, as there have often been assumptions made about children's poor memory and their conse-quent unreliability as witnesses. Psychological research has been able to challenge these assumptions.

INTRODUCTION

In spite of some early links between research on perception and memory and evaluation of eyewitness testimony, it was not until the 1950s that the law began to make use of social and behavioural science research to inform its policy making and to make judgements in individual cases. There then followed a growth in psychological research, some dealing with offending behaviour and some dealing with courtroom issues. Blackburn (1993), however, argues that forensic psychology is quite specific in its focus, drawing on the American Psychological Association's definition of forensic psychology as:

" ... all forms of professional psychological conduct when acting, with definable foreknowledge, as a psychological expert on explicitly psycho-legal issues, in direct assistance to courts, parties to legal proceedings, correctional and forensic mental health facilities, and administrative, judicial, and legislative agencies, acting in an adjudicative capacity." (Committee on Ethical Guidelines for Forensic Psychologists, 1991)

Thus, the forensic psychologist will offer advice in areas where substantial academic research has developed understanding of psychological processes relevant to the courtroom. These areas would include juries, eyewitness testimony and child witnesses.

JURIES

In the United Kingdom no qualifications are required other than age and the right to vote in order to sit on a jury. Juries deliberate in secret and are therefore accountable to no one, though they may seek advice. They are, however, obliged to honour an oath to 'faithfully try the defendant or defendants and give a true verdict according to the evidence'. Whilst a jury may not be able to reach full agreement, jurors once sworn cannot refuse to come to a decision and in March 1997 two jurors, including the foreperson, were jailed for contempt after they said they could not make a decision in relation to the defendants in a British fraud trial because of their 'personal beliefs'. These were revealed later to be confusion about the evidence and an unwillingness to 'judge' anyone.

There have been cases, however, when jurors have brought in 'perverse' verdicts against the weight of the evidence in order to reflect their disapproval of the prosecution. This happened in the case of Clive Ponting, the civil servant who was charged with breaches of the Official Secrets Act for leaking information about the Falklands war, when the jury refused to convict. Jurors in the UK are in fact entitled to vote according to their conscience, despite the evidence presented. Although the verdicts which juries do reach can often appear to the public or to the police as irrational, the British jury system is admired and emulated throughout the world.

Selecting jurors

Whilst no qualifications are required to sit on a jury and one might therefore assume that the first 12 people selected would form the jury, there are procedures by which objections may be made to a limited number of potential individual jurors. In Britain these are called peremptory challenges, whilst in America the process is called *voir dire* and has become a significant feature in the run-up to a trial. Objections are often based on assumptions about the personalities, attitudes and beliefs of potential jurors which legal professionals think may influence their judgement about the defendant.

Lawyers, in common with many other people, tend to rely on implicit personality theories and cultural stereotypes in order to form their impressions of others. Lawyers want to use this information to select jurors who will be sympathetic to their client and in America, a small industry has developed advising lawyers on how to select or reject prospective jurors. Thus, it has been suggested, for instance, that occupation is an important influence with, for example, engineering types likely to be unemotional, athletes lacking in sympathy for victims and butchers very unlikely to be shocked by violent crime (Fulero and Penrod, 1990).

Not surprisingly, social psychologists have conducted extensive research in the area of juror variables which might affect decision making and it would seem that demographic factors such as sex, age, race, income, education and occupation are unlikely to help predict juror decisions (Hastie et al., 1983). Neither do personality factors play an important part (Kassin and Wrightsman, 1983). The one factor which does seem to have some predictive power relates to the American legal system, where in several states the death penalty operates. A special jury selection practice exists which is known as the death qualification clause. Under this procedure, judges may exclude all prospective jurors who say they could not support the death penalty. Ellsworth (1993) has shown that people who do not oppose the death penalty tend to be prosecution minded, i.e. they are more concerned about crime, more trusting of police practice and more cynical about defendants. Moreover, when she asked 288 people to participate in a mock jury concerning a murder trial, those who were willing to impose the death penalty were more likely to vote guilty before deliberating than those who would have actually been excluded from jury service because of their refusal to impose a death sentence. This practice may thus in itself act as a bias in the performance of juries, making findings of guilt more likely.

How do juries reach their decisions?

Judges and jurors tend to reach their decisions in different ways: judges offer an individual and professional view based on legal experience, whilst jurors offer group decisions based on their own general knowledge and life experience. Juries exist to make decisions and thus provide a valuable opportunity for the study of decision making in small groups, particularly the potential shift between individuals' early decisions and the subsequent collective decision of the group. Initially, the juror is listening to evidence as an individual jury member and then enters the jury room with some ideas which are subsequently subjected to group scrutiny. It is clear that different jurors draw different conclusions on the basis of having heard exactly the same evidence. So, how does this occur?

It has been suggested that the processes which occur when juries deliberate to reach their decisions are similar to the small group dynamics which are well documented by social psychologists. However, since it is illegal in this country to question jurors about their experiences, one of the only ways to explore this possibility is to study mock juries and their deliberations. Whilst this can be informative, particularly if the reconstruction is as realistic as possible, the jurors will always be aware that the defendant's fate is not actually going to be determined by their decisions. However, other countries have more liberal laws and one of the largest and most influential studies of real-life juries was conducted in 1966 by Kalven and Zeisel in the United States. They compared jury verdicts with the trial judges' views in 3576 criminal cases and found agreement in 78% of cases. Following the publication of this study, however, many American states passed laws forbidding jurors to participate in future studies of this kind, presumably because of fears that the justice system might be compromised.

The decision-making process is said to pass through three stages (Hastie et al., 1983). In common with other problem-solving groups, juries begin in a relaxed, open-ended 'orientation period' during which they set an agenda, raise questions and explore the facts. Differences of opinion then start to become apparent, usually when the first vote is taken, and factions may develop. The group then slips quite quickly into a period of 'open conflict' where the debate may become fierce and begins to focus on quite detailed aspects of the case and the different interpretations possible. There is still a common objective, however, and the jurors look together at the facts before them and discuss the judge's instructions. If all the jurors agree, they can return a verdict but if they do not agree the majority may try to convert the others through social pressure. At that point the group enters a period of 'reconciliation', during which an attempt is made to smooth over previous conflicts.

What happens when jurors disagree?

Kalven and Zeisel (1966) interviewed the members of 225 criminal juries in order to compare their first votes with the eventual outcomes. Out of 215 juries which opened with an initial majority, 209 reached a final verdict which was consistent with this vote. So, in the main the majority tends to get its way, but there is one reliable exception to the majority-wins rule. Deliberation tends to produce a leniency bias which favours the defendant. Individual jurors are more likely to vote guilty on their own than in a group. If juries are initially split they are more likely to return a not-guilty verdict – it seems to be easier to raise a reasonable doubt in people's minds than it is to remove such a doubt.

Psychologists who have studied decision making using jury simulation concluded that if two-thirds of the jury (8 of 12) agreed initially about the best outcome (whether that was acquittal or conviction) it was likely that an agreed verdict would eventually be reached. If, however, the number of jurors initially in agreement is less than eight it is very likely that the jury will be deadlocked and unable to reach a collective decision (Davis, 1980). This research also demonstrated that in any given jury it is likely that most of the jurors will be inclined towards acquittal.

FIGURE 7.1 *Even a minority of one, in this case Henry Fonda in the film* Twelve Angry Men, *can sometimes sway the opinion of the rest of a twelve person jury*

The process of resolving disagreements has merited special attention. From social psychologists' research on conformity, it would seem that there are two possibilities. Sometimes people conform because, through a process of 'informational influence', they are genuinely persuaded by what others say. They listen to other people's opinions and use that information as the basis on which to reach their own judgement. At other times, however, people seem to yield to the pressures of 'normative influence' by changing their stated view in the majority's direction even though they may privately disagree. They go along with the group norms because they do not want to appear deviant. Other studies indicate that consensus is usually achieved by a vigorous exchange of views and information, but occasionally heavy-handed social pressure can be brought to bear and, as Asch (1956) showed, it can be very difficult to resist intense pressure publicly. His studies showed that participants were inclined to go along with a majority view (in this case, the estimate of a line's length) even though they could see that the estimate was incorrect.

Offences which carry stiff penalties may actually discourage jurors from convicting, which presumably is not what legislators intend (Kerr, 1978). Thus, demands for a mandatory life sentence for rape may in fact result in fewer convictions and might even lead to some rapists murdering their victims, since murder might eliminate a witness and is not going to result in a longer sentence.

139

Should jury verdicts always be unanimous?

In Britain a majority verdict secures a conviction, whilst in America all but two states require a unanimous verdict. As a result of this, a phenomenon called 'jury nullification' has emerged whereby an individual juror who for personal reasons wants to protest against particular prosecutions can vote against the other jurors and a mistrial will have to be declared. In fact, all jurors are entitled to ignore a judge's directions and vote according to their conscience even if this goes against the evidence, but in America not only is this not generally known but courts are actually prevented from informing jurors of this right under a Supreme Court ruling made in the 1890s. In 1997 Laura Kriho was a juror in a drugs trial and when she told her fellow jurors of their right to acquit even if they believed the accused had broken the law, she was herself convicted of contempt and fined $1200. Kriho is associated with the Fully Informed Jury Association (FIJA), an organisation which believes that juries should be allowed to exercise their right to veto the law. FIJA are also opposed to the use of *voir dire* in order to exclude anyone with forceful opinions or extra knowledge of a case in its social or political context. They operate against a powerful American campaign to reduce the powers of juries substantially by exchanging ordinary citizens for retired lawyers and judges.

How long does it take juries to reach a decision?

Psychologists have been concerned with whether the need for unanimity or majority decisions influences the time taken to reach a verdict. Common sense would indicate that if a majority verdict is acceptable, discussion time will be reduced. Research tends to support this: Hastie et al. (1983) recruited 800 people to take part in mock juries and after watching a re-enactment of a murder trial, the groups were instructed to reach a verdict by a 12:0, a 10:2 or a 8:4 margin. The differences were quite marked. Compared to juries needing unanimous decisions, the others spent less time discussing the case and more time voting. After reaching the required margin they often ended the discussion abruptly and returned a verdict. When Hastie et al. (1983) watched tapes of the juries reaching their decisions, they observed that majority-rule juries tended to adopt 'a more forceful, bullying, persuasive style' than did juries instructed to reach a unanimous decision.

Are juries conservative or radical?

In some jury situations members may share the same idea but differ in terms of the extremity of this position, e.g. they may all agree that compensation should be awarded but differ in relation to the amount. Research in this area shows that in group decision making, extreme positions tend to carry a lot of weight (Kaplan and Schersching, 1981). Thus the decision reached by the group tends to be more extreme than the average of the initial views expressed by individual members. This effect was initially known as the 'risky shift' phenomenon, after work by Stoner (1968), and tends to be counter-intuitive in the sense that committees are often viewed stereotypically as inherently conservative. Stoner, however, by presenting life dilemmas to people on their own initially and then in a small group situation, was able to demonstrate that their decisions became riskier. This effect is now called group polarisation since the tendency for exaggeration of initial views after group discussion can lean in the direction of conservatism or radicalism depending on the initial views expressed. The more group discussion occurs and the more persuasive arguments used, the more extreme attitudes become (Kerr, 1992). Thus, the early period when jury members first begin to express their views is crucial to the eventual outcome.

Leadership within the jury

If juries are essentially small groups of decision makers, what else can social psychologists tell us about the process of their decision making? In theory, all the jurors are equal, but in practice they have to elect a foreperson who will relay their decision back to the court. This person may or may not be the actual leader of the group, however, and dominance hierarchies soon develop with a handful of individuals tending to control the discussion. Others participate at a much lower rate and some merely watch from the sidelines. This phenomenon – allowing some people to do all the work – has been called 'social loafing' (Latané et al., 1979).

The jury foreperson occupies a crucial role in the decision-making process and research suggests that this role is most likely to be occupied by someone of higher socioeconomic status, someone who has had previous experience as a juror, someone who simply sits at the head of the table the first time the jury meets, or who speaks first (Strodtbeck and Lipinski, 1985). How is the foreperson elected? It is usually by vote within a few minutes of the jury beginning their deliberations, but the outcome tends to follow a predictable pattern. Men tend to be chosen more often than women. When Kerr et al. (1982) examined the records of 179 trials in San Diego, they found that 50% of jurors were female, but 90% of the forepersons were male. Since men are more likely to speak first and to take the prominent seats (Nemeth et al., 1976), this may explain the sex difference in the selection of a foreperson.

Does the size of the jury make a difference?

In keeping with the British tradition, 12 has tended to be the ideal number, but in the United States there have been a number of initiatives to vary jury size. In 1985 a defendant in Boulder, Colorado, 'fearing the mob mentality of 12 people', successfully argued for a one-person jury but this was overturned on appeal. Since 1970, however, American courts are allowed to use six-person juries except in cases which involve the possibility of the death penalty. In fact, the Supreme Court cited the work of Asch (1956) to conclude that reducing the number of jury members would not affect a minority's ability to resist normative pressure because a juror's resistance depends on the proportional size of the majority. They felt that a lone dissenter in a 5:1 situation was in an identical position to the minority in a 10:2 split. In fact, Asch's research demonstrated that these situations are very different – the presence of just one ally can enable a dissenter to maintain their independence quite fiercely.

The size of a jury can also make a difference in other ways too: the smaller the jury, the less likely it is to represent minority groups in society and the more likely it is to begin deliberating at a near-unanimity position (Roper, 1980). Smaller juries spend less time discussing the evidence and are less likely to declare themselves undecided (Saks, 1977). This may save the courts time and money, but may not always be in the best interests of justice.

Factors which influence jurors

There are some factors which seem to influence jurors quite markedly in their decision making. Three which have been revealed by research include the perceived attractiveness of defendants, the race or ethnicity of defendants and pretrial publicity.

Attractiveness of defendants

A range of studies indicate that when defendants are physically attractive they tend to be sentenced less harshly (Sigall and Ostrove, 1975), unless they are deemed to have used their attractiveness to secure their ends, e.g. fraud. Similarly, Dane and Wrightsman (1982) suggest that in the courtroom, stereotypes are imported which predict that villains are unattractive, of low socioeconomic status, of dubious moral character and from a powerless minority group. Thus, when attractive, high status, majority group members of previously good character appear in the dock, the temptation to find reasons for acquittal is strong.

Race of defendants

The race or ethnicity of the defendant is also an issue for juries, with studies which have used mock jurors revealing that a racial bias does operate. Thus, Pfeifer and Ogloff (1991) showed that white university students rated black defendants more guilty than white defendants charged with the same crime, especially when the victim was white. In real life the consequences of a racial bias can be severe. Thus, black defendants are more likely than white defendants to receive prison sentences for similar offences (Stewart, 1980) and defendants who murder a white victim are more likely to receive the death penalty than those whose victim is black (Henderson and Taylor, 1985).

Pretrial publicity

Pretrial publicity can be very influential too and difficult for juries to ignore. Examples of this would include the media attention surrounding the case in which several Los Angeles police officers were charged with beating Rodney King, the outcome of which – a not-guilty verdict – led to the Los Angeles riots; and the extensive media coverage of both the criminal and civil trials of O.J. Simpson in connection with the death of his ex-wife. More recently, the Oklahoma Bomber, Timothy MacVeigh, appealed against the death sentence imposed on him in June 1997 on the grounds that 'emotive' pretrial publicity influenced jurors against him.

In Britain the press attention given to Frederick West, the alleged serial killer, particularly following his suicide in 1995, seemed likely to prejudice the case against his wife, Rosemary West, though she eventually received several life sentences of imprisonment in 1996. Mr West's brother was subsequently charged with sexual offences concerning one of the West children, but before a verdict was reached he too committed suicide. In such high-profile cases, it is almost impossible for jurors to remain neutral and only consider the information presented to them at trial when attempting to reach a verdict. It can also prove extremely stressful if jurors involved in long, high-profile cases are unable to discuss their views or their feelings with anyone other than their fellow jurors.

Pretrial publicity can also influence the fate of the victim as well as the accused. Before the ruling of no publicity, victims of rape often suffered from negative media coverage and an example is provided by Benedict (1993), who analyses the way the media covers sex crimes and focuses on the adverse publicity which the victim of a New Bedford gang rape suffered – her story was subsequently filmed as *The Accused* (1987).

CASE STUDY 7.1
Media influence on trials

All these factors may have played a part in the Louise Woodward trial in October 1997. Louise was a young English au pair working in America and looking after two children, a toddler and a baby. The baby, Matthew Eappen, died as a result of a massive brain haemorrhage and Louise was charged with first-degree murder. The prosecution alleged that Louise, in a state of frustration after her employers had restricted her free time, shook the infant so vigorously that he suffered fatal injuries. The defence argued that there was no medical evidence to support this allegation and that the injury could have occurred accidentally some weeks previously.

In the months before the trial there was considerable speculation in the media about this case which the jurors, when asked, claimed had not influenced them. Matthew's parents, both doctors, were criticised for working full-time and employing an inexperienced young woman to care for two demanding children. Louise was portrayed alternately as an 'innocent abroad', and someone who lied about her age to drink alcohol and had 'cybersex' on the Internet. During the trial expert witnesses appeared for both prosecution and defence, presenting conflicting medical evidence, and the testimony of Louise Woodward herself began to assume more and more significance in terms of influencing the jurors. When she gave her evidence she appeared to be calm and composed apart from some rather incongruous incidents of nervous smiling. Her vulnerability because of her youth was apparent, but not her physical attractiveness — she appeared awkward, gauche, plump and plain. More importantly, her Englishness was paramount, no hysteria, no great show of emotion, no playing to the gallery. This may well have appeared to the jurors, confused by the medical evidence, as a display of indifference intended to cover lies. The end result was that after 26 hours of deliberation the jury returned a verdict of second-degree murder, believing that Louise had intentionally and maliciously inflicted fatal injuries on Matthew Eappen on a set day.

This unexpected verdict caused uproar in America, and also in the UK, because the overwhelming view was that the prosecution had not presented a case beyond reasonable doubt. Moreover, the jury was seen as having attempted to solve the mystery of the infant's death rather than critically evaluating the evidence. Assertions were made that the verdict was an almost unconscious atonement for the equally unexpected not-guilty verdict in the 1996 O.J. Simpson murder trial (see Chapter 6), and significantly the same defence lawyer appeared in both cases. The reputation of American justice took centre stage as the decision of 12 jurors, required to bring in a unanimous verdict and undoubtedly influenced by pretrial publicity, the appearance of the defendant and the victim's parents, cultural expectations of appropriate displays of emotion, and conflicting expert evidence, increasingly came under scrutiny. Legal appeals were made, and a week later the jury's decision was overturned by the judge who ruled that a verdict of manslaughter would be more appropriate. He then sentenced Louise to 279 days imprisonment, the exact time she had already served, allowing her to be released immediately.

During the short period of appeal there was massive media coverage of the case, with Matthew Eappen's parents appearing on live TV shows repeating their belief in Louise's guilt, and Louise's parents and supporters protesting her innocence. Although the judge said he had not been influenced by any of this, it is clear that the issues raised by the Louise Woodward case would not have received such attention if the trial had not been televised. These issues include:

- the right of mothers to work (Dr Deborah Eappen in particular was vilified for her decision to pursue her career whilst her children were so young);
- the value of childcare (there seems to be a tradition in the USA of not employing professionally trained nannies, and opting for the cheaper alternative of non-American au pairs who may have little experience of childcare);
- xenophobia on both sides of the Atlantic (curiously this anti-foreign feeling seemed to reverse after Louise was free, with her English supporters expressing new-found sympathy for the Eappen family and the American legal system, and a backlash in America because of the apparent leniency in Louise's immediate release);

- attitudes towards mixed-race children (Dr Sunil Eappen is Indian, and although Matthew being the product of a mixed-race marriage was never explicitly referred to in the legal proceedings it undoubtedly played a part in the public's response to the case);

- disbelief in the potential of women to be violent (the firm belief that women, especially mothers, cannot be violent, especially towards children, is flawed and yet continues to influence objective evaluation of the evidence);

- the 'showmanship' of lawyers (the contrast between the expensive and out-of-town 'dreamteam' defence, and the homegrown prosecution team, became less marked as all key players began to perform for the jury, calling on high emotion and persuasive techniques to influence the outcome);

- the ability of jurors to evaluate complex evidence (the difference of opinion between the medical experts called by the prosecution and the defence, and the complexity of their evidence, clearly caused confusion for the jurors, yet when they asked for advice on this issue they were refused)

The media influence on such high-profile cases deserves rigorous scrutiny.

FIGURE 7.2 *Did the media coverage of Louise Woodward's trial in 1997 help or hinder her quest to prove her innocence?*

EYEWITNESS TESTIMONY

One of the most important areas in which psychology has been applied to the courtroom is eyewitness testimony. The accuracy of memory is important in many situations but it is absolutely critical in one, namely a courtroom, where the very life of the defendant may depend on the accuracy of a witness's or a victim's recall of events and a jury's willingness to believe them. Eyewitness testimony and eyewitness identification play profoundly important roles in the apprehension and prosecution of criminal offenders. Jurors attach considerable importance to the evidence of eyewitnesses despite generally accepted knowledge that there have been many cases of mistaken identification. Why should this be so? Jurors want hard evidence and they also want to believe the words of someone who was there at the time of the offence – who else knows better than an eyewitness? Unfortunately, as Cutler and Penrod (1995) point out, eyewitnesses can be '100% confident and still be 100% wrong'.

Loftus (1974) investigated the significance given to eyewitness testimony in an experimental setting. In one study she had participants play the role of jurors by listening to evidence in a criminal case of robbery-murder in a grocery store. The mock jurors had to decide whether or not the defendant was guilty. Circumstantial evidence was presented to a group of 50 mock jurors:

- the fact that the robber ran into the defendant's apartment block;
- money was found in the defendant's room;
- tests revealed there was a slight chance the defendant had fired a gun on the day of the robbery-murder.

Only 18% of participants hearing just this information said the defendant was guilty. Another group of 50 subjects was given the circumstantial evidence plus another piece of evidence – the store clerk's eyewitness identification of the defendant. Of these, 72% were prepared to convict the defendant, demonstrating the powerful effect of eyewitness testimony. Nothing that surprising? Rather more striking were the results of a third condition in Loftus's study in which 50 participants received the circumstantial evidence, plus the eyewitness testimony, plus information *discrediting* the witness, i.e. that he was shortsighted, he was not wearing his glasses at the time of the offence and he could not have seen the robber's face from where he was standing. Nevertheless, 60% of the mock jurors still convicted.

The error rate of eyewitness testimony

The possibility of error in eyewitness testimony has been demonstrated in experimental studies and also in real life. In 1980, Buckhout showed a 13-second film of a mock mugging on prime-time TV, then showed an identity parade of six men and asked viewers to phone in and identify the offender. Over 2000 viewers responded, but picked the mugger correctly only 14% of the time, which is slightly worse than a random guess (with six possibilities 16.67% should be right by chance alone).

What is the extent of error in eyewitness identification in real life when the consequences for individuals and their families are enormous? Huff (1987) estimates that although the error rate in American criminal convictions may be as low as 0.5%, in real terms this translates into 7500 erroneous convictions per year in the serious offences category. When Huff looked in detail at 500 cases of wrongful conviction he found that the single leading cause (60%) was erroneous eyewitness identification of the defendants. This figure is all the more remarkable since eyewitness identifications feature in only 5% of criminal cases (Loh, 1981). Within Huff's own parameters these figures suggest that there may be as many as 4500 wrongful convictions based on mistaken eyewitness testimony.

Loftus (1979) cites an American case of mistaken identity in 1975 when the assistant manager of a store was kidnapped at gunpoint in an attempted robbery. He saw his two kidnappers only briefly but gave the police a description and two local men, Sandie and Lonnie Sawyer, were arrested. They both had alibis and yet when the case went to trial they were found guilty and sentenced to a total of 32 years in prison. A year later they were released after the confession of another prisoner that he and another man had actually committed the crime was brought to the attention of the authorities.

In the United Kingdom one of the most notable cases of mistaken identity was that of James Hanratty who was hanged for the A6 murder in 1962 and is now being considered for an official pardon. However, a recommendation in a 1976 report by Lord Devlin that trials based solely on identification evidence should not proceed has still to be implemented. The report was prepared after a miscarriage of justice in 1969 when Laso Virag was wrongly convicted of the attempted murder of a policeman on the basis of eyewitness identification. He was subsequently pardoned in 1974 and received substantial compensation. The Devlin Committee looked at all identification parades held in 1973 in England and Wales and found that 45% led to a suspect being picked out and 82% of these people were subsequently convicted. In more than 300 cases eyewitness testimony was the only evidence of guilt but still produced a conviction in 74% of cases, suggesting that enormous weight is given to this type of evidence.

Graham Davies (1994), Professor of Psychology at Leicester University and an expert in eyewitness testimony, has argued strongly for a change in the law to prevent people from being convicted on the basis of identification without corroborating evidence. He argues that research clearly shows that most people remember faces poorly and recall details not from memory but from stereotypes of what they think criminals should look like. Yarmey (1982) found that elderly participants were more likely than younger participants to identify an innocent bystander as an offender if that bystander 'looked like a criminal', whilst Yarmey et al. (1984) found that younger participants recalled more details when the observed offender wore jeans and a leather jacket, presumably because they identified with him more closely or because these clothes fit a stereotype. Bull (1982), for instance, found that people were quite prepared to identify criminals by their appearance alone, presumably on the basis of quite firmly held stereotypes.

One potential explanation for mistaken convictions seems to be the importance attached to eyewitness identification by jurors who seem prepared to believe this sort of testimony above all others. This may be because intuitively we think of memory and perception as passive copying processes, rather like a camera or a tape recorder which provides a permanent record of events. Most modern psychological research in fact shows both memory and perception to be active and constructive processes. Perception does not produce a record but an interpretation, whilst memory is susceptible to both deterioration and reconstruction.

Research on memory

Memory has been a solid area of research for psychologists for many years. The classic work of Bartlett (1932) on the reconstructive nature of memory is a prime example of how this research can be applied to an understanding of eyewitness testimony. Bartlett concluded on the basis of his work that interpretation plays a key role in how people recall previous events. We tend to rewrite history in some ways by trying to fit memories into existing systems and the more difficult this is, the more likely it is that we will distort our memories in order to make them fit. Bartlett called this making 'efforts after meaning' and described memory as an 'imaginative reconstruction' of experience. He felt that we try to make the past more coherent and logical and that can involve making deductions about what should have happened rather than what actually did happen.

Belief in the accuracy of eyewitness testimony may fail to take into account such developments in the field of perception and memory. Doubts about the accuracy of human memory were noted as long ago as 1895 when Cattell asked his students questions about the previous week's weather, when it had snowed. Of 56 people asked, only seven mentioned the snow, which prompted Cattell to remark:

> "(people) cannot state much better what the weather was a week ago than what it will be a week hence."

More recently, in 1982 Nickerson and Adams asked Americans to draw from memory what they would expect to find on each side of a US coin. On average, people recalled correctly only three of the eight critical features of the coin and even these were often mislocated and this was an object with which they were very familiar.

Contemporary research highlights the dynamic and fluid quality of perception and memory, especially over time. Researchers find it useful to view memory as a three-stage process involving:

1 *acquisition* – the witness's perception at the time of the event;
2 *storage* – when the witness stores the information in order to prevent forgetting;
3 *retrieval* – when the information is needed, e.g. in court, the witness has to retrieve it from storage.

This model suggests that errors can occur at all of these three different points. During the original event an individual perceives it and encodes it in memory but many factors influence this process. It is suggested that a combination of witness factors (e.g. age, gender, individual responses to stress, beliefs, etc.) and event factors (e.g. duration, level of violence, etc.) influences the perception and memory of criminal events.

Witness factors

Age

Memory for witnessed events does vary with age, so children's recall tends to be less accurate than adults, (Dent and Flin, 1992) and they are slightly more suggestible to leading questions (Goodman and Reed, 1986). Similarly, older people may recall fewer details of witnessed events (List, 1986).

Occupation

Despite the fact that police witnesses do not recall details of witnessed events more accurately than non-police observers (Ainsworth, 1981), and in some instances perform less well (Clifford, 1976), the public tends to believe that police officers will have better recall (Loftus and Davis, 1984) and they are therefore more likely to be believed.

Stress

There also seems to be a relationship between stress and perception, namely the Yerkes–Dodson Law, which states that perception, learning and performance are best at moderate levels of arousal and worst at very high and very low levels of arousal. This may well seem counter-intuitive, in that subjective recall of personal events indicates that high emotion often produces very clear and vivid memories. In fact, psychologists have lent credence to this – Brown and Kulik (1977) investigated people's memories of the assassination of President Kennedy in 1963, and found that a phenomenon called 'flashbulb memory' existed. Their participants could remember – as if a camera flash had gone off and preserved the details – where they were and what they were doing when they had heard the news. The trouble with this is that although recall may be vivid, there is no guarantee that it is accurate and current research would indicate that stress can impair a witness's recall in a variety of ways.

Beliefs

People's expectations and beliefs inevitably influence their reports. A classic study by Hastorf and Cantril (1954) demonstrates this. They showed a film of a football game to fans from both sides and asked them to count instances of inappropriate behaviour and fouls. Guess the result? Each group of fans reported many more fouls from the opposing side.

Event factors

Duration

People almost always overestimate the amount of time events take (time seems to stand still or events take place in slow motion). Buckhout et al. (1975) staged an assault on a professor in front of 141 students. The attack only lasted 34 seconds, but the average estimate of the event's duration was 81 seconds.

Violence

Clifford and Scott (1978) demonstrated that people's recollection of non-violent events was superior to their memory of violent events. Violence in particular seems to interfere with recall, causing witnesses to focus on one aspect of the situation to the detriment of more general observation. This is known as 'weapon focus' which allows the witness to provide lots of details about the weapon used, but virtually nothing about the user of the weapon. Loftus et al. (1987) showed that people viewing a film will focus on a gun held by a customer in a restaurant, rather than (in an alternative version of the film) on a cheque in his hand. Identification of the suspect in an identity parade and the answers to more specific questions were more accurate in the 'cheque' condition than in the 'gun' condition. Maass and Kohnken (1989) also demonstrated the effects of weapon focus: participants approached by a white-coated female experimenter with a syringe in her hand were less accurate at subsequently identifying her than those who saw her with a pen in her hand. This appears to contradict the 'emotion heightens accuracy' claim inherent in Brown and Kulik's (1977) 'flashbulb memory' study.

The possibility of contamination

Once an event has occurred the details of that event are not inviolable. The individual will be receiving a variety of information subsequent to the event which may influence the memory trace and contaminate it. Postevent information can affect recall quite significantly, as Loftus and Palmer (1974) vividly demonstrated. In one study participants watched a film of a car accident and filled in a questionnaire afterwards. Some of them were asked:

"About how fast were the cars going when they *hit* each other?"

whilst others were asked:

"About how fast were the cars going when they *smashed* into each other?"

The second group made significantly higher estimates of the speed of the cars. One week later all participants were brought back and asked:

"Did you see any broken glass?"

There was in fact no broken glass, but those who had received the question with 'smashed' in it were more likely to say they had indeed seen some glass (32% versus 14%).

Even very subtle changes in wording can have an effect. Loftus and Zanni (1975) showed subjects a short film of a road accident. Some of them were asked:

"Did you see *a* broken headlight?"

whilst others were asked:

"Did you see *the* broken headlight?"

In fact, there was no broken headlight in the film but 7% of those asked about a broken headlight said they had seen it and 17% asked about *the* broken headlight said they had seen it.

The work of Loftus seems to support the assertions made by Bartlett (1932) in relation to the 'effort after meaning' which we tend to employ when remembering past events, but there is not total agreement with this view. Bekarian and Bowers (1983) have suggested that the method of questioning is crucial in producing accurate recall. If questions are structured and follow the order of events in such a way that retrieval is not interfered with, then it is less likely that the introduction of bias will influence recall. Indeed, Loftus (1979) found that if the misleading information introduced was 'blatantly incorrect' it had little effect on recall.

Recognition of faces

The recognition and identification of faces is a very specific area of research in eyewitness testimony. In 1971, Goldstein and Chance tested subjects for their recall of photos of women's faces, snowflakes and inkblots. Subjects were shown 14 photos from each set and tested immediately afterwards and then again after 48 hours. The results showed that accuracy of recall for the faces was good – 71% – as against 48% for the inkblots and 33% for the snowflakes.

The trouble is that when this translates into real life recall can be both subjective and subject to distortion. A vivid example concerns an Australian psychologist, Donald Thompson, whose research attracted some media attention and he appeared in several TV programmes to discuss his findings. A few weeks later, however, he was picked up by the police, put in a line-up and was identified by a woman who claimed he had raped her. It subsequently emerged that the time of the rape coincided with Thompson's appearance on a live TV discussion programme so he had an excellent alibi. The woman had been raped whilst this programme was on TV and although she correctly identified Thompson's face, having associated it with the event, she wrongly assigned it to the rapist.

The cognitive interview

The most notable development in research involving eyewitness testimony has been that which examines the use of a technique called the cognitive interview (CI) which is used to assist witnesses' recall of events. Traditionally police officers and lawyers use the Standard Interview Procedure which involves a period of free recall about the event followed by specific questions on the information which is revealed during the free recall stage. Geiselman et al. (1986) suggested that using the cognitive interview instead would result in a 30% improvement in recall, with no increase in the number of incorrect responses. A revised version of the cognitive interview produced a 45% improvement on the original technique and is described in Fisher and Geiselman (1992). Compared to a standard police interview, the revised cognitive interview elicits almost twice as much information with no loss of accuracy. The technique involves:

- mentally reinstating the context of the event, i.e. the sounds, smells, feelings experienced during the event;
- asking witnesses to recall the event in various orders or in reverse order;
- asking witnesses to report absolutely everything, regardless of the perceived importance of the information;
- recalling the event from a variety of perspectives, e.g. imagining what the scene must have looked like from the point of view of several characters there at the time.

Each of these retrieval mnemonics allows the witness to re-view the event without the interference of leading questions but forces them to scrutinise their memory record. The technique aims to maximise the number of potential retrieval routes and to benefit from overlaps, hopefully triggering otherwise unrecalled details of the event.

Mackinnon et al. (1990) developed supplementary techniques to the cognitive interview to assist recall of car number plates. The techniques involved asking the witness to form an image of the scene in which the car appears, then to focus on the rear end of the car, looking at the lights, the bumper and finally the number plate. Witnesses are then asked, did the plate have any special characteristics? Do you think the numbers were high or low? Did the letters or numbers remind you of any words or things? This type of questioning tends to elicit more detail than the free recall technique normally used.

The cognitive interview procedure may have special benefits for those interviewing child witnesses, especially those who may have been the victims of physical or sexual abuse (Westcott, 1992). Children have traditionally been viewed as unreliable witnesses (Goodman et al., 1987), but Chapman and Perry (1992) found that children produced more accurate recall of a road accident when interviewed with the cognitive interview procedure than when a standard interviewing procedure was used. Using the cognitive interview technique with child witnesses requires certain refinements. When it has been used (e.g. Geiselman and Padilla, 1988; McCauley and Fisher, 1992), there have been improvements in recall but not as great as with adults and individual differences (on the part of both interviewers and children) have produced inconsistencies. It seems clear that the CI technique has potential in relation to child witnesses, but that the interviewer needs also to be trained in assessing the linguistic and cognitive competence of each child interviewee and be able to adapt the cognitive interview accordingly. It is clear that this is an area which should yield useful applications of psychological research.

Criticisms of the cognitive interview include the suggestion that the benefits may simply be the result of more attention and time having been given the witness, leading to higher motivation and the opportunity for more questions to be asked. In addition it is suggested that use of the cognitive interview can make witnesses more susceptible to leading/misleading questions. However, when Geiselman et al. (1986) looked into this they found that the cognitive interview procedure provided a degree of insulation to biased questions.

Conclusions

Research seems to demonstrate, therefore, that eyewitness testimony is not always as reliable as both jurors and courts believe. Witnesses are susceptible to influences at various stages during their observation of an event and are also vulnerable to incorrect postevent information. In view of this, it seems clear that eyewitness testimony should never be allowed to be the sole evidence supporting a conviction, but that psychologists can greatly assist in interviewing techniques which can improve the extent and the accuracy of witnesses' recall of events. They should also perhaps appear as expert witnesses to advise jurors of the dangers of accepting too readily the testimony of eyewitnesses.

The assumption, however, that eyewitnesses are uniformly unreliable has also been challenged. Stephenson (1992) suggests that since most of the research relating to eyewitness memory has taken place in the laboratory its low ecological validity must be borne in mind when considering the conclusions. He then refers to a study which involved recall of a real crime and which demonstrated the accuracy of eyewitness testimony. Yuille and Cutshall (1986) describe interviews conducted with 13 witnesses of a violent street crime 4–5 months after they had been interviewed by the police. The results of both interviews were then compared and revealed considerable accuracy, despite the introduction of two misleading questions. Significantly those witnesses who appeared to be the most distressed by their experience (e.g. they reported suffering nightmares) were the most accurate in their recall.

CHILD WITNESSES

Whereas adult eyewitnesses tend to be believed, often in situations where a healthy scepticism might be more appropriate, the case is very different for child witnesses. Various surveys show that most adults believe that children under the age of nine or ten have poorer memories and are more suggestible than adults (e.g. Leippe et al., 1989). Moreover, when Leippe et al. (1992) asked subjects to assess the accuracy of child and adult witnesses they found that the children were judged to be less consistent and less believable than the adults, even though the reports of the children and adults were in fact equally accurate. These beliefs are particularly pertinent in view of the increasing number of allegations of child sexual abuse where the word of a child may be the only evidence of long-standing episodes of abuse and this testimony has to convince a judge and jury.

Regrettably, however, stereotypical beliefs about children's recall abilities often hold true in court too. Thus, in a legal textbook on evidence published in 1984, Heydon stated:

> "First, a child's powers of observation and memory are less reliable than an adult's. Secondly, children are prone to live in a make-believe world, so that they magnify incidents which happen to them or invent them completely ... children sometimes behave in a way evil beyond their years. They may consent to sexual offences against themselves and then deny consent. They may completely invent sexual offences."
> (p.84)

In view of current knowledge about the extent of child sexual abuse and the difficulty in securing prosecutions, especially where very young children are involved, it is astonishing that such statements could be made in the form of advice to lawyers. A resistance to listening to children has been a significant feature of many of the notorious child sex abuse scandals which have occurred over the last ten years. In 1987, 121 children were removed from their homes in Cleveland because they were believed to be victims of sexual abuse. Many of these children were very young, so young they could not really say what had happened to them. However, two paediatricians, Dr Marietta Higgs and Dr Geoffrey Wyatt, began using a technique called the anal dilatation reflex which they felt was able to reliably indicate sexual interference. They discovered a scale of abuse which completely confounded the authorities and their ability to deal with the issue and, as a result of professional rivalry and a media furore about parental rights, the majority of these children were returned home without their cases being adequately examined. It is now thought that 70–75% of the initial diagnoses of sexual abuse were in fact correct and the authorities returned children to continuing abuse. At the time, however, it was the two paediatricians who were vilified and the horrors of child sexual abuse were conveniently pushed away (see Campbell, 1988).

There have been many cases of child sexual abuse trials 'folding' because of doubts about the evidence of the child victims. Thus, in 1994 two Newcastle nursery school workers were charged with rape and indecent assault, after several young children reported abuse. The police considered that six of these children were capable of giving evidence in court, but the judge halted the trial because he felt, after viewing the video interview with the eldest child (aged five), that the children were too young to give an intelligible account. He also had the 'gravest worry' as to whether he would allow his own young children to undergo cross-examination in similar circumstances. The two defendants were discharged, to the horror of the children's parents and indeed the children themselves who had been told they would be believed and protected if only they told the truth about what had happened to them.

Even the successful prosecutions are characterised by a 're-victimising' of the victims. In 1994 five defendants were found guilty of systematic and horrific sexual abuse which had taken place over a period of years but during the trial, which lasted eight months, the children's evidence was consistently described as 'pure fantasy' and one 11-year-old victim 'endured six days of crossexamination and frequently broke down in tears' (*Daily Telegraph*, June 13, 1994).

Many of the doubts about the quality of children's evidence centre on the way they have been interviewed by social workers, doctors and police officers and various judicial inquiries have criticised the professionals involved in interviewing children. This has been particularly true when there have been suggestions of ritualistic or satanic abuse, to such an extent that the possibility of such abuse occurring has virtually been dismissed. This is despite the common-sense understanding that so-called 'magical' practices of a group of adults can undoubtedly silence children who have been victims of their abuse and thus effectively prevent prosecution. Any child who speaks of black robes, chanting, animal sacrifices and murdered babies will automatically be viewed with considerable caution and anyone determined to abuse children is well aware of this. Psychological research has been used, however, to inform the development of good practice in listening to children and together with some changes in legislation, the experiences of child witnesses have slowly begun to improve, though there is still a considerable way to go.

Psychological research and child witnesses

As Naylor (1989) points out:

> "It has been conventional wisdom that young children have poor recall, and are therefore inaccurate; that they are more open to suggestion; and that they have difficulty distinguishing fantasy and reality." (p.395)

For these reasons their testimony in court has been regarded as unreliable and inaccurate. However, current psychological research has shown that these beliefs may themselves be inaccurate.

Most of the experimental studies in this area are forced to use certain paradigms to explore the accuracy of recall and you might feel this sometimes reduces their credibility. From an ethical point of view, it would be unacceptable to subject children to traumatic events and then interview them and so experimenters either have to question children about fairly mundane events and bear in mind the effects of stress in the real world (if, for instance, the child were being questioned about abuse) or the experimenter can try to be really innovative and construct situations which do have an element of stress in them, e.g. a visit to the dentist or a situation in which children are touched in a non-intimate way within a safe medical setting and then asked about the incident.

Accuracy

Although Freud (1924) pointed out that adults may repress their early memories, he noted that children do often recall events from their younger lives in some detail. This ability seems to have been borne out in a number of dramatic real-life cases, e.g. Jones and Krugman (1986) report how a three-year-old girl was abducted by a man in a car and was not found for three days. She had been pushed into a cupboard six feet below the ground in a house miles from anywhere and had survived by perching on a rim above the mud. She was only found when two hikers happened along and heard her cries for help. When she was interviewed by a child psychiatrist she gave details which enabled the police to arrest her abductor. He eventually pleaded guilty and corroborated the details the little girl had provided. If, however, he had contested the allegations, the child's testimony would undoubtedly have been subjected to considerable scrutiny and might not have withstood such an examination.

Most of the studies carried out confirm that whilst children's recall improves with age (possibly because they have had more experience of the world and have been able to develop various cognitive strategies to assist recall), even young children can accurately recall information, especially if it is within a familiar context. For instance, children will always outperform adults if the memory test is on toys! Young children tend to recall significantly less information than adults in a free recall situation, yet when they are provided with prompts and cues (not leading questions) their recall improves dramatically. Davies and Brown (1978) found that reminding five-year-olds of the categories from which 'to-be-remembered' items had been drawn increased average recall by 53%.

This research suggests that when children are interviewed a free recall approach should be used, followed by verbal prompts or the use of props for very young children, but no specific or leading questions.

Suggestibility

In some ways it is not surprising that children being interviewed by adults might be suggestible. The power differential is readily apparent and children tend to want to please adults, who they believe know everything already. For instance, if a child is being interviewed by an adult and is asked to pick out a photograph of someone they have met, they are likely to assume that if the grown-up has gone to the trouble of setting out a display of photographs the correct one will probably be there. Peters (1987) found exactly that. He asked children who had visited the dentist (a situation of mild stress) to pick out from a range of photographs someone they had seen there. In one condition the target photograph was present but the children selected a different photograph 31% of the time. However, when the target photograph was not included in the selection the children picked one of the photographs 71% of the time. Very few of them were prepared to say they were not sure and then pick none.

Social conformity can also increase suggestibility. In a study by Baxter (1990), children aged 7–13 watched an incident on video before answering a series of questions about the content. Whilst they waited to be questioned some of the children heard other children giving misleading answers (these children had actually watched a different version of the same film). As a result these children tended to introduce this new material into their answers, presumably because they wanted to conform and possibly also to please the experimenter.

This suggests that when children are interviewed considerable care needs to be taken that the interviewer does not have prior knowledge which might lead the interview in a particular direction. Poole (1992) devised a felt board which could be used by interviewers to enable this to occur. The board has the outline of a child's head and an adult's head and initially a large number of felt triangles is placed inside the outline of the child's head. These triangles represent what the child knows of the incident in question and the interviewer explains that the adult's head is empty because at the start of the interview, the adult does not know anything about the incident. The child can then be encouraged to provide information which can be symbolised by the triangles moving from the child's head to the adult's head. Poole found that this procedure resulted in children giving longer accounts.

There is little doubt that children, and adults, are influenced by leading questions and assisting children to resist inappropriate and misleading questions is therefore vital. Warren et al. (1991) found that misleading questions resulted in less accurate recall and more story changes, but that giving children a warning that some of the questions they would face were likely to be 'tricky' reduced this effect.

Fantasy/reality

Freud (1966) suggested that the claims of childhood sexual abuse made by his female adult patients were false, reflecting their inability as children to distinguish between fantasy and reality. This view has been largely accepted, despite claims that Freud's theory was a response to widespread disbelief that child sexual abuse occurs on a massive scale (Masson, 1984). Perhaps now we should know better.

It has sometimes been suggested that children will make up stories of abuse in order to get attention, but King and Yuille (1987) found that in a survey of 576 cases of sexual abuse only 8% of these were based on fictitious allegations and 6% of these had been generated by adults, not children. Thus, whilst children are certainly capable of lying, as are adults, the occurrence in relation to allegations of abuse seems to be rare.

A technique called statement validity analysis has been developed to assess the veracity of children's evidence by examining the structure and content of the child's report (Steller and Koenken, 1989). It involves the analysis of each statement made by the child according to a set of 19 reality criteria, the underlying theory suggesting that a child would be unable to fabricate a statement with these qualities. Several studies (e.g. Anson et al., 1993) have assessed the effectiveness of SVA and conclude that the procedure has good validity and reliability.

Changes in the law

Improvements in legislation have only taken place in recent years. Thus, until 1990, the criminal justice system in England and Wales assumed that a child under the age of six was an incompetent witness and therefore his or her testimony had to be corroborated by an adult. However, under the Criminal

Justice Act (1991) it was proposed that all children have the potential to give evidence provided the judge considers them sufficiently intelligent and able to tell and distinguish the truth. Until 1993 judges were also obliged to warn juries of the danger of believing sexual complaints. Other improvements include the practice of allowing children to give their evidence from behind a screen or via a live video link, so that they do not have to face the defendant.

Many of these changes arose from the recommendations of the 1988 Pigot Committee, though its more radical proposals were resisted by the Home Office. The committee's report proposed that the evidence of children should be obtained prior to court and recorded on videotape. This recording of the initial interview, plus a subsequent recording of a cross-examination held in chambers, could then replace live testimony. These proposals acknowledged the dangers of contaminating evidence because of the delay in cases coming to court and repeat interviews with children and it also aimed to protect children from the trauma of court appearances. What was eventually implemented in 1992, though, was a conservative interpretation of these recommendations. Thus, the recording of the child's initial interview can be used as evidence, but the child must still attend court and undergo live cross-examination, though if the resources are available and the judge permits it, this can be conducted via a live video link. If, however, the judge considers the initial interview with the child to have been unfairly conducted, the video of the interview, or parts of it, can be excluded.

In order to ensure that interviews are conducted properly and to provide criteria for judges to evaluate this, the Home Office published in 1992 the Memorandum of Good Practice on Video Recorded Interviews with Child Witnesses for Criminal Proceedings.

Memorandum of Good Practice

In order to compile this document, Home Office officials consulted with lawyers, social workers, police officers, psychologists and psychiatrists. In its foreword the Home Office Minister states:

> "The interests of justice and the interests of the child are not alternatives. Children have a right to justice, and their evidence is essential if society is to protect their interests and deal effectively with those who would harm them."

The finished work provides advice on the issues which practitioners need to address in order to provide recordings of interviews which will be acceptable in court. A preliminary planning meeting prior to the interview and a pattern of interviewing is recommended which follows a sequence of:

- establishing rapport;
- allowing the child a period of free recall;

- questioning using open-ended, not leading questions;
- ending the interview in a reassuring way.

Whilst the Memorandum is based on research available at the time (Bull, 1992) and is clearly well intentioned, its focus on legal constraints and its assumption that the child being interviewed actually wants to tell and will tell in the recommended one-hour interview severely restricts its application. Moreover, there is little guidance on how to interview very young children or those with learning difficulties (Bull, 1995).

The use of video technology in relation to child witnesses

The Criminal Justice Act (1991) allows a video of a child's initial interview to be presented as prosecution evidence, though this is only possible for children under 14 years in physical assault cases and under 17 years for sexual offences and is subject to the judge's agreement. The interview will normally have been conducted in accordance with the Memorandum of Good Practice soon after an allegation has been made and compliance with the guidelines will be checked by the lawyers concerned.

This facility would seem to be particularly useful in cases involving very young or very nervous children and as Davies and Westcott (1992) point out, the advantages are as follows.

- The interview can take place in a safe and supportive setting.
- Early recording can preserve accuracy, whilst the event is still fresh in the child's mind.
- The viewer is able to hear the account in the child's own words and can also observe the non-verbal behaviour.
- Multiple interviews are avoided, thus reducing stress and possible confabulation.
- If the video is shown to the defendant it might encourage a change of plea which might save the child having to go to court at all.

There are, however, also some disadvantages.

- Defendants are deprived of their natural entitlement to confront the witness.
- The use of videotapes might implicitly suggest the guilt of the defendant and thus impair his right to a fair trial.
- If leading questions have been used, albeit for therapeutic purposes, the evidence in court will be weakened.

In spite of the innovative nature of the use of video interviews and the intention to spare children unnecessary trauma, it is clear that the procedure is not being used as much as had been anticipated. Some 14,000 children have been interviewed on video since October 1992 but by February 1994, only 116 of these interviews had been shown in court. It may be that the restrictions placed on interviewing procedure and the focus on presenting sound legal evidence conflict with the therapeutic ideals of practitioners and the needs of children. Bilton (1994) points out that the need for the child to mention the name of the accused or the nature of the offence before the interviewer may lead the child to believe that their story is in doubt, whilst Wattam (1992) suggests that the practical restriction to a single one-hour disclosure interview does not sit well with the practice of building up trust over several interviews.

A recognition that fear of the accused and uncertainty in the arena of the courtroom might contribute to stress for child witnesses led to the introduction of closed-circuit television in 1989 in an effort to allow children to give their evidence in a different part of the court setting. Although not all courts have the necessary resources, this facility has been used sufficiently to allow evaluation. Davies and Noon (1991) and Noon and Davies (1993) found that judges and other legal professionals felt that the consequent reduction in stress on the part of child witnesses had significantly improved the quality of their evidence, but that the impact of live testimony was reduced for the jury.

Conclusion

Most of the evidence suggests that children's ability to recall events and give evidence in court has been seriously underestimated in the past and this has led to welcome innovations within the criminal justice system, e.g. the introduction of video links in court, the installation of video recording interview suites, more preparation of child witnesses and an appreciation of their possible trauma. A fundamental question in relation to child witnesses, however, is whether the welfare of damaged children and the interests of justice can ever be compatible? Whilst psychological research might suggest better, possibly more therapeutic, ways of dealing with child witnesses, there will always be a legal pull towards ensuring that the defendant receives a fair hearing and this may seriously hamper any attempts to improve practice.

chapter eight

TREATING CRIME

CHAPTER OVERVIEW

This chapter examines how psychologists can contribute to the treatment of offenders in an attempt to reduce the risk of further offending. There is also coverage of the debate over whether offenders should be offered treatment at all or whether the 'nothing works' perspective is true and all attempts at rehabilitation should be abandoned, with offenders simply locked up in prison. Particular attention will be paid to treatment programmes designed by psychologists which focus on identified problem areas, such as anger control, or which target specific groups of offenders, such as paedophiles. This provides the opportunity for a more detailed examination of paedophilia in terms of how treatment is informed by theoretical explanations of offending behaviour.

INTRODUCTION

It is usually taken for granted that crime is a 'bad thing' and that something should be done about it, but opinion varies quite markedly over whether offenders should simply be locked up and thereby prevented from offending or whether there should be a meaningful attempt at rehabilitation which endeavours to help offenders reduce the likelihood of recidivism. Moreover, even if the concept of rehabilitation is accepted, Chapter 2 will hopefully have convinced you that there is no single cause of crime and it is therefore unlikely that one rehabilitative approach is likely to be successful with a diverse population of offenders.

Psychologists have nonetheless attempted to develop intervention programmes which are designed to promote rehabilitation either in the community or in prisons. The overriding objective of these programmes is to enable offenders to avoid further offending by increasing their own personal effectiveness. There is thus an inherent belief that some individuals can change and that given the right approach, they can be responsive to intervention. More global attempts to change the social environment of offenders are left to other disciplines such as sociology, though the work of psychologists in the area of crime prevention has made a valuable contribution (see Chapter 10).

In July 1997 the British prison population reached 62,067, with numbers rising at a rate of 300 a week. Even the building of several new prisons and the costly purchase of an American prison ship, the Resolution, which took its first inmates in June 1997 as HMP Weare, will not accommodate the dramatic rise in the number of prisoners if this rate continues. The 30% increase in the prison population since 1992 (when it was 42,000) has been explained in terms of judicial responses to the then Home Secretary, Michael Howard, calling for harsher sentences because 'prison works'. However, judges themselves have indicated that they felt under considerable public and media pressure to impose prison sentences in a climate where faith in community sentences was being systematically reduced and they were being urged to be punitive in an attempt to restore moral order.

Whatever the explanation, the increase in the British prison population has presented the prison service with a massive problem of management and there have been various suggestions about how to deal with this crisis. For instance, it has been suggested that up to 4000 non-violent prisoners should be released from their sentences early as long as they agree to electronic tagging in order to reduce the pressure (Jack Straw, Home Secretary, July 1997). There is clearly a crisis in terms of containment, despite some politicians'

FIGURE 8.1 *HMP Weare, a prison ship bought from America to ease the serious problem of prison over-crowding on the mainland, and a relic from more 'primitive' times*

views that increasing the likelihood and length of prison sentences is the only way to reduce crime. But does imprisonment actually work as a deterrent? Research would suggest not, either in terms of deterring the individual or deterring others. Lipsey (1992) found that imprisonment, boot camps and intense surveillance on average resulted in a 25% increase in recidivism, whilst Home Office statistics reveal a high reconviction rate over a four-year period for offenders discharged in 1987 and for young adult males, who commit the majority of recorded crimes, the reconviction rate was 82% (Home Office, 1994). Clearly, then, action needs to be taken not only to prevent new offenders embarking on a life of crime, but to offer alternative opportunities to those who have already chosen a criminal career.

The picture for female offenders is no better. Since 1993 the female prison population has risen by 76% (compared to 35% for men) and two-thirds of female prisoners received short sentences for non-violent property offences, those offences which used to attract community penalties. A recent report from the National Association of Probation Officers (1997) suggests that:

> "A harsher sentencing climate has evolved, even though there has been no discernible increase in female crime."

What can psychologists do?

Traditionally, psychologists working within the penal system have been involved in assessment, treatment and research with a very specific client group, namely convicted offenders. In many ways these psychologists do not 'treat' their clients in a 'pure' clinical sense; rather, they try to identify problems which can be addressed in such a way that offenders can manage these problems in the community without reoffending. Thus, teaching social skills, coping skills and new strategies for dealing with difficult situations may ultimately enable an offender to make a choice not to offend when he is released.

The long-term savings which could result from such intervention, both financial and psychological, have unfortunately not convinced the authorities that appropriate funding should be provided for the development and implementation of treatment programmes for offenders. Politicians feel they must respond to the public, whose interest, more often than not, lies in retribution and the punishment of offenders rather than their rehabilitation. The debate about the viability of rehabilitation has also taken place in the academic arena.

During the 1970s the appropriateness of pursuing rehabilitation was subjected to scrutiny. Research papers began to appear which suggested that 'nothing works' in terms of reducing recidivism, especially if reoffending is considered to have more to do with social factors such as peer pressure and disadvantage than with the personal problems which are the focus of most treatment programmes. Thus, in 1974 when Martinson examined 231 controlled outcome studies (1945–67), covering a range of interventions including counselling, probation, and parole, he concluded that:

> "With few and isolated exceptions, the rehabilitative efforts that have been reported so far have had no appreciable effect on recidivism." (p.33)

Whilst Martinson's views did not go unchallenged, with critics pointing out that 48% of the studies he reviewed showed positive or 'partly positive' effects, an encouraging outcome considering that most rehabilitation services receive very little funding or support (e.g. Palmer, 1975), the slogan 'nothing works' did appeal to those on the political right who had already been critical of rehabilitation attempts (especially in the aftermath of rising crime rates in the 1970s) but also to those at the other end of the political continuum who argued that addressing the problems of individual offenders was futile. Either way it looked as if the future of psychologically based treatment programmes was bleak.

Later evaluations of outcome studies were rather more optimistic, with Gendreau and Ross (1979) reporting 86% successful outcomes from their review of 95 intervention programmes for alcoholism, drug abuse and sex offending. By the 1980s, though, the rehabilitation ideal was still under threat, with calls for more rigorous scrutiny and evaluation of treatment programmes. Subsequently meta-analyses of intervention programmes concluded that most treatments are better than no treatment and the main characteristics of successful offender rehabilitation programmes can be identified (Andrews et al., 1990). They include a substantial psychological component, but in addition they will:

- contain a high degree of structure and focus, e.g. a particular approach (behavioural) to a particular type of behaviour (violence);
- be operated by staff who use authority in a 'firm but fair' fashion and who model and reinforce anticriminal values;
- have enthusiastic and committed staff, supported by management;
- target attitudes and values which support offending behaviour;
- employ problem-solving procedures based on cognitive and social learning principles;
- match the programme to offender characteristics;
- evaluate the success of their programmes not simply in terms of recidivism but also in terms of personal growth;
- focus on medium- to high-risk offenders;
- attempt to generalise beyond the institutional setting.

Hollin (1995) describes such programmes as having high treatment 'integrity' and suggests they are likely to produce a decrease in recidivism 20–40% above the normal baseline levels. He points to three threats to programme integrity:

1 *programme drift* – where there is a gradual drift away from the aims of the programme over a period of time;
2 *programme reversal* – when staff inadvertently model inappropriate responses, e.g. becoming aggressive when involved in an anger management course;
3 *programme non-compliance* – when, despite planning, practitioners change the programme halfway through, introducing new methods or adding extra targets.

Types of treatment programme

There are many types of treatment programme, each driven by a particular theoretical psychological perspective.

Psychoanalytic/psychodynamic approaches

This perspective is probably the least favoured in contemporary approaches to working with offenders, though those who do practise it believe that gaining insight and self-knowledge via analysis is the only route to successful rehabilitation. In contrast, Andrews et al. (1990) argue that:

> "Traditional psychodynamic and nondirective client-centred therapies are to be avoided within general samples of offenders" (p.376)

and Blackburn (1993) points out that there are very few evaluations of classic psychoanalysis as a treatment method with offenders, though psychodynamically oriented approaches are often used in programmes which offer some form of counselling. To dismiss the potential contribution of psychodynamically based therapy may therefore be rather premature, especially in view of the accepted need for rapport with a warm and genuine therapist/carer as a prerequisite for all successful treatment.

Behaviour therapy

Based on classical and operant learning principles, this approach aims to reinforce socially acceptable behaviour in an attempt to discourage further offending behaviour. Thus, Fo and O'Donnell (1975) describe a 'buddy system' in which adult volunteers were paired with young offenders on a regular and frequent basis so that they could both model appropriate behaviour and reinforce imitation. The alternative approach is to focus on selected negative aspects of offending in an effort to discourage reoffending whilst at the same time securing some acceptance of responsibility. Thus, reparation and restitution programmes require offenders to make a personal apology to the victims of their crimes, which makes them feel very uncomfortable. They are also required to offer some financial compensation. Evidence from diversion schemes which operate this policy suggests that this very practical approach can have successful outcomes and is moreover considerably less expensive than incarceration (Dignan, 1992).

Cognitive behavioural therapy

This approach draws on cognitive theory and social learning theory and is based on the premise that thoughts influence behaviour and so changing the nature of thoughts (or cognitions) will also effect behavioural change. There are some theorists who believe that many offenders have deficits in social cognitions which result in an egocentric perspective (Ross and Fabiano, 1985). An example of this would be the young man who believes that when certain individuals look at him in a social setting such as a pub they are inviting him to fight them, otherwise why would they be looking specifically at him? Teaching such a person to consider other, less confrontational roles others might be adopting can enable a repertoire of possible responses to be constructed. This teaching can take the form of 'self-instructional training' (Goldstein and Keller, 1987). We all use inner speech to evaluate our own actions and intended actions, though we are mostly unaware of this. Modifying the statements we make to ourselves in order to increase positive evaluations and reduce self-criticism can increase self-control. Other techniques used within cognitive behavioural programmes include modelling, role play and rehearsal in order to enable individuals to build up a range of responses from which they can choose when faced with a potentially difficult situation.

Social skills training

The technique of social skills training with young offenders became popular during the 1970s, although the seminal work was largely in the clinical field and based on the analogy drawn by Argyle (1967) between social skills and motor skills. Argyle suggested that both sets of skills can be learned in the same way so if offenders are seen to have a deficit in social competence which contributes to their offending, maybe they can be trained in such a way as to improve their social skills. Social skills include the range of behaviours which we absorb as children then take for granted as adults but which make social interaction run smoothly. They cover basic skills such as listening, looking and smiling at each other appropriately, conversational rules and how to read the intentions of others. Patterns of non-verbal communication are just as important as speech, particularly in relation to cultural, class, status and gender differences.

A combination of techniques is used in social skills training, based on behavioural methods. They include instruction (clear description of appropriate behaviour), modelling of the social behaviour by another person, practice and rehearsal of those skills via role play, feedback on performance and contingent reinforcement for the skill (praise as the required behaviour is shaped). In addition, homework tasks are often set so that the behaviour can be generalised to real-life situations outside group sessions and then practised. The focus is usually on developing micro-skills such as appropriate eye contact and gestures and then moving towards specific skills of negotiation and communication with particular categories of people and in particular

Social skills checklist

Here is a list of things that people have to do nearly every day when they meet other people. Which of them are you good at? and which of them are you not so good at? Look at each item in turn and decide how good you are at doing it; then put a tick in the space opposite which is nearest to how good or bad you think you are.

	I am good at this	I am not bad at this	I am not very good at this	I am bad at this
A				
1. Looking people in the face				
2. Being watched by lots of people				
3. Staring people out				
4. Smiling at people I fancy				
5. Keeping a straight face				
6. Not blushing when I am caught out				
7. Looking angry when I feel it				
8. Hiding my disappointment				
9. Knowing what other people are feeling				
10. Standing close to other people				
B				
1. Joining a group of people already talking				
2. Having to tell people who I am				
3. Going into a room full of people				
4. Being interviewed				
5. Starting a conversation with a stranger				
6. Giving people directions in the street				
7. Carrying messages				
8. Saying what I want to say				
9. Understanding what other people say				
10. Answering questions/asking questions				
C				
1. Having an argument				
2. Being told off				
3. Being ordered about				
4. Making a complaint				
5. Refusing to do something				
6. Apologizing, making excuses				
7. Giving someone bad news				
8. Praising someone				
9. Responding to praise				
10. Asking for help				

FIGURE 8.2 *An example of a social skills training exercise (taken with permission from Maguire & Priestley, 1985) which requires offenders to evaluate their own competence in relation to very basic interpersonal skills*

situations. Areas for work might include resisting pressure to have more to drink, refusing an invitation to a potentially violent venue or explaining one's presence at a troublespot to a police officer.

Evaluations of social skills training programmes have been positive in terms of improved performance and self-esteem in the short term (Goldstein, 1986) but there have been criticisms because of a lack of evidence of transferability of these skills beyond the training context and also a lack of durability. A more serious criticism is a questioning of the assumption that social skills deficits do contribute to offending behaviour. As Hollin (1990) points out, it is inappropriate to assume that the link is so simple, though this is not to suggest that social skills training does not have a part to play in treatment programmes. It just may be unwise to assume that an improvement in social skills will lead directly to an immediate reduction in offending, though any change which leads to more positive self-appraisal must be worthwhile. As Spence and Marzillier (1981) discovered, a group of young offenders who had undergone social skills training did appear six months later to have a lower level of convictions than a control group, but when both groups produced self-reports of offending behaviour the SST group's tally was actually higher. It could be concluded, therefore, that social skills training had really worked in that these individuals were clearly more able to negotiate successfully in their encounters with authority, but if the measure of success was involvement in crime, SST was a spectacular failure. Hollin remarks:

> "Social skills training is not a cure for crime (though) it may be a powerful method of personal change." (p.491)

Moral reasoning development

The assumption behind programmes which focus on moral reasoning is that offending behaviour is the result of a lack of appropriate development through the stages of moral judgement identified by Kohlberg (1976), leading to a lack of empathy and egocentricism. Involving young offenders in small group discussions about a range of moral dilemmas and requiring them not only to justify their views but to achieve consensus within the group on the best solution to the dilemma is thought to lead to an improvement in moral reasoning ability. The aims of the sessions are to improve the ability of participants to take another's perspective, to engage in active listening and to acquire problem-solving skills. Gibbs et al. (1984) describe such a programme which consisted of eight 40-minute sessions and resulted in 88% of those at stage 2 (within Kohlberg's framework) shifting to stage 3, compared with only 14% of a no-treatment control group.

Multimodal programmes

Some of the most successful treatment programmes have incorporated a number of the approaches described above, particularly social skills training, behavioural therapy and self-management training, and they have produced impressive results in terms of not only personal growth but also reduced recidivism (e.g. Ross et al., 1988; Goldstein et al.,1989). These multimodal programmes are attractive because the techniques used can be readily taught to practitioners within the criminal justice system, though Blackburn (1993) warns of the dangers of a 'shotgun empiricism' approach in blending a range of interventions rather haphazardly on intuitive grounds which may not always be justified.

Specialist treatment programmes

There are also successful treatment programmes which focus on particular types of offending behaviour. The success of these programmes relies on comprehensive assessment of potential participants in order to identify those individuals most likely to benefit from intervention. Working in groups seems to be the favoured approach since not only is this economical but it allows opportunities for sharing experience and rehearsal of coping strategies in a safe but certainly not uncritical environment. Other group members can be extremely accurate in recognising faking and will not be afraid to challenge. The two types of specialist treatment programmes which will be described in detail are anger control, or anger management, groups and sex offender groups.

ANGER CONTROL GROUPS

One of the most critical areas for intervention in relation to young offenders is that of anger and aggression. Problems in these areas can interfere with schooling, family and peer relationships and may propel adolescents into an escalating spiral in which they lose control and become enmeshed in a pattern of behaviour from which they feel unable to escape. Aggression seems to loom large in the lives of adolescents, possibly because of a need to establish a new identity and a lack of confidence about both existing and future relationships which can lead to an overcompensation for insecurity which reveals itself in aggressive words or behaviour. As Novaco and Welsh (1989) explain, however:

"Paradoxically anger is both satisfying and frightening." (p.129)

both qualities likely to ensure that an aggressive pattern of behaviour continues.

In his original formulation of the theory of anger control, Novaco (1975) emphasised the role of cognition in the process of emotional arousal which precedes aggression. He suggested that anger often occurs because the individual is already upset about other matters. There is therefore a tendency to displace angry feelings onto inappropriate but available targets. The expression of anger may then present itself as a method of taking charge or assuming control when things appear to be getting out of hand. It then follows that anger is more likely to occur when people feel unsure and threatened and this may be particularly true for young men who can feel that their masculinity depends on an exaggerated display of outrage which confirms their control of the situation and discounts any possibility of fear. In this kind of situation, being aggressive can be experienced as very reinforcing and is therefore likely to be repeated.

Novaco also stressed that anger is not necessarily all bad – we all experience it and anger can serve a useful function, not least in that it can alert us and others to the possibility of anger turning into aggression. Thus the objective of any treatment targeting anger is effective control and management of the emotion in order to enable the individual to achieve their objectives success-fully. As Aristotle said in *The Nicomachean Ethics*:

> "Anyone can become angry – that is easy. But to be angry with the right person, to the right degree, at the right time, for the right purpose, and in the right way – this is not easy."

The route by which Novaco suggests anger can be managed is through the acquisition of strategies of self-control, techniques which will allow the individual to deal with a potentially violent situation without becoming aggressive and without any loss of face. Paradoxically, the use of assertiveness training can ensure that anger is used in a controlled way, whilst the use of 'stress inoculation' ensures that the individual is exposed to small doses of provocation in such a way that they can develop and practise the necessary skills to cope with such situations in real life. Tackling these situations within a group of peers not only provides authenticity but can prove an effective reinforcer for the transfer of newly acquired skills into other situations too.

A typical anger management programme would consist of three stages: cognitive preparation, skill acquisition and application practice.

Cognitive preparation

In this stage group members are helped to recognise their own personal anger patterns by carefully analysing previous incidents in which they have lost their temper. They are encouraged to 'brainstorm' short-term and long-term consequences of being angry and to recognise that the former tend to be positive and the latter negative. (Think of the last time you were really angry with someone. What were the immediate and subsequent consequences? Probably a brief sense of satisfaction, followed by guilt, self-recrimination and the loss of friendship.) By identifying the various cues or 'triggers' for their anger, group members can begin to collect information which can in the future help them to realise when aggression is likely to occur. The clear links between cognitive, physiological and behaviour components in the

HEY YOU!   Write this on a card and put it up on a wall, with plenty of space above and below and to the right of it.

Ask the group to discuss and agree three possible responses to this opening shot. One reply should be conciliatory or neutral, i.e. not intended to lead to violence. One should be such as to lead almost certainly to violence; and the third should be problematical, not necessarily provocative, but not conciliatory either. These should be written on separate cards and displayed in a column just to the right of HEY YOU! e.g.:

'GET STUFFED' leads to violence – fix a red star to that card; or another card marked 'POW' in red ink.

The groups then consider the likely next move of the aggressor for each of the other two replies, and write a likely response from someone who is clearly bent on provoking a violent retaliation; e.g.

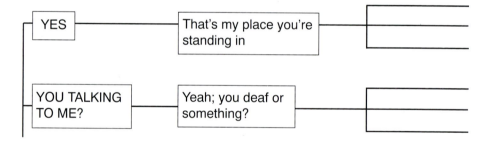

For each of the replies 'That's my place', and 'You deaf?', the groups devise three further ripostes in the categories used for the first, i.e.
     conciliatory
     ambiguous
     provocative

In both cases the 'provocative' reply is assumed to lead to instant violence and is marked with a POW! card. For each of the other two responses, further replies from the adversary are invited, both in a provocative vein; to each of which three further responses are invented, to each of which.... The process can go on indefinitely, but the wall-space will almost certainly give out after three or four rounds.

FIGURE 8.3 *An example of an exercise used in anger control groups (taken with permission from Maguire & Priestley, 1985) when offenders are asked to construct scenarios which might lead to aggression, and then consider alternative avoidance strategies*

anger pattern will be identified in this stage. For example, the individual might recognise that in an anger situation he or she begins to think negative thoughts not only about others but also about themselves and what others might be thinking of them. They might then begin to experience shallow and rapid breathing, sweaty palms, flushed skin and they may begin flexing their muscles, tapping their feet or fingers and forming a fist. All of these reactions may occur in a very short period and may appear to be beyond conscious control, but recognising the pattern enables the individual to gain some control.

Skill acquisition

During this stage members of the group learn a range of coping skills which they can employ to deal more effectively with anger-provoking situations. These skills can usefully be divided into cognitive and behavioural skills. Cognitive skills include refining attention in order to identify potential triggers accurately; the use of thought-stopping techniques (yes, literally saying to yourself 'STOP!') which will enable individuals to restructure their immediate angry and often irrational thoughts into something more adaptive and positive; and self-instruction strategies which will provide controlled direction through anger situations. For instance, when an individual recognises that an unhelpful sequence of events is beginning, they can interrupt themselves with a statement such as, 'Calm down, there's a way to avoid this, and it will lead to a positive result' or, 'I can handle this without losing my temper'. These cognitive skills may initially have to be practised out loud until they become familiar.

Behavioural skills include relaxation training, assertiveness training, refinement of communication skills and problem-solving strategies. Paradoxically, relaxation training is a potent device for illustrating the possibility of self-control. Many athletes use the techniques involved in relaxation training, such as the progressive tensing and relaxing of specific muscle groups, deep breathing and visualisation of success. Not only do these techniques reduce physiological tension (thereby reducing some of the antecedent cues to aggression), they also provide a time delay before a choice has to be made about how to respond and they refocus attention from external cues to internal control. Assertiveness training allows individuals to defuse conflict situations whilst maintaining personal rights and a level of self-control. It involves the acquisition of strategies such as the 'broken record' (simply repeating a request calmly without escalation but with perseverance), 'empathic assertion' (recognising someone else's feelings but repeating the request nonetheless) and 'fogging' (confusing the provoker by agreeing with their insult). All these skills are taught using modelling and role play, with positive feedback so that rehearsal can become self-reinforcing.

Application practice

In this final stage group members have the opportunity to put their newly acquired skills to the test. They are exposed to graduated, stressful, anger-provoking situations so that their anger control skills can be applied, refined, reinforced and eventually generalised beyond role play into the real world. There should be monitoring of progress and also cognitive self-monitoring along the lines of 'I handled that pretty well without getting angry' or, 'I tried my best, but I'm not going to get down about it, I'll just try harder next time'. Once the group programme has ended individual group members may need support to ensure that they transfer their skills to real life.

SEX OFFENDER GROUPS

The treatment of sex offenders is controversial. Many would argue that this group of offenders, perhaps more than any other, deserves punishment and that the offer of treatment whilst they are incarcerated is pointless since they clearly either do not wish or are unable to change their behaviour. Moreover, they may opt for treatment quite cynically in order to facilitate earlier release or less intrusive supervision in the community. Perkins (1990), however, strongly argues the case for treating sex offenders on the following grounds.

- Treatment may enable sex offenders to modify their behaviour, whilst no treatment clearly will effect no change.
- Treatment may counteract the negative influences of imprisonment, e.g. confined contact with other sex offenders which might lead to a strengthening of sexual deviation and long periods of incarceration which may further impair offenders' social competence.
- Treatment may enable researchers to build up a body of knowledge which might help to reduce the possibility of sexual offences.
- Treatment may be entirely appropriate for those individuals whose offending could be related to their own sexual victimisation as children.
- Where sexual abuse has occurred within a family setting and there is a possibility of reintegration, treatment will be essential.

Perkins also points out that criticisms of treatment programmes for sex offenders based on less than impressive recidivism rates often fail to take into account the number of further offences which have been prevented since these are inevitably 'invisible'. We only usually know when offences have been committed, not when potential offences are successfully resisted. The provision of treatment programmes for sex offenders is limited – currently 25 prisons run such programmes (attended by about 600 prisoners) and the

Probation Service has established 90 programmes throughout the country, treating almost 2000 offenders each year.

What are sex offences?

Since 'normal' sexual activity is a social construction which varies according to time and cultural mores, it is perhaps not surprising that defining 'abnormal' sexual activity is problematic. For instance, acts of sadism between consenting adults are illegal in the UK and the age of consent for heterosexual intercourse is 16 years, but 18 years for homosexual intercourse. Defining current legal categories of sexual offences is relatively simple – attempted rape, rape, indecent assault, gross indecency, soliciting, unlawful intercourse, incest, procuration and indecent exposure – but not all forms of sexual deviation are against the law. Prins (1991) suggests that a useful classification of sexual deviation would include the following.

- Sexual activity which does not require a human partner, e.g. the use of animals (zoophilia) or objects (fetishism).
- Sexual activity which does not require a willing partner, e.g. rape, necrophilia, voyeurism or indecent exposure.
- Sexual activity which occurs under unusual conditions, e.g. with the very young or the very old, within the family or with excessive violence.
- Activity which is sexually motivated but presents in 'masked form', e.g. stealing female underwear, excessive interest in bodily secretions or pyromania (fire setting).

All or some of these types of behaviour may appear in the sexual history of sex offenders but in terms of sex offences, it is perhaps helpful to concern ourselves with sexual behaviour which victimises others who do not or cannot, consent. Since the theories of rape and the motivation of rapists were discussed in Chapter 4, the focus here will be on paedophilia, a type of paraphilia (see Chapter 3) which involves sexual assault of children by adults.

PAEDOPHILIA

If you were asked to describe a typical paedophile, what adjectives would you use? The chances are that a stereotypical picture of a 'dirty old man' hanging around outside a school would be provided, someone who is rather lonely and inadequate, sexually frustrated and ready to pounce on an unwilling victim, using force. The evidence available, however, would suggest that most child victims of sexual assault are abused by someone they know and that perpetrators are often quite young, sexually active and may have 'targeted' and 'groomed' their likely victim for several months. Force may not always be necessary, particularly if a child is vulnerable, and indeed the child may experience some sexual arousal which makes their victimisation even more traumatic and difficult to disclose. Whilst most perpetrators will indeed be male, there is growing concern about the number of women who sexually abuse children.

Paedophilia is defined as an enduring and exclusive sexual interest in children, though some paedophiles may have sexual fantasies about children yet never molest them. So, not all paedophiles are child molesters. Similarly, not all child molesters are paedophiles. A person who prefers to have sex with adults may decide, for a number of reasons, to have sex with a child. Those reasons might include availability, curiosity or a desire to hurt someone who is associated with the child (see Case Study 8.1).

Thus, child molesters are not a homogeneous group, in spite of the stereotypical image often projected by the media. Those who commit sexual offences against children vary in terms of age and gender, the age and gender of their preferred victims, their relationship to the victim, the extent and nature of sexual contact involved and the degree of force used.

CASE STUDY 8.1
Child sexual abuse as revenge

Andrew Pountly was jailed in 1997 for the abduction, rape and murder of five-year-old Rosemary McCann, the daughter of his girlfriend. Pountley was described as a jealous man who after an argument with his girlfriend in a pub, got drunk and told her 'You are going to be sorry'. He then took a taxi to the little girl's home and abducted her, still in her pyjamas. She accompanied him willingly because she knew him. Her body was found seven weeks later in a holdall on waste ground. (reported in *The Guardian*, 16th January 1997, p.4)

What is the scale of the problem?

A Home Office study has revealed that there are 110,000 men who have been convicted of sexual offences against children currently living in England and Wales (Marshall, 1997). These 110,000 paedophiles are amongst an estimated 260,000 men classified as sex offenders because they have been convicted of offences such as rape, indecent assault, incest or sex with a minor. The same study, partly based on tracing the criminal careers of a sample of men born in 1953, estimates that one in 60 of all men have been convicted of a sex crime by the time they are aged 40 and one in 90 has been convicted of a serious sex offence (rape, incest or gross indecency with a child) by the same age. The majority of convicted paedophiles are aged over 40 (see Box 8.1).

Box 8.1 Official estimate of men with paedophile convictions, by age (Home Office, 1997)

20–24 years	4000
25–29 years	6000
30–34 years	10,000
35–39 years	11,000
40+ years	79,000
Total	110,000

Another source which can be used to estimate the extent of the problem comes from victim surveys and random samples. When Finkelhor (1986) interviewed 530 female students and 266 male students he found that 11% of the women and 4% of the men said they had experienced unwanted sexual contacts with adults before the age of 12.

Typologies

Acknowledging the heterogeneity of paedophiles has led to attempts to produce typologies of paedophiles in order to identify common elements within subgroups. The most common division is the one which divides paedophiles into *fixated* offenders, who prefer and feel more comfortable with children, and *regressed* offenders who have some adult heterosexual interest but who also have feelings of inadequacy and may react sexually to a child following a threat to their masculinity (Groth and Birnbaum, 1978).

Fixated offenders are described as individuals who have never matured sexually to the point where they can relate effectively to adult partners. They have a strong exclusive preference for children, interacting with whom brings sexual satisfaction. At the onset of sexual development they have become fixated on children. They are often immature and may have been abused themselves in childhood. They may then have incorporated their experience of abuse into their own sexuality.

Regressed offenders are described as individuals with normal sexual orientation who generally relate sexually to adults. Under certain circumstances, however, e.g. stress, alcohol, drugs, etc., they may choose a sexual partner who is a child. The onset of inappropriate sexual behaviour is thus a response to a trigger and in order to come to terms with their own guilt they may view their victim as more mature and more complicit than they could ever be.

Howitt (1995) points out that this distinction allows responsibility to be somehow deflected away from regressed offenders who are described as 'normal' heterosexual men who, under pressure, turn to children for sexual 'comfort'. This tends to disguise the fact that some sexual interest in children must have existed prior to the stress. There is also an assumption that sexual offending which occurs in the family – incest – is essentially different from extrafamilial abuse and yet Abel et al. (1987) found that in a sample of 142 men who had abused their daughters, 44% of them had also abused female children outside the home and 11% had abused other male children.

Dietz (1983) provides a more detailed typology, dividing individuals who sexually molest children into two broad categories – *preferential* and *situational* offenders.

Preferential offenders have a definite sexual preference for children. Their sexual fantasies focus on children and they have sex with children not because of some situational stress but because they are sexually attracted to children. Whilst this group is smaller in number than situational child molesters, potentially they can target many more victims. Within this category there are three major patterns of behaviour.

1 *Seduction* – the offender courts his target with attention, affection and gifts over a period of time and may choose victims who are the subject of emotional or physical neglect. Multiple targeting can occur, e.g. a group of children at the same school. This type of offender is skilled, he can identify with children and knows how to listen to them.
2 *Introverted* – this offender lacks social skills so cannot seduce. He therefore targets very young children or strangers. He fits the 'dirty old man' stereotype more closely than any of the others but he may marry and produce children whom he can then molest.
3 *Sadistic* – this offender has a sexual preference for children but also needs to inflict pain and suffering in order to be gratified. He uses force to gain access to his victims and may even murder them to avoid detection. An example is Robert Black, who sexually assaulted and killed three little girls between 1982 and 1986, dumping their bodies in an area known as the Midlands triangle. He said he killed his victims so they would not have to suffer the pain he was going to inflict on them, but it is highly likely that they were alive when he assaulted them.

Situational child molesters do not necessarily have a sexual preference for children and their offences may be one-off incidents or become part of a long-term pattern. Their offending falls into four major types.

1 *Regressed* – this offender has low self-esteem and poor coping skills. He may turn to children as a substitute and use coercion. The main criterion for targeting victims may be availability, so his own children are vulnerable.
2 *Morally indiscriminate* – for this offender the sexual abuse of children is simply part of a general pattern of abuse in his life. He may lie and cheat in all aspects of his life and may molest children for a simple reason – why not? He may abuse his own children and typically uses manipulation or force.

3 *Sexually indiscriminate* – this offender is prepared to try anything to secure sexual gratification, but in other areas of his life may appear to be quite normal. His basic motivation is sexual experimentation and he may abuse his own children or their friends and may get involved in group sex with children.

4 *Inadequate* – this category would include withdrawn isolates and those suffering from mental disorder. Involvement with children may be the result of curiosity or insecurity, but inability to cope with frustration may lead to excessive use of force.

Adolescent offenders

In the past adolescents who molested younger children were often dismissed as 'just going through a stage of sexual experimentation' and yet it is now increasingly recognised that not only should sexual abuse of younger children always be viewed as an indicator that the older child was sexually abused, but it is during adolescence that a pattern of deviant sexual arousal is often established. It is therefore vital that adolescent sex offenders should be carefully evaluated for appropriate intervention (Ryan, 1987). The extent of involvement in sexual abuse of children by other children is not known, though Smith and Bentovim (1994) estimate that between 25% and 50% of reported cases of sexual abuse are committed by individuals under the age of 18 years.

Female sex offenders

"A bogus woman social worker who sexually attacked a baby boy was today being hunted by police. The trickster indecently assaulted the eight-month-old infant after conning her way into his family home." (reported in the *Leicester Mercury*, 9th March 1993, p.3)

Whilst convicted female sex offenders are statistically rare, it is now recognised that serious under-reporting may have led to a tendency to assume they are non-existent. This may have been the result of different attitudes to male and female sexuality, so that a woman having intercourse with a 13-year old boy is seen as 'initiating' a willing partner who will suffer no distress. Or it could be an unwillingness to even contemplate women, particularly mothers, engaging in such behaviour. Thus, as Matravers (1997) says:

"The common-sense view – namely, that women simply don't do those kinds of things – is grounded in cherished notions about the maternal bonds so compellingly familiar that, even if it appears likely that a woman may indeed have done some of those things, the sexual threat she is perceived to present is outweighed by the harm that would be caused by separating a child from its mother." (p.9.)

The extent of the problem may be quite large, however, especially in comparison to rates of female offending in general. Thus, Risin and Koss (1987) found that over 40% of sex offenders against boys were female, often in caring roles such as teachers, babysitters and parents' friends, whilst about 30% of a sample of college males said they had been sexually abused by females (Urquiza, 1988).

Matthews et al. (1990) differentiate between female sex offenders who act alone and those who offend with others. Lone offenders are described as falling into one of three patterns:

1 *intergenerationally predisposed* – those women who have suffered extensive sexual and physical abuse themselves in childhood and who tend to choose girl victims, often their daughters, in a re-enactment of their own abuse;
2 *experimenter/exploiter* – adolescent girls who victimise young boys when they are babysitting, often out of curiosity and fear of adult sexuality;
3 *teacher/lover* – women who become involved in what they describe as a normal love affair but which happens to be with a boy in the 11–16-year-old range.

Accompanied offenders are either:

1 *male-coerced* – women who come under the influence of a male abuser, and begin abusing children, sometimes their own; or
2 *psychologically disturbed* – women who, because of their own dependency needs, create situations in which they know abuse of their children will occur, e.g. becoming involved with convicted sex offenders.

One area in which sexual abuse by females has been researched quite thoroughly is in American daycare. Finkelhor et al. (1988) found that women who sexually abused children in this setting were less likely to be single or to be socially isolated compared to male sex offenders. They were also less likely to have problem histories in relation to schooling, employment, drugs, crime or psychiatric intervention. The most striking feature of sexual abuse by women in daycare settings was that it was frequently committed with others – 73% had acted in the company of others, sometimes all-female groups but more commonly mixed gender groups.

Theories attempting to explain paedophilia

There are a range of theories which attempt to explain paedophilia, some of which complement rather than compete with each other, but none of which is able to offer a comprehensive explanation of this type of behaviour. An acceptance of these theories will, however, determine the treatment offered in an attempt to reduce further offending. Theories include the following.

Sexual learning theory

Here the suggestion is made that all children engage in various forms of sexual activity during childhood and early adolescence and this is often with peers. For some individuals the association between intense sexual pleasure and the immature body characteristics of perhaps prepubescent peers might set into motion an inappropriate cycle of arousal, especially if the prospect or reality of grown-up sex has some negative associations (Howells, 1981). Such individuals may then rely on fantasies about other children during masturbation, which will reinforce this inappropriate imagery. Whilst this theory seems plausible in explaining sexual attraction to children, it cannot explain why only some children who experience pleasurable sex with peers go on to become adult paedophiles.

Preconditions theory

Finkelhor's (1984) precondition model of child sexual abuse is probably the most widely known and was described in Chapter 6. It assumes that paedophiles are diverted from adult relationships and that if preconditions of emotional congruence, sexual arousal to children, blockage to alternative sources of satisfaction and disinhibition exist there is a high probability that sexual offences against children will occur. Each of these preconditions presents an opportunity for treatment; for example, if relationships with adults are blocked then social skills training will be useful.

Cognitive distortion theory

A set of distorted beliefs, supported and reinforced by pornography, is held by some to account for paedophilia (Wyre and Tate, 1995). These beliefs would include blaming the child for seducing the offender, verbally sanitising the actual behaviour in such a way that it appears accidental or harmless and maintaining that incidents of child molestation are one-offs, the result of stress. Wyre, who was responsible for setting up one of the first sex offenders' treatment centres in Britain, Gracewell Clinic, maintains that these beliefs must be confronted and challenged if treatment is to have any chance of success. He believes that paedophiles are very often highly manipulative and adept at concealing their true feelings and since they are virtually 'addicted' to their offending, the methods required to break this addiction are inevitably severe.

Psychodynamic theory

For Freud, those who sexually abuse children are aberrations who turn to children for gratification as a result of cowardice, impotence or sexual privation and they are not treatable. Subsequent psychodynamic theorists have blamed either seductive children, alcohol and societal permissiveness (Socarides, 1988) or a tendency to idealise the innocence and purity of childhood (Gordon, 1976) or even the mother who fails to facilitate appropriate separation between herself and her child (Kraemer, 1976). None of these theories can adequately explain why only some individuals develop such a strong attraction to having sex with children.

Biological theory

Whilst there has been research which suggests that structural abnormalities are commoner in the brains of sex offenders, with a significant proportion having smaller left brain hemispheres (Wright et al., 1990), or that dysfunctional communication between the two halves of the brain encourages abnormal sexual ideas (Flor Henry et al., 1991), there is little substantial evidence which would indicate that all paedophilia can be explained in this way.

Gender politics

As with feminist explanations of rape (see Chapter 4), feminists who attempt to explain paedophilia relate this behaviour to the fundamentals of masculinity.

> "Generally boys and men learn to experience their sexuality as an overwhelming and uncontrollable force; they learn to focus their sexual feelings on submissive objects, and they learn the assertion of their sexual desires, the expectation of having them serviced." (MacLeod and Saraga, 1988, p.41).

A society which infantilises women, pornography which portrays women as compliant and seductive children and a view of male sexuality as driven all feed into a set of cultural expectations whereby some men fail to differentiate between the affection and intimacy within appropriately consensual sex and a desire for sexual power and gratification at any cost.

However, the existence of women who sexually abuse children poses something of a problem in relation to feminist analyses of child abuse which locate sexual violence in the patriarchal power held over women and children by men. Some have suggested that a feminist conspiracy exists to mask the extent of female sexual abuse (e.g. Young, 1993), and that this is unhelpful in terms of developing a coherent framework in which to develop our understanding of child sexual abuse.

Treatment programmes

As stated earlier, a belief in what contributes to sex offending will determine the nature and content of treatment programmes. But before treatment can begin sex offenders have to present themselves for treatment and many sex offenders either deny their offence or do not see their behaviour as a problem. They do not therefore readily engage in therapy and their treatment then presents a number of practical and ethical problems. Do you make treatment compulsory? If so, how do you ensure that it works? There is some difference of opinion amongst the experts so, for instance, Groth (1983) feels that if offenders are already incarcerated inducements in the form of privileges may be necessary, whilst Perkins (1987) believes that informed consent is essential for success. Some offenders may give this consent if they feel that by doing so they might avoid prison, but their commitment to the programme may then be half-hearted. The result is that the drop-out rate from sex offender treatment programmes is high (about one-third). There is also often disapproval of treatment programmes designed for sex offenders, because it is felt the nature of their offences is so repugnant that they should simply be punished and kept out of society for as long as possible. The difficulty with this approach is that not attempting to address the problem in any way probably increases the likelihood of further offences being committed.

For many people the most obvious treatment for paedophiles would be castration and some would argue that recidivism rates following surgical castration are very low, under 4% (Bradford, 1985), though in the studies cited most of the men were volunteers. Similarly, chemical castration, using synthetic steroids to reduce testosterone, has produced mixed results (Hucker et al., 1988). Whilst castration might have emotive appeal, its effects are by no means certain. Sexual satisfaction can be obtained without an erection and since many sex offenders do not wish to change their behaviour, they are unlikely to volunteer for castration. Any move to impose surgical or chemical castration on convicted offenders would be strongly resisted by civil liberties groups.

Discounting this possibility then leaves us with the design and content of effective treatment programmes for sex offenders, to be used within an institutional setting or in the community. Effective and comprehensive assessment of sex offenders is vital before treatment can begin. This will cover social, cognitive, affective and physiological levels of functioning and initial interviews will involve systematic analysis of the events surrounding the offence, such as the element of planning, the role of disinhibitors such as drugs or alcohol, the nature and severity of the assault and the offender's feelings about the victim. A full social and sexual history will also be taken, which will include details of early family relationships, the frequency and type of sexual activity and fantasy. Personality measures may also be taken, levels of social competence assessed and cognitive style explored, e.g. the prevalence of distorted beliefs about children or women.

One of the most difficult aspects of this early assessment is coping with denial. Most sex offenders will either totally or partially deny their offences and the interviewer may need to use a range of strategies to confront their denial. The most effective include emphasising the positive potential of truthfulness and assumptive questioning whereby, for instance, the offender is asked when he committed the offence rather than if he did (see Towl and Crighton, 1996). Once the assessment is complete this can be used to inform the design of the treatment programme and to decide whether the individual should be part of a group programme. Sex offender groups (of 6–10 individuals) are usually the preferred option because continued denial can be confronted by other offenders as well as therapists and offenders can begin to recognise that others have similar problems in controlling their sexual behaviour.

In terms of the content of treatment programmes, Prentky (1995) provides a useful summary of the target areas for treatment which include impaired relationships with adults, lack of empathy, anger, cognitive distortions, deviant sexual arousal and antisocial personality. He then suggests strategies for dealing with each of these areas.

Impaired adult relationships

It is recognised that many paedophiles lack competence in their social and interpersonal skills, feeling awkward with adults and much more comfortable with children. Addressing this via social skills training, sex education, self-esteem enhancement, relaxation training and assertiveness training may help such individuals improve their expertise in the area of interpersonal relationships with adults, though they may need substantial rehearsal opportunities and positive feedback.

Lack of empathy

A lack of empathic concern for victims is a significant feature of all interpersonal violence. Thus, providing offenders with the opportunity to develop empathy may enable them to recognise the pain their victims will suffer and then desist from hurting them. This can be accomplished by exposing offenders to videos of victims describing their feelings and experiences following abuse, enabling them to visualise themselves in a similar situation of betrayal and violation, role play and role reversal taking the role of their victim and writing letters of apology to their victims (which will not be sent). Many offenders will themselves have experienced victimisation as children but may need help to develop more affective appreciation, in order to generalise these feelings towards their own victims. Pithers (1993) believes that developing empathy is crucial in treatment programmes for sex offenders:

> "If empathy can be established, significant effects may be observed in sexual arousal, cognitive distortions, intimacy within interpersonal relationships, realistic self-esteem, and motivation to change and maintain change." (p.190)

Establishing empathy with victims is a vital part of early treatment because it significantly shifts perception so that denial of pain becomes impossible. The offender can then be assisted to resist the urge towards denial.

Anger

Not all paedophiles will use anger and force to subdue their victims, but it is clearly an element in the more serious cases of assault and may readily arise if a child refuses to comply. Early and unresolved experience of victimisation can create a depth of anger which may need to be addressed, otherwise the techniques used in the anger management programmes described earlier in this chapter will be appropriate in order to increase self-control.

Cognitive distortions

Most sex offenders justify their behaviour by the use of cognitive distortions, or irrational ideas, which minimise the degree of force used, the impact on their victims, their role in the offence or the inappropriateness of their behaviour. Since these cognitive distortions are often learned attitudes, supported by societal and cultural systems which tend to perpetuate misogyny and the exploitation of children, they have to be confronted and challenged in a systematic way known as cognitive restructuring. This involves providing accurate information about sexual abuse and its consequences and helping to reveal the functional role of distorted attitudes, how they allow the offender to avoid responsibility, and facing up to his actions. It also includes creating discomfort in the offender by emphasising the victim's response to abuse – their shame, fear, pain and humiliation – in an attempt to help the offender 'own' his behaviour and its dreadful consequences rather than hiding behind convenient cognitive distortions.

Deviant sexual arousal

There is a clear link between deviant sexual fantasy and deviant sexual arousal which may lead to inappropriate and unacceptable behaviour. Sexual arousal is usually measured using an instrument called a plethysmograph which measures penile volume changes in response to a range of auditory and visual stimuli. This provides a baseline against which to assess changes in arousal which follow treatment. Once a pattern of deviant sexual arousal has been identified, for example to photographs of children, then behavioural techniques can be employed either to decrease deviant arousal or to increase more appropriate arousal. Those techniques designed to reduce deviant arousal include covert sensitisation, aversion and masturbatory satiation, whilst those which aim to shape the individual's arousal pattern towards more appropriate targets include systematic desensitisation, fantasy modification and orgasmic reconditioning.

All these techniques rely on basic classical and operant conditioning principles and the most commonly used involve some element of aversion therapy, whereby an unpleasant stimulus is paired with the visual stimulus which produces deviant sexual arousal. Early examples of unpleasant stimuli included brief electric shocks or nausea-inducing chemicals, though it is now more likely that noxious smells will be used. When covert sensitisation is used, the offender is told to imagine his deviant activity resulting in unpleasant consequences such as being arrested at work and humiliated or assaulted. 'Assisted' covert sensitisation involves pairing arousal with an imagined aversive event such as vomiting or having a tooth filled without anaesthetic. The technique of satiation involves the offender being told to masturbate to orgasm using a non-deviant fantasy (e.g. consensual sex with an adult) and then to continue masturbating after ejaculation whilst verbalising deviant fantasies. The idea is that the unpleasant experience will become associated with deviant fantasies and a consequent reduction of sexual arousal to those fantasies. This activity is undertaken in private but the offender is obliged to make audio tapes of his experiences which will be checked for authenticity by the therapists.

The most popular technique for increasing non-deviant arousal is orgasmic reconditioning, whereby the offender is instructed to masturbate to his preferred deviant fantasy but must switch to a non-deviant fantasy at the point of orgasm, thus taking away the satisfaction of the deviant fantasy. The non-deviant fantasy is then progressively moved back in time towards the start of masturbation. Fantasy modification involves gradually reducing the inappropriate elements of a deviant fantasy and moving the offender toward a more acceptable fantasy which can be associated with sexual satisfaction.

Antisocial personality

There would appear to be a link between the characteristic behaviours associated with antisocial personality, in particular impulsivity, and sexual assault. This is particularly important when considering the possibility of relapse or recidivism following treatment and release. Attempts to address impulsivity include identifying the 'assault cycle', i.e. the chain of events and emotions which lead up to offending behaviour, so that the offender can develop strategies to avoid high-risk situations. Families can also be involved in this aspect of treatment so that they can identify predictors which might suggest that further offending behaviour is likely to occur and inform the appropriate authorities.

Evaluation – how do we know when treatment programmes are successful?

Some therapists will argue that any treatment of sex offenders is better than none since no form of treatment makes offenders more deviant (Laws, 1985), but evaluating the success of treatment programmes is particularly difficult because of under-reporting of offences (by victims and offenders) and the timescale necessary to be sure of effective rehabilitation. Dwyer and Myers (1990) report a ten-year follow-up of a particular group of sex offenders who had volunteered to undergo a particularly comprehensive treatment programme. Recidivism was under 4%, although over two-thirds of the offenders reported experiencing urges to reoffend. Abel et al. (1988) carried out a similar study and found a recidivism rate of 12% after one year. When comparing untreated sex offenders with treated sex offenders, Marshall et al. (1991) claim that 20–60% of untreated offenders reoffend in the five years following release from prison, whereas typically only 15% of treated offenders repeat their offences. They thus offer strong support for the continuation of treatment programmes for sex offenders, particularly those with a cognitive behavioural perspective.

What happens when sex offenders are released?

Doubts about the effectiveness of treatment programmes for sex offenders have led to calls to publish the names of known offenders so that their new neighbours are aware of the potential dangers. Whilst the Sex Offenders Act 1997 has established a register of all convicted paedophiles in England and Wales and has required all on the register to inform the police of their addresses, access to this register is restricted and some newspapers have taken the step of 'outing' convicted sex offenders living in the community. The results have been forced evictions, arson and severe beatings, sometimes involving innocent men.

The move towards releasing information on sex offenders stems from legislation in America following a particularly horrifying crime. In 1994 Jesse Timmendequas sexually assaulted and murdered Megan Kanka, aged seven, in New Jersey. He had previous convictions for sex offences but when he moved into Megan's neighbourhood no one knew about his past. After Megan's death her mother campaigned vigorously for the right to know if paedophiles move into a community and her efforts resulted in 'Megan's Law' whereby this information has to be made public. Unfortunately, this legislation has not reduced the rate of child sex offences and critics of 'Megan's Law' point out that not only does the majority of child sexual abuse occur in the home, but if paedophiles are hounded out of communities they may have to go underground and conceal their identities, making it more difficult for them to continue treatment and maybe even increasing the possibility of relapse.

A more extreme response to the potential for sex offenders to reoffend lies in the decision made by the American Supreme Court in June 1997 that repeat sex offenders can be detained indefinitely if a doctor reports a likelihood of recidivism. Whilst civil liberties groups have protested, this legislation has been seen as one which will be popular with the general public, though understandably less popular with the medical profession upon whose judgement the public will rely for the protection of children.

CONCLUSION

It seems clear that whilst locking offenders up for long periods may satisfy some primitive urge for retribution, a more humane and realistic plan for the future must involve investment in the development of treatment programmes for offenders, including very dangerous offenders, such as paedophiles. The research indicates that psychologists have a pivotal role in the development of such programmes, the most effective of which rely on cognitive behavioural techniques which challenge egocentric and distorted attitudes, and training offenders to develop a range of cognitive and interpersonal skills which should enable them to choose an escape route from a life of crime.

chapter nine

RESPONDING TO CRIME

CHAPTER OVERVIEW

In this final chapter we will look at how psychologists have responded to crime in terms of offering practical strategies for primary and secondary crime prevention. People tend to be fearful of crime and this can affect their behaviour in terms of a perceived vulnerability. Strategies for crime prevention, crime reduction and risk assessment can empower people to regain control and not suffer the psychological consequences of victimisation, which will also be reviewed. Finally, the future of criminological psychology will be discussed in terms of new directions based on a solid, empirically based foundation.

INTRODUCTION

As you will recall from Chapter 1, although it is problematic to estimate accurately how much crime there is, it is undoubtedly clear that people today are much more frightened of the possibility of becoming a victim of crime than was ever previously the case. Interestingly, although violent crime only accounts for a small percentage of all offences it is the fear of becoming a victim of violence which seems to determine most people's attitude to crime generally, their behaviour and their view of society. The 1996 British Crime Survey revealed that more than one in ten women and one in 20 men said they never went out after dark and one-third of the women who stayed in cited fear of crime as the reason. According to the 1997 International Crime Victimisation Survey, the fear of crime in England and Wales is so great that people are more anxious about going out alone on the streets after dark than people in any of the other ten countries surveyed, including the USA.

As Hollin (1992) points out, the fear of crime may not correlate with the actual risk of crime. Thus, the elderly tend to be very fearful of 'street crime' such as robbery and assault and yet are the least likely victims of such crimes, whilst those who are likely to be the victims of 'street crime', men aged

16–30 years, do not appear to be worried about the possibility of this type of attack. Nevertheless, the fear of crime does have an impact on people's behaviour in that they may curtail their activities at certain times or not attend particular events and in so doing, maintain their fear via the process of negative reinforcement (e.g. 'I didn't go to the pub on Friday night, so I didn't get picked on – maybe not going out is a good thing').

This is not in any way to suggest that fear of crime is irrational. In spite of official pronouncements of dramatic reductions in crime rates, the rise in crime during the last 15 years has affected the everyday lives of millions of people. For example, in one year (1991) the rise in reported crime was 1.25 times that of the total crime rate in 1950 (Young, 1995). Moreover, it seems that some people have every reason to be worried about victimisation. Home Office research shows that whilst 60% of the population do not experience crime in any one year, 40% suffer one or more crimes, and 4% of these victims suffer about 44% of all crimes. There appears to be a category of individuals – repeat victims – who because of a chaotic lifestyle, an occupation which increases vulnerability or, most likely, the area in which they live seem to be extremely vulnerable to victimisation. Farrell and Pease (1995) suggest that analysing repeat victimisation would provide strategies for crime prevention which would not only protect the most vulnerable groups but would also dramatically reduce crime. Women have often been advised to modify their behaviour in order to reduce the risk of sexual assault and yet the rate of reported rapes continues to rise and this type of offence is one of the least likely to be reported in the first place. Between 1979 and 1988, there was a 144% increase in the number of rapes reported to the police (Home Office, 1989). Presumably, then, women too do realistically have something to worry about in relation to possible victimisation.

WHAT ARE THE CONSEQUENCES OF BECOMING A VICTIM OF CRIME?

Whilst irritation, inconvenience and some anger may characterise the response of victims to minor crime, it is clear that for more serious crimes the consequences for victims can be very severe. This seems particularly so when an individual's safety and security have been threatened, leaving the victim feeling vulnerable and helpless. The growth of victim support schemes in the last few years has undoubtedly helped many victims of crime begin to come to terms with their trauma.

The American Psychological Association Task Force on the Victims of Crime and Violence listed the following as potential psychological consequences of being a victim: depression, anxiety, paranoia, loss of control, shame, embarrassment, vulnerability, helplessness, humiliation, anger, shock, feelings of inequity, increased awareness of mortality, tension, malaise and fear (Kahn, 1984). Although the intensity of these symptoms will vary for individuals and will undoubtedly be more severe for those who already suffer from mental health problems, it is clear that victimisation can produce short-term and long-term consequences with which it may be very difficult to cope without professional help.

In cases of sexual assault the subsequent trauma experienced by victims may last several months and appears to follow a recognised pattern, not dissimilar to the experience of post-traumatic stress syndrome. Resick and Markaway (1991) report an initial reaction of shaking, trembling, confusion and restlessness which may last in a quite intense form for the first week following an assault and subside in the second, only to return in the third week. Victims may also experience depression, fatigue and problems with social adjustment. Although levels of anxiety and fear remain high, the other symptoms may begin to subside after 2–3 months. Psychological problems may continue for some individuals for many years following a sexual assault, often as a result of self-blame and self-protective avoidance strategies, which can lead to difficulties in intimate relationships (Resick, 1993).

The consequences of child sexual abuse can be both short-term and long-term and are often devastating. Adult women survivors of child sexual abuse may experience revictimisation, suffering further incidents of sexual assault, rape, or 'unwanted' pregnancies (Wyatt et al., 1992), whilst male survivors can experience disturbed adult sexual functioning which seriously impairs self-esteem and can damage personal relationships (Roesler and McKenzie, 1994). The incidence of child sexual abuse in the life histories of many sex offenders testifies to the most severe consequences.

Smith and Bentovim (1994) describe five categories of possible effects following sexual abuse.

1 Sexualising effects, e.g. increased sexual activity, deviant sexual fantasies and activities, confusion and anxiety about sexual identity, withdrawal from sexual activity, sexual dysfunction.
2 Emotional effects, e.g. guilt, shame, self-blame, powerlessness, isolation, dependency.
3 Depressed mood, e.g. helplessness, hopelessness, anger, sleep and appetite disturbance, suicidal feelings, vulnerability, fear of the future.
4 Anxiety effects, e.g. dreams, flashbacks, intrusive thoughts, relationship problems.
5 Behavioural effects, e.g. aggression, a need to control, self-harm, phobias, eating disorders.

When Ussher and Dewberry (1995) asked 775 women survivors of child sexual abuse to describe their feelings as adults in relation to the abuse, 68% reported anger, 66% shame, 60% guilt, 51% anxiety and 31% fear of sex.

Only 2% of the respondents claimed that the abuse had had no effects. Clearly, the degree of trauma experienced by survivors of sexual abuse differs between individuals and being believed and supported by other family members can dramatically reduce the severity of the emotional consequences. The major predictors of serious consequences of child sexual abuse appear to be an element of violence (actual or potential), blaming the child, penetration, abuse by a father or stepfather and long-term abuse (Mannarino et al., 1992).

In view of the severe consequences for the victims of crime, the costs of incarceration and the effect on the general population in terms of fear of crime, it is perhaps not surprising that attention has turned towards crime prevention and crime reduction, with varying degrees of success.

CRIME PREVENTION

It is not simply a truism to say that the most effective way of preventing crime is to decriminalise particular offences, e.g. when sex between consenting adult males in private became legal in 1967 this offence disappeared overnight. Alternatively, the law can be strengthened as was the case in October 1997 when Part IV of the Family Law Act (1996) came into effect, allowing the victims of domestic violence and child abuse much more effective protection. This new law provides additional powers for the police and the courts, so that arrest for breach of non-molestation orders is automatic and individuals who are suspected of having abused children will have to leave the home, rather than the children being removed, as was the case previously. These changes should prevent offences being committed.

When criminal behaviour is as diverse as serial murder and attempting to steal a bar of chocolate, however, then strategies for preventing crime need to be equally diverse. Interestingly, the area of crime prevention is the most fertile for co-operation between psychologists and sociologists, since although some sociologists have argued that social institutions rather than at-risk individuals should be targeted, there is increasing recognition that understanding the origins of crime is not simply a matter of choosing between social or individual determinants and that there is room for productive dialogue between the two disciplines.

In relation to particular offences, such as date rape, there have been impressive advances in prevention work. Thus, all American students are issued with a comprehensive pamphlet from the American College Health Association, which warns them of the dangers associated with the offence of date rape, e.g. alcohol and miscommunication, whilst at the same time challenging the stereotypes about rape and providing typical scenarios which could occur and cause real harm. Preventing sexual violence has always been difficult and the literature has often been inconsistent, urging women to be passive *and* aggressive, to cry *and* not show weakness, to scream *and* not to scream (see Morgan, 1986). Much of the confusion stemmed from a tendency to focus on an individualised response to rape, whereas more modern approaches (Parrot, 1991) emphasise the situation (e.g. ensuring an escape route) and the responsibility society has in ensuring rape myths are challenged and awareness increased of the trauma associated with sexual assault. How might you attempt this in your institution?

There are four broad approaches to crime prevention:

1 primary prevention which attempts to reduce the opportunity for crime developing in the individual;
2 secondary prevention which tries to prevent the development of criminality, targeting individuals who may be vulnerable because they have already committed an offence;
3 tertiary prevention which focuses on chronic offenders, offering treatment in an attempt to prevent a return to crime;
4 situational crime prevention which attempts to reduce opportunities for crime in the environment.

Primary prevention

Within this approach energies are directed towards preventing the onset of criminality, so the target population may be non-criminal though there will be identified risk factors. Since various studies have identified the early characteristics of antisocial behaviour (see the work of Farrington, 1994, which is also discussed in Chapter 2) it would seem reasonable to suggest that intervention in at-risk families should prevent the development of delinquent behaviour. However, when this was attempted in the 1940s and two groups of 'difficult' young boys were compared after 30 years, one of which had received personal and social counselling from social workers plus additional academic tutoring over a period of five years, there were no differences between the two groups in terms of their adult criminal history, though more of the experimental group (the one receiving counselling) had committed at least two offences (McCord, 1978). Maybe it was already too late for these individuals or the potential stigma of being involved in the programme led to a self-fulfilling prophecy or perhaps the 'treatment integrity' of the intervention was not all it could have been.

Certainly there is evidence that earlier intervention at the preschool or initial school level seems to be more successful, whether the focus is on the children (providing training in social cognitive skills in order to reduce impulsivity) or on parental training to encourage more effective attachment (Spivack et al., 1976; Hawkins et al., 1987). The best-known preschool intervention is

Operation Headstart which was introduced in America in the 1960s and attempted to accelerate cognitive development in children from high-risk families before their entry to school. Although the evidence for sustained cognitive gains is limited, what these children did seem to gain was enhanced social competence, including reduced aggression and the ability to defer gratification (Zigler and Hall, 1987). In view of research on the backgrounds of offenders, this might be seen as a clear step in the right direction.

Factors which have been identified in the backgrounds of offenders include impulsivity and lack of empathy, characteristics which could be addressed in early childhood, particularly those children deemed vulnerable because of family disruption or disadvantage which may interfere with their ability to form stable attachments. In the 1960s Mischel and his colleagues devised a study which could measure impulse control in small children. It became known as the 'marshmallow test' because four-year-olds were confronted with a dilemma: they were told by the experimenter that he had to run an errand but if they waited until his return they could have two marshmallows. If they felt unable to wait they could have one marshmallow and have it straight away. Some of the children did wait, and it was often quite a struggle, but their reward was two marshmallows when the experimenter returned, whilst other children could hardly wait for the experimenter to leave the room before they ate the single marshmallow available. When these children were traced as adolescents those who had resisted temptation at four were more socially competent, confident and successful at school, whilst those who had been unable to resist seemed to be more troubled both socially and academically (Shoda et al., 1990). Studies of empathy have also shown that its development can be tracked in very small children (e.g. Hoffman, 1984). If the abilities to defer gratification and to empathise with others are recognised not only as effective barriers to the development of antisocial behaviours but also as positive characteristics in their own right, it would seem essential that training be offered alongside conventional academic subjects.

Other areas for intervention include the provision of parental training for school children, information packs for practitioners in spotting early indicators of domestic and child abuse and support groups for new and possibly unskilled mothers. The problems which affect any of the primary interventions described include the costs of spreading the net wide, i.e. involving large numbers of individuals who may or may not become involved in or associated with crime, and perhaps more significantly, the dangers of labelling the selected group in such a way as to hasten their involvement in crime.

Secondary prevention

Here the intervention is ideally prompt and early, when an individual may show some signs of antisocial behaviour and have already committed a single or minor offence. The aim is to minimise legal intervention in recognition that being 'processed' within the criminal justice system is likely to increase the probability of further offending. Since official labelling is seen as possibly helping to create a criminal identity young offenders may be diverted away from the courts. The main forms such diversion takes are intermediate treatment and reparation.

Intermediate treatment was introduced in the early 1970s and the idea was to attach the opportunity for recreational and educational activities to a super-vision order under the control of the social and probation services. The provision of structured schemes designed to remove youngsters from their immediate environment and open up opportunities for personal development seemed important for disadvantaged and deprived children without stigmatising them. This work could then be continued with groups in their own neighbourhood, activities being supervised by youth workers. Unfortunately, the success of intermediate treatment programmes has been varied, particularly since success-ful implementation is so reliant on effective planning, support and adequate resources. A review of IT in England found that schemes lacked consistent goals and procedures and were not managed effectively in spite of the enthusiasm of most staff (Bottoms and McWilliams, 1990). Media exposés of intermediate 'treats' in the form of 'trips abroad for delinquents funded by the taxpayer' did not particularly encourage the public to understand the preventive nature of much of this work.

Reparation was briefly mentioned in Chapter 8 and involves diverting offenders from court and involving them in a process whereby they quite literally make reparation to their victims by apologising and offering some financial compen-sation or even repair of damage done. The rationale behind such schemes, the most well established of which operates in Northamptonshire, is that offenders have to reflect on their actions and the consequences of those actions, facing their victim and trying to make amends. Whilst it may sound exceedingly simple, it is clear that not only is such a scheme inexpensive but it can be very effective in terms of reducing recidivism and also in helping the victims of crime.

Tertiary prevention

Providing treatment for chronic and serious offenders falls into this category and has already been covered in Chapter 8. However, harsher forms of tertiary prevention would include selective incapacitation, keeping high-rate offenders out of circulation altogether, as has been suggested in relation to serious sex offenders and repeat offenders ('three strikes and you're out'), or rather severe intervention for young offenders in the form of military-style training, e.g. 'boot camps' and 'secure training centres'. Whilst there may be instinctive appeal in some of these options there are no guarantees of success; not all high-rate offenders are correctly classified and the removal of criminally active individuals from the street may well simply open up criminal opportunities for others eager to step into their shoes.

Situational crime prevention

This approach takes a radical move away from the individual and looks closely at the environment. If opportunities to offend are reduced then the individual may just weigh up the risks and make a choice not to commit crime. The initial impetus for this thinking in the UK stemmed from the observation that substituting natural gas for toxic gas in British homes was followed by a reduction in the number of suicides. When people who were suicidal were denied a popular method of suicide, some of them did not choose an alternative but chose instead to live. It was then argued that removing some of the opportunities to commit crime might reduce the total number of crimes. This view resonated with an emerging explanation of criminal behaviour in the 1980s called the rational choice model (Cornish and Clarke, 1986) and provided the stimulus for a number of new initiatives. Mayhew et al. (1976) had pointed out how the compulsory fitting of steering-column locks to all cars in West Germany during the 1960s led to a 60% reduction in car theft. Similar legislation in relation to new British cars led to a reduction in the theft of new cars and a rather surprising reduction in motorbike thefts followed the introduction of compulsory crash helmets, presumably because potential thieves realised they might become rather noticeable (Mayhew et al., 1989a)!

The most common form of environmental intervention is target hardening, making the target of crime more difficult and thus altering the balance of perceived costs and benefits for the would-be offender making a choice. Examples would include strengthening coin boxes in public telephone kiosks or making them usable by credit card only, making burglar alarms very obvious, security lighting, car immobilisation systems, lockable wheel nuts, etc. Many of these techniques can be used by the general public, and are often contained in crime prevention leaflets distributed by the police. An alternative approach is to remove the target altogether. Target removal would include the use of credit cards instead of cash, the payment of wages by direct transfer to bank accounts and the provision of late night transport systems. These strategies have all contributed to a reduction in the opportunity to commit theft, robbery or assault.

Whilst the results of these types of intervention can look quite impressive, there have been criticisms. They can be very costly but more importantly, reducing criminal opportunities in one area may result in displacement, whereby criminals turn their attention to other types of crime. So, for example, although thefts of new cars did drop following the introduction of steering locks in 1971, thefts of older cars increased (Mayhew et al.,1980). As Heal and Laycock (1986) warned:

> "There is little point in the policy-maker investing resources and effort into situational (crime) prevention if by doing so he merely shuffles crime from one area to the next but never reduces it." (p.123)

Pease (1994), however, feels this view may be a little pessimistic, especially since introducing crime prevention techniques in specific communities may also provide protection which is much valued in those areas which are particularly beset by crime problems. The pattern of crime ensures that some areas are significantly more at risk than others and it is there that attention needs to be focused in an attempt to discover what factors make an area more vulnerable. The work of Wilson (1980) identified a correlation between child density and high levels of vandalism – an obvious point maybe, but it should perhaps call into question the policy of most housing departments in relation to allocating families to homes.

Another approach to crime prevention involves increasing the risk of detection and this can be done by using cameras to monitor activity in specific areas such as car parks or town centres. The presence of this kind of formal surveillance, closed circuit television or CCTV, is thought to deter criminal activity and a controlled study of its use on the London underground did demonstrate a 70% reduction in crimes of robbery and theft in the year after the system was installed (Burrows, 1980). CCTV has now become big business in terms of security, though it is costly. In Kings Lynn, the first British town to adopt CCTV, its introduction was partly funded by raising the fees in city centre car parks, but this did not bring complaints because of the results. In 1991 there were 200 cases of car theft or damage and in 1992 after CCTV was introduced, the number of cases was down to ten. Northampton introduced CCTV in 1993 and has 120 individual cameras in its town centre. Local police claim that there has been a 27% decrease in crime as a result, with the exception of house burglaries which have increased. Critics might argue that this is clear evidence of displacement.

A perhaps more insidious use of surveillance is electronic tagging, which has been introduced rather gently in the UK though it seems likely that in view of prison overcrowding, it may now be used more extensively. The principle is that the offender wears a small transmitter, or tag, on his or her ankle and the signal from this transmitter can be picked up at the monitoring centre. The offender's whereabouts can then be logged and if a curfew has been imposed, any violation will become apparent. As Nellis (1991) has noted, there are several problems with this kind of intervention, not the least of which is technological meltdown. The questionable reliability of the equipment, the effectiveness of monitoring and the infringement of civil liberties would all appear to present difficulties which have not as yet been adequately addressed.

Informal surveillance undertaken by volunteers seems to be both inexpensive and reasonably effective. The introduction of Neighbourhood Watch schemes has proved popular and Mayhew et al. (1989b) describe such schemes as:

> "... (having) made more of an impact, in terms of visibility if nothing else, than any other community crime prevention effort in Britain." (p.51)

FIGURE 9.1 *CCTV has significantly reduced crime in town centres, though it is expensive and there are concerns about possible infringements of civil liberties*

Members of these schemes are encouraged and supported by the police to keep an eye out for any suspicious activity in their community and to inform the authorities if they do see anything untoward. This activity is very much seen as a partnership with the police, as evidenced by the slogan 'Crime – together we'll crack it'. The effectiveness of Neighbourhood Watch schemes, however, seems to lie more in the fostering of community spirit and reducing fear of crime than in reducing crime itself (Brantingham and Brantingham, 1990) and there is a danger of an overzealous commitment to Neighbourhood Watch leading to an element of vigilantism. This has been particularly true in area where communities have wanted to get rid of prostitution.

Probably the most well-known example of situational crime prevention involves architectural design and environmental psychology. Common sense alone might tell us that the physical environment is related to the risk of crime – why else would we avoid dark streets and run-down areas? Why do we feel safer and less vulnerable in communities of people who look out for each other? According to architect Oscar Newman (1972), responding to these everyday observations and drawing on the seminal work of Jane Jacobs (1961), crime can be reduced by designing the built environment in such a way as to increase defensible space or areas for which residents feel some sort of ownership. He pointed out that in many public housing projects, such as high-rise blocks of flats, there are large areas which no one owns or controls. Because nobody takes responsibility for maintaining these areas they can become magnets for criminal activity and the general effect is a reduction of community activity because people are afraid and there is a consequent deterioration in the quality of life. Whilst offenders are unlikely to stand around in someone's front garden, they are likely to occupy open spaces where no one is going to tell them to move on. Newman suggested that three environmental features contribute to defensible space.

Zones of territorial influence

Based on ethological theories of territoriality is the notion that if people perceive certain areas as their own space they will take a pride in and defend them. Additionally, a community which has a shared sense of territoriality is more likely to repel intruders. Architectural design can take account of this by establishing real or symbolic barriers, for example fencing, which should encourage territoriality.

Opportunities for surveillance

If buildings are designed in such a way as to allow residents to naturally observe areas, and to recognise outsiders, it is more probable that any offences will be noticed early and reported.

Image and milieu

The design of buildings conveys a visual image and an identity, as does the setting. For instance, high-rise blocks all look the same whereas signs of individuality tends to signal a private area. Similarly, a vandalised area can convey disorder and apathy.

Whilst Newman's approach has been criticised (e.g. Mawby, 1977), mainly on the grounds that it suggested that residents would change their behaviour in defending their space and this has not generally been the case, its potential remains attractive because theory can be applied optimistically. It is now accepted that the wrong physical environment may indeed deter people from acting against crime, though a better one may not necessarily produce new behaviours. Rubenstein et al. (1980) have identified the major design approaches which can be used to make space more defensible:

- improving external lighting;
- reducing opportunities for offender concealment;
- reducing unassigned open spaces;
- locating outdoor activities in sight of windows;
- increasing the number of designated walkways or paths;
- increasing pedestrian activity

whilst Poyner (1991) adds the elements of fencing, house improvements, road closure and landscaping. All of these variables can contribute to a reduction

FIGURE 9.2 *To what extent does the physical environment influence crime? If an area begins to look run-down does this then lead to vandalism and further deterioration?*

in crime in terms of increased commitment to the community, increased likelihood of reporting and a higher risk of detection acting as a deterrent. Moreover, they can add to the quality of life experienced by residents.

In relation to house burglaries, Brown and Altman (1983) suggest the use of three features which can help deter burglars in addition to the normal security measures – barriers, markers and traces. Barriers can be fences, hedges, walls and gates, whilst markers and traces include indications of occupation, for example house name plates and garden furniture. Garages also help prevent burglaries because they make it hard for potential burglars to know whether anyone is home.

Most of the environmental approaches to crime prevention rely very much on the principle of informal social controls operating in cohesive communities and the idea that environmental design can help to encourage a sense of cohesion. As Murray (1995) points out, however, improved environmental and building design can enhance the quality of life in a community, but if there are elements within that community which continue to contribute to a pattern of disorder or there are serious rifts within a community, then no amount of environmental intervention will produce a reduction in crime. Thus, those areas which could most benefit from crime prevention strategies are probably the least likely to show an improvement. Skogan (1990) feels that these areas are characterised by disorder and he distinguishes between physical disorder (abandoned or neglected buildings, broken streetlights, litter, etc.) and social disorder (public drinking, prostitution, sexual innuendo, etc.). Whilst this might sound rather judgemental in the sense that disorder is presumably perceived differently by different people, Skogan found that the area in which people lived was a more significant indicator of the number of disorders they reported than any other personal characteristic. Skogan went on to identify disorders as being most numerous in areas with low neigh-bourhood stability, poverty and a high ethnic minority population. He suggested that the significant consequences of disorder included less willing-ness by residents to help one another, higher crime rates and a desire to leave the neighbourhood.

Whilst situational crime prevention tries to change the environment, another approach is to target potential victims, changing their behaviour in such a way as to reduce the likelihood of their victimisation. Women and children have tended to be the main targets of such intervention because of their vulnerability in relation to interpersonal violence and campaigns providing information and advice have become very popular. Perhaps not surprisingly, there have been criticisms from feminists because of the assumption behind these campaigns that those who need to change are the likely victims rather than the perpetrators, but more informed campaigns also call on men to change their attitudes and behaviour. The most well known of these is the impressive zero tolerance campaign against domestic violence which was introduced in Edinburgh during 1992 by the council's women's unit. The campaign was unusual because, although hard-hitting, it was both educational and empathic, appealing to the whole community to do something about violence in the family. What the numerous posters and leaflets signalled was that the time to tolerate such abuse was over and that without demonising perpetrators or sensationalising victims, the power to end it lay in the community.

ZERO TOLERANCE

The concept of zero tolerance has gained increasing significance in the 1990s as a result of apparently falling crime rates in American cities, which have been presented as the outcome of police forces being encouraged to crack down hard on seemingly minor offences, such as begging, dodging fares and public urination. This strategy is based on the principle that acting swiftly against small crimes helps reduce the bigger ones too. It stems from the work of Wilson and Kelling (1982) who argued that allowing a climate of disorder to develop leads to more serious crimes, so for instance leaving a broken window in a building and not repairing it will inspire some individuals to vandalise the rest of the building. From small beginnings, these vandals may turn to more serious crimes.

> "A piece of property is abandoned, weeds grow up, a window is smashed ... Adults stop scolding rowdy children; the children, emboldened, become more rowdy. Families move out ... many residents will think that crime, especially violent crime, is on the rise and they will modify their behaviour accordingly. They will use the streets less often, and when on the streets will stay apart from their fellows ... It is more likely that here, rather than in places where people are confident they can regulate behaviour by informal controls, drugs will change hands, prostitutes will solicit, and cars will be stripped." (Wilson and Kelling, 1982)

Other academics supported this theory, for instance Lavrakas (1982), who pointed out that the presence of litter, abandoned cars and graffiti in neighbourhoods can lead people to conclude that those who live there do not care enough to defend their homes and gardens and that vandalism and crime are commonplace. There are then fewer inhibitions in those who wish to add to the disorder.

When a zero tolerance policy was introduced in New York in 1992 it led to a 25% increase in arrests but the number of serious crimes, especially those of violence, markedly decreased. There were extra benefits too, as many arrests for minor offences led to the clearing up of other unresolved crimes or hastened the subsequent arrest of people for very serious crimes. One example was John Royster, whose fingerprints had been taken after an arrest for fare dodging, an offence for which previously he would probably have not been arrested. His fingerprints were subsequently found at a murder scene where a 65-year-old woman had been battered to death and he was arrested shortly afterwards.

In the USA reported crime dropped 3% in 1996, the fifth consecutive annual decrease, and murder rates showed the greatest reduction – 11% (FBI, 1997). Most of the major cities reported a decline in serious crime and whilst the policy of zero tolerance was presented as the major reason for this, criminologists suggested that the answer might lie in a mixture of factors such as:

- intensified police efforts and increased resources;
- demographic shifts with people moving away from cities;
- increased numbers of incarcerated offenders;
- fewer people in the crime-committing age group of 16–23 years.

McCord (1995) added:

"It's possible that the increasing concern people are showing about crime is helping to define better values, as people speak more loudly on the issue. As far as advances in policing go, there are so many experiments around the country that it's hard to tell which ones are effective." (p. 14)

She also pointed out that whilst crimes committed by people over the age of 35 are indeed decreasing, teenage crime remains high and the fear of crime remains static because it is exactly these crimes which are both unpredictable and sometimes vicious.

Attempts to introduce zero tolerance strategies in the UK have been welcomed by politicians anxious to reduce crime rates, but some senior police officers have urged caution. The Chief Constable of Thames Valley Police, Charles Pollard (1997), has suggested that zero tolerance policies can bring short-term gains but it would be naive to assume that this is the only reason why, for instance, New York seems to have enjoyed such a reduction in crime. He points out that New York was given an extra 7000 police officers on top of an already high ratio of police to public and that the new Police Commissioner introduced a raft of new policies, all stressing increased co-operation between the police, local communities, local businesses and local government agencies. Moreover, a system of accountability was introduced whereby local precinct commanders were held responsible for crime rates in their area and required to explain them and their planned response during weekly strategy meetings at central headquarters. Pollard goes on to argue that introducing a zero tolerance policy in the UK without thinking through the implications might result in a targeting of minority groups within communities and the possibility of riots.

RISK ASSESSMENT

Psychologists working in the field of prevention attempt not only to reduce the risk of crime, but also the risk of harm. Their work might involve assessing an individual in terms of their likelihood to commit further crime or to behave in a way which might harm themselves or others. This might occur at the sentencing stage or whilst a person is in custody or when contemplating release from prison or special hospital and can involve making important decisions about 'dangerousness'. The assessment is thus made not only in terms of the individual but also in relation to likely consequences; in other words, it concerns probability and outcomes. Perhaps not surprisingly, risk assessment is often associated with negative consequences – for example, the early release into the community of an individual who then commits a serious offence. However, unless a policy of permanent incarceration is adopted alongside a belief that attempts at rehabilitation are futile, risk assessment is an essential part of working with offenders and one to which psychologists can make a useful contribution.

There are several stages for practitioners to consider in the process of risk assessment.

1 Identify the target behaviour.
2 Evaluate existing knowledge in relation to this behaviour, e.g. previous offending pattern, academic work in the area (e.g. characteristics of offenders who have committed the same type of offences, base rates, reoffending rates, response to specific treatment, etc.).
3 Establish a match with the literature based on the individual's account of himself and his behaviour and any corroborative documentation, e.g. accounts from the individual's wife/partner, case records, etc.
4 Use this information to identify factors which would decrease the likelihood of the target behaviour being displayed and the factors which would increase that probability.
5 An estimate of the probability and likely consequences of the target behaviour occurring should now be possible, alongside an assessment of the acceptability or otherwise of this risk.
6 Finally, a monitoring and review programme needs to be set in place.

(See Towl and Crighton (1996) for a fuller account.)

The emphasis is very much on a systematic and informed analysis of information, but inevitably the risk assessment process involves some use of subjective judgements. Consequently psychologists compiling risk assessment reports need to be circumspect in the evidence they present to support their conclusions and avoid overconfidence in their predictions.

CASE STUDY 9.1
Risk assessment

You are a prison psychologist and you need to provide a risk assessment report in relation to 'Stuart' and the likelihood of a suicide attempt. You should prepare a list of questions to ask Stuart in interview before you compile your report. You will then need to identify the factors which might increase the probability of the target behaviour occurring and those which might decrease this.

Stuart is 20 years old and is on remand in relation to an alleged offence of burglary. He is of slight build and can be quick-tempered. He has been in custody before on several occasions and has a history of self-harm. He was taken into care when he was 14, but still has contact with some members of his family. Before his arrest Stuart was working on a building site. His girlfriend is pregnant and lives some distance from the prison. Stuart has been lethargic over the last few days and rather uncommunicative. One of the prison officers has reported a rumour about Stuart being picked on by other inmates in relation to debts and is concerned about his welfare.

Information you might like to consider before preparing your report.

- Rates of suicide for young males have increased over the last few years.
- Rates of suicide in prisons in England and Wales have risen in recent years, e.g. between 1984 and 1994 there were 387 deaths in custody and in 1994 there were 60 such deaths.
- Suicide rates in prison are about four times the rates in the community and the response of staff to inmate distress is crucial (Dexter, 1993).
- Research indicates that bullying in prison

can contribute to distress and depression (Inch et al., 1995), as can 'institutionally legitimised humiliation rituals' such as strip searches (Dexter and Towl, 1995).

- An analysis of several studies pinpoints specific risk factors in relation to suicide and these include membership of disrupted families which may have a history of suicide, drug and alcohol abuse, school failure, unemployment and depression (Diekstra and Hawton, 1987).
- Certain events can 'trigger' suicide attempts, e.g. the ending of a relationship, anniversaries, provocation, social isolation, frustration, etc.

What do you think is the likelihood of Stuart making a suicide attempt and how might a programme of intervention be designed to reduce the risk? Would you want to suggest to the prison governor any policy changes which might reduce the overall risk of suicide?

THE FUTURE OF CRIMINOLOGICAL PSYCHOLOGY

The future of criminological psychology looks extremely promising, with undergraduate and postgraduate courses flourishing at several colleges and universities and a very credible range of academic journals being published, reflecting the empirical work going on in the field. The background of criminological psychologists remains varied, with expertise and knowledge emanating from specialisms within clinical psychology, educational psychology, social, cognitive and biological psychology and also from specific practitioner experience and research. This is the real strength of criminological psychology – its basis in both intellectual and practical endeavour which can be used not only to develop theory but to inform policy.

What has psychology got to offer to our understanding of crime? Hopefully, by now you should be convinced that the contribution can be a positive and productive one. A psychological model of criminal behaviour does not have to depend on assumptions of psychopathology. Instead, it can draw on a whole range of theories of behaviour – biological, cognitive and social – placing them in the context of class, race and gender. Moreover, rather than simply concentrating on the offender, psychologists can make a valuable contribution to rehabilitation efforts, crime prevention and the treatment of victims.

Although the gulf between the disciplines of law and psychology has significantly narrowed since the early part of the century and there are now productive links between the two, there is still unresolved debate about the role of the 'expert witness' in British courts. In America criminological psychologists from the academic sphere but also from within the ranks of the police force are routinely called upon to provide expert witness testimony in legal cases. In this country there is still suspicion that introducing academics into the criminal justice system will be a challenge to the rights of defendants and the evidence introduced will not be subject to sufficient scrutiny. It goes without saying that the rights of defendants need to be protected, but the rights of alleged victims also need to be defended, particularly, for instance, in cases of child sexual abuse. This would seem to be an area where further work is needed in order to disseminate appropriate knowledge to key members of the legal profession, including the judiciary.

There would appear to be several important directions in which criminological psychology can proceed. Traditionally, psychological knowledge has been used *post hoc*, to understand why offenders have committed their offences, to predict degrees of dangerousness in order to ascertain whether certain offenders should be released into the community and, importantly, to develop appropriate treatment programmes which will help to rehabilitate convicted offenders. An important area where research needs to be directed in order to make full use of psychological expertise and to demonstrate its utility is that of prevention. If crime and violence can be prevented or reduced then the benefits for society will be considerable. This need not necessarily involve the dubious use of early screening to detect potential offenders, but could be in the form of environmental shaping which reduces the opportunity for crime or increasing use of parental training and recognition of the crucial importance of early childhood. This work would necessarily involve working closely with other disciplines, in itself a fruitful endeavour with mutual benefits.

Another worthwhile direction would be a move towards assisting the police service, not necessarily in the dramatic form of offender profiling or crime scene analysis. This is well established and will hopefully grow but in a less public way and be supported by rigorous empirical investigation. The areas for co-operative work would be in relation to police recruitment and training and the interrogation of suspects, leading to the collection of sound and untainted evidence which will secure convictions.

The future for criminological psychology looks exciting, particularly in view of the number of students who want to enter the field and are prepared to work extremely hard to achieve their ambitions. Their enthusiasm and their valuing of empirical research should ensure that criminological psychology grows in a systematic way and is recognised as a truly applied science.

RECOMMENDED
FURTHER READING

Allison, J. and Wrightsman, L. (1992) *Rape: the Misunderstood Crime*. London: Sage.

Barker, M. and Petley, J. (eds.) (1997) *Ill Effects: the Media/Violence Debate*. London: Routledge.

Blackburn, R. (1993) *The Psychology of Criminal Conduct*. Chichester: John Wiley.

Bottoms, B.L. and Goodman, G.S. (eds.) (1996) *International Perspectives on Child Abuse and Children's Testimony: Psychology, Research and Law*. Newbury Park: Sage.

Britton, P. (1997) *The Jigsaw Man*. London: Bantam Press.

Browne, K. and Herbert, M. (1997) *Preventing Family Violence*. Chichester: John Wiley.

Cahn, D.D. and Lloyd, S.A. (1996) *Family Violence from a Communication Perspective*. Thousand Oaks: Sage.

Canter, D. (1994) *Criminal Shadows*. London: Harper Collins.

Clarke, R.V. (ed.) (1992) *Situational Crime Prevention: Successful Case Studies*. New York: Harrow and Heston.

Cumberbatch, G. and Howitt, D. (1989) *A Measure of Uncertainty; the Effects of the Mass Media*. London: Libbey.

Cutler, B.L. and Penrod, S.D. (eds.) (1995) *Mistaken Identification: the Eyewitness, Psychology and the Law*. New York: Cambridge University Press.

Gauntlett, D. (1995) *Moving Experiences: Understanding Television's Influences and Effects*. London: John Libbey.

Gibson, P.C. and Gibson, R. (eds.) (1993) *Dirty Looks: Women, Pornography, Power*. London: BFI.

Glaser, C. and Frosh, S. (1988) *Child Sexual Abuse*. Basingstoke: Macmillan.

Gunter, B. and McAleer, J.L. (1997) *Children and Television: the One-eyed Monster?* 2nd edn. London: Routledge.

Hazelwood, R. and Burgess, A.W. (eds.) (1995) *Practical Aspects of Rape Investigation*, 2nd edn. Boca Raton: CRC Press.

Hickey, E.H. (1991) *Serial Murderers and their Victims*. Belmont: Wadsworth.

Hodge, J., McMurran, M. and Hollin, C.R. (eds.) (1997) *Addicted to Crime?* Chichester: John Wiley.

Hollin, C.R. (1992) *Criminal Behaviour*. Basingstoke: Falmer Press.

Hollin, C.R. (ed.) (1997) *Working with Offenders*. Chichester: John Wiley.

Hollin, C.R. and Howells, K. (eds.) (1991) *Clinical Approaches to Sex Offenders and their Victims*. Chichester: John Wiley.

Howitt, D. and Cumberbatch, G. (1990) *Pornography: Impacts and Influences*. London: Home Office Research Unit.

Itzen, C. (ed.) (1992) *Pornography: Women, Violence and Civil Liberties*. Oxford: Oxford University Press.

Jupp, V. (1993) *Methods of Criminological Research*. London: Routledge.

Maguire, M., Morgan, R. and Reiner, R. (eds.) (1997) *The Oxford Handbook of Criminology*, 2nd edn. London: Oxford University Press.

McGuire, J. (ed.) (1995) *What Works? Reducing Offending*. Chichester: John Wiley.

Messerschmidt, J.W. (1993) *Masculinities and Crime: Critique and Reconceptualisation of Theory*. Lanham: Rowman and Littlefield.

National Television Violence Study (1996) Los Angeles: Mediascope.

Norris, J. (1988) *Serial Killers*. Reading: Arrow Books.

Parrot, A. and Bechofer, L. (eds.) (1991) *Acquaintance Rape: the Hidden Crime*. New York: John Wiley.

Prins, H. (1994) *Offenders, Deviants or Patients?* London: Routledge.

Radford, J. and Russell, D. (eds.) (1992) *Femicide: the Politics of Woman Killing*. Milton Keynes: Open University Press.

Ressler, R.K., Burgess, A.W. and Douglas, J. (1988) *Sexual Homicide: Patterns and Motives*. Lexington: Lexington Books.

Ross, D.F., Read, J.D. and Toglia, M.P. (1994) *Adult Eyewitness Testimony: Current Trends and Developments*. Cambridge: Cambridge University Press.

Scully, D. (1990) *Understanding Sexual Violence: a Study of Convicted Rapists*. Boston: Unwin hyman.

Stephenson, G.M. (1993) *The Psychology of Criminal Justice*. Oxford: Blackwell.

Towl, G.J. and Crighton, D.A. (1996) *Handbook of Psychology for Forensic Practitioners*. London: Sage.

Walklate, S. (1995) *Gender and Crime: An Introduction*. London: Prentice-Hall.

Ward, C. (1996) *Attitudes to Rape*. London: Sage.

Internet

There are many crime-related sites on the worldwide web. You can find some of them via my web page at:

http://www.nene.ac.uk/ass/behav/crim/crim.html.

REFERENCES

Abbey, A. (1991) Misperception as an antecedent of acquaintance rape: a consequence of ambiguity in communication between women and men. In Parrot, A. and Bechofer, L. (eds.) *Acquaintance Rape: the Hidden Crime.* New York: John Wiley.

Abel, G.G., Becker, J.V., Mittelman, M. et al. (1987) Self-reported sex crimes of non-incarcerated paraphiliacs. *Journal of Interpersonal Violence,* **2**(1), 3–25.

Abel, G.G., Mittelman, M., Becker, J.V., Rathner, J. and Rouleau, J.L. (1988) Predicting child molesters' responses to treatment. *Annals of the New York Academy of Sciences,* **528**, 223–234.

Abrahamsen, D. (1973) *The Murdering Mind.* New York: Harper and Row.

Abrahamson, D. (1960) *The Psychology of Crime.* New York: John Wiley.

AGB Cable and Satellite Yearbook (1995). London: BARB/Taylor Nelson AGB plc.

Ageton, S.S. (1983) *Sexual Assault among Adolescents.* Lexington: D.C. Heath.

Agnew, R. (1990) The origins of delinquent events: an examination of offender accounts. *Journal of Research in Crime and Delinquency,* **27**, 267–294.

Aichorn, A. (1925) *Wayward Youth.* New York: Meridian Books.

Ainsworth, P.B. (1981) Incident perception by British police officers. *Law and Human Behaviour,* **5**, 231–236.

Akers, R. (1990) Rational choice, deterrence, and social learning theories in criminology: the path not taken. *Journal of Criminal Law and Criminology,* **81**, 653–676.

Allen, K., Caslyn, D.A., Fehrenbach, P.A. and Benton, G. (1989) A study of interpersonal behaviors of male batterers. *Journal of Interpersonal Violence,* **4**, 79–89.

Allison, J.A. and Branscombe, N.R. (1992) The influence of affective and general personality factors on the likelihood of sexual aggression. Unpublished manuscript, Pittsburg State University, Pittsburg.

Amir, M. (1971) *Patterns in Forcible Rape.* Chicago: University of Chicago Press.

Andrews, D.A., Zinger, I., Hoge, R.D. et al. (1990) Does correctional treatment work? A clinically relevant and psychologically informed meta-analysis. *Criminology,* **28**, 369–404.

Anson, D., Golding, S. and Gully, K. (1993) Child sexual abuse allegations: reliability of criteria-based content analysis. *Law and Human Behaviour,* **17**, 331–341.

Argyle, M. (1967) *The Psychology of Interpersonal Behaviour.* Harmondsworth: Penguin.

Asch, S. (1951) Effects of group pressure upon the modification and distortion of judgments. In Guetzkow, H. (ed.) *Groups, Leadership and Men.* Pittsburgh: Carnegie Press.

Asch, S.E (1956) Studies of independence and conformity: a minority of one against a unanimous majority. *Psychological Monographs,* **70**, 416.

Ault, R.L. and Reese, J.T. (1980) A psychological assessment of crime profiling. *FBI Law Enforcement Bulletin,* **49**(3), 22–25.

Baddeley, A. (1993) *Human Memory.* London: Routledge.

Bailey, S. (1996) Adolescents who murder. *Journal of Adolescence,* **19**, 19–39.

Baker, A. and Duncan, S. (1985) Child sexual abuse: a study of prevalence in Great Britain. *Child Abuse and Neglect,* **9**, 457–467.

Bandura, A. (1977) *Social Learning Theory.* Englewood Cliffs: Prentice-Hall.

Bandura, A. and Walters, R.H. (1959) *Adolescent Aggression.* New York: Ronald Press.

Bandura, A. and Walters, R.H. (1963) *Social Learning and Personality Development.* New York: Holt, Rinehart and Winston.

Bandura, A. Ross, D. and Ross, S.A. (1963) Imitation of film mediated aggression models. *Journal of Abnormal and Social Psychology,* **66**, 3–11.

Barker, M. and Petley, J. (eds.) (1997) *Ill Effects: the Media/Violence Debate.* London: Routledge.

Barnett, N. and Feild, H.S. (1977) Sex differences in attitudes to rape. *Journal of College Student Personnel,* **18**, 93–96.

Barnett, O.W. and LaViolette, A.D. (1993) It Could Happen to Anyone: Why Battered Women Stay. Newbury Park, CA: Sage.

Barnett, O.W., Miller-Perrin, C.L. and Perrin, R.D. (1997) Family Violence across the Lifespan. Thousand Oaks, CA; Sage.

Baron, R. and Bell, P. (1973) Sexual arousal and aggression by males: effects of type of erotic stimuli and prior provocation. Journal of Personality and Social Psychology, 35, 79–87.

Bartlett, F.C. (1932) Remembering. Cambridge: Cambridge University Press.

Bartol, C.R. (1980) Criminal Behaviour: a Psychosocial Approach. Englewood Cliffs: Prentice-Hall.

Baumgardner, S.R., Becker, C.S, Beaulieu, D. and Kenniston, A. (1988) Cause, responsibility, blame for rape: do we blame the victim? Paper presented at the August meeting of the American Psychological Association, Atlanta.

Baxter, J. (1990) The suggestibility of child witnesses: a review. Journal of Applied Cognitive Psychology, 3, 1–15.

Bee, H. (1995) The Developing Child. New York: Harper and Row.

Bekarian, D.A. and Bowers, J.M. (1983) Eyewitness testimony: were we misled? Journal of Experimental Psychology, Learning, Memory and Cognition, 9, 139–145.

Benatar, P., Geraldo, N. and Capps, R. (1981) Hell is for Children. Rare Blue Music Inc.

Benedict, H. (1993) Virgin or Vamp. London: Routledge.

Benyan, J. (1994) Law and Order Review 1993: an Audit of Crime, Policing and Criminal Justice Issues. Centre for the Study of Public Order, University of Leicester.

Berkowitz, L. (1965) Some aspects of observed aggression. Journal of Personality and Social Psychology, 2, 359–369.

Bilton, K. (1994) Child Protection Practice and the Memorandum of Good Practice: a Discussion Paper. London: British Association of Social Workers.

Binney, V., Harkell, G. and Nixon, J. (1981) Leaving Violent Men: a Study of Refuges and Housing for Battered Women. London: Women's Aid Federation.

Birns, B., Cascardi, M. and Meyer, S. (1994) Sex-role socialisation: developmental influences on wife abuse. American Journal of Orthopsychiatry, 64, 50–59.

Blackburn, R. (1983) Psychopathy, delinquency and crime. In Gale, A. and Edwards, J.A. (eds.) Physiological Correlates of Human Behaviour, Vol. 3: Individual Differences and Psychopathology. London: Academic Press.

Blackburn, R. (1993) The Psychology of Criminal Conduct. Chichester: John Wiley.

Blair, R.J.R., Jones, L., Clark, E. and Smith, M. (1997) The psychopathic individual: a lack of responsiveness to distress cues? Psychophysiology, 34, 192–198.

Bohman, M. (1995) Predisposition to criminality: Swedish adoption studies in retrospect. In Genetics of Criminal and Antisocial Behaviour, Ciba Foundation Symposium 194. Chichester: John Wiley.

Bonger, W.A. (1916) Criminality and Economic Conditions. Bloomington: Indiana University Press.

Boon, J. and Davies, G. (1992) Fact and fiction in offender profiling. Issues in Legal and Criminological Psychology, 32, 3–9.

Borkowski, M., Murch, M. and Walter, V. (1983) Marital Violence: the Community Response. London: Tavistock Press.

Bostwick, T.D. and Delucia, J.L. (1992) Effects of gender and specific dating behaviors on perceptions of sex willingness and date rape. Journal of Social and Clinical Psychology, 11(1), 14–25.

Bottomley, A.K. (1979) Criminology in Focus. London: M. Robertson.

Bottoms, A. and McWilliams, W. (1990) Evaluating intermediate treatment. In Robbins, D. and Walters, A. (eds.) Department of Health Yearbook of Research and Development. London: HMSO.

Bouchard, T.J., Lykken, D.T., McGue, M., Segal, N.L. and Tellegen, A. (1990) Sources of human psychological differences: the Minneapolis study of twins reared apart. Science, 250, 223–228.

Bowlby, J. (1944) Forty-four juvenile thieves. International Journal of Psychoanalysis, 25, 1–57.

Bradford, J.M.W. (1985) Organic treatment for the male sexual offender. Behavioural Sciences and the Law, 3, 355–375. New York: New York Academy of Science.

Branscombe, N.R. and Weir, J.A. (1992) Resistance as stereotype inconsistency: consequences for judgments of rape victims. Journal of Social and Clinical Psychology, 11, 1–23.

Brantingham, P.L. and Brantingham, P.J. (1990) Situational crime prevention in practice. *Canadian Journal of Criminology*, **32**, 17–40.

Briere, J. (1987) Predicting self-reported likelihood of battering: attitudes and childhood experiences. *Research in Personality*, **21**, 61–69.

Briere, J. and Conte, J. (1993) Self-reported amnesia for abuse in adults molested as children. *Journal of Traumatic Stress*, **6**, 21–31.

Briere, J. and Runtz, M. (1989) The Trauma Symptoms Checklist: early data on a new scale. *Journal of Interpersonal Violence*, **4**, 151–163.

Brittain, R.P. (1970) The sadistic murderer. *Medicine, Science and the Law*, **10**, 198–207.

Britton, P. (1997) *The Jigsaw Man*. London: Bantam Press.

Broude, G.J. and Greene, S.J. (1983) Cross-cultural codes on husband-wife relationships. *Ethnology*, **22**, 263–280.

Brown, B.A. and Altman, I. (1983) Territoriality, defensible space, and residential burglary: an environmental analysis. *Journal of Environmental Psychology*, **3**, 203–220.

Brown, R. and Kulik, J. (1977) Flashbulb memories. *Cognition*, **5**, 73–99.

Browne, K.D. and Pennell, A.E. (1998) Film Violence and Young Offenders. *Aggression and Violent Behaviour*, 3, 27–35.

Brownmiller, S. (1975) *Against Our Will: Men, Women and Rape*. New York: Simon and Schuster.

Brush, L.D. (1990) Violent acts and injurious outcomes in married couples: methodological issues in the National Survey of Families and Households. *Gender and Society*, **4**, 56–67.

Brussel, J.A. (1969) *Casebook of a Crime Psychiatrist*. London: New English Library.

Buckhout, R. (1980) Nearly 2000 witnesses can be wrong. *Bulletin of the Psychonomic Society*, **16**, 307–310.

Buckhout, R., Figueroa, D. and Hoff, E. (1975) Eyewitness identification: effects of suggestion and bias in identification from photographs. *Bulletin of the Psychonomic Society*, **6**, 71–74.

Bull, R. (1982) Physical appearance and criminality. *Current Psychological Reviews*, **2**, 269–281.

Bull, R. (1992) Obtaining evidence expertly: the reliability of interviews with child witnesses. *Expert Evidence*, **1**, 5–12.

Bull, R. (1995) Innovative techniques for the questioning of child witnesses, especially those who are young and those with learning disability. In Zaragoza, M.S., Hall, G.C.N., Hirschman, R. and Ben-Porath, Y.S. (eds.) *Memory and Testimony in the Child Witness*. Thousand Oaks: Sage.

Burgess, A.W., Hartmen, C.R., Ressler, R.K., Douglas, J.E. and McCormack, A. (1986) Sexual homicide: a motivational model. *Journal of Interpersonal Violence*, **1**, 251–272.

Burman, B., Margolin, G. and John, R.S. (1993) America's angriest home videos: behavioural contingencies observed in home reenactment of marital conflict. *Journal of Consulting and Clinical Psychology*, **61**, 28–59.

Burns, G. (1985) *Somebody's Husband, Somebody's Son*. London: Pan.

Burrows, J. (1980) Closed circuit television and crime on the London Underground. In Clarke, R.V. and Mayhew, P. (eds.) *Designing Out Crime*. London: HMSO.

Burt, C. (1925) *The Young Delinquent*. London: University of London Press.

Burt, M.R. (1980) Cultural myths and supports for rape. *Journal of Personality and Social Psychology*, **38**, 217–230.

Byrne, D. and Lamberth, J. (1970) The effect of erotic stimuli on sex arousal, evaluative responses, and subsequent behaviour. In *Technical Reports of the Presidential Commission on Obscenity and Pornography (Vol.8)*. Washington: Government Printing Office.

Cain, M. (1989) Feminists transgress criminology. In Cain, M. (ed.) *Growing Up Good*. London: Sage.

Cameron, D. and Frazer, E. (1987) *The Lust to Kill: a Feminist Investigation of Sexual Murder*. New York: New York University Press.

Campbell, B. (1988) *Unofficial Secrets*. London: Virago.

Campbell, B. (1993) *Goliath: Britain's Dangerous Places*. London: Virago Press.

Canter, D. (1989) Offender profiles. *Psychologist*, **2**(1), 12–16.

Canter, D. (1994) *Criminal Shadows*. London: Harper Collins.

Caplan, P. (1986) The myth of women's masochism. In Walsh, M.R. (ed.) *The Psychology of Women*. Yale: Yale University Press.

Caputi, J. (1987) *The Age of Sex Crime*. Bowling Green: Bowling Green State University Press.

Cattell, R. (1895) Measurement of the accuracy of recollection. *Science*, **20**, 761–776.

Chapman, A.J. and Perry, D.J. (1992) Applying the cognitive interview procedure to road accident witnesses. *Psychologist*, **5**, 55–56.

Check, J. (1985) *The effects of Violent and Nonviolent Pornography*. Ottawa: Department of Justice.

Check, J.V.P. and Malamuth, N.M. (1983) Sex role stereotyping and reactions to depictions of stranger versus acquaintance rape. *Journal of Personality and Social Psychology*, **45**, 344–356.

Chess, S. and Thomas, A. (1984) *Origins and Evolution of Behavior Disorders*. New York: Brunner/Mazel.

Christiansen, K.O. (1977) A preliminary study of criminality among twins. In Mednick, S. and Christiansen, K.O. (eds.) *Biosocial Bases of Criminal Behavior*. New York: Gardner Press.

Christie, R. and Geis, F.L. (1970) *Studies in Machiavellianism*. New York: Academic Press.

Claussen, A.H. and Crittenden, P.M. (1991) Physical and psychological maltreatment: relations among types of maltreatment. *Child Abuse and Neglect*, **15**, 5–18.

Cleckley, H. (1976) *The Mask of Sanity*. St. Louis: Mosby.

Clifford, B.R. (1976) *The Psychology of Person Identification*. Chichester: John Wiley.

Clifford, B.R. and Scott, J. (1978) Individual and situational factors in eyewitness testimony. *Journal of Applied Psychology*, **63**, 352–359.

Clover, C. (1989) Her body, himself: gender in the slasher film. In Donald, J. (ed.) *Fantasy and the Cinema*. London: BFI Publishing.

Clover, C. (1992) *Men, Women and Chain Saws*. London: BFI Publishing.

Cohen, D. (1990) *Being a Man*. London: Routledge.

Conduit, E. (1993) *Angry Violence and Television Influence*. Division of Criminological and Legal Psychology, Newsletter No. 34. Leicester: British Psychological Society.

Copson, G. (1996) At last some facts about offender profiling in Britain. *Forensic Update*, **46**, Division of Criminological and Legal Psychology. Leicester: British Psychological Society.

Copson, G. and Holloway, K. (1997) *Offender profiling*. Paper presented to the annual conference of the Division of Criminological and Legal Psychology, British Psychological Society (October).

Cornish, D.B. and Clarke, R.V. (eds.) (1986) *The Reasoning Criminal: Rational Choice Perspectives on Offending*. New York: Springer-Verlag.

Cortés, J.B. and Gatti, F.M. (1972) *Delinquency and Crime: a Biopsychosocial Approach*. New York: Seminar Press.

Crowe, R.R. (1974) An adoption study of antisocial personality. *Archives of General Psychiatry*, **31**, 785–791.

Cumberbatch, G. (1992) Is television violence harmful? In Cochrane, R. and Carroll, D. (eds.) *Psychology and Social Issues*. London: Falmer Press.

Cumberbatch, G. (1994) Legislating mythology: video violence and children. *Journal of Mental Health*, **3**, 485–494.

Cutler, B.L. and Penrod, S. (1995) *Mistaken Identification: The Eyewitness, Psychology and the Law*. New York: Cambridge University Press.

Daly, M. and Wilson, M. (1988) *Homicide*. New York: Aldine Press.

Dane, F.C. and Wrightsman, L.S. (1982) Effects of defendants' and victims' characteristics on jurors' verdicts. In Kerr, N.L. and Bray, R.M. (eds.) *The Psychology of the Courtroom*. London: Academic Press.

Davies, G. (1994) Witness error still convicts the innocent. *The Guardian*, 10th September.

Davies, G. and Brown, L. (1978) Recall and organisation in five-year old children. *British Journal of Psychology*, **69**, 343–349.

Davies, G. and Noon, E. (1991) *An Evaluation of the Live Link for Child Witnesses*. London: Home Office.

Davies, G. and Westcott, H. (1992) Videotechnology and the child witness. In Dent, H. and Flin, R. (eds.) *Children as Witnesses*. Chichester: John Wiley.

Davis, J.H. (1980) Group decision and procedural justice. In Fishbein, M. (ed.) *Progress in Social Psychology*. Hillsdale: Erlbaum.

De River, J.P. (1950) *Crime and the Sexual Psychopath*. Springfield: C.C. Thomas.

De Young, M. (1982) *The Sexual Victimisation of Children*. Jefferson: McFarland.

Delgado, J. (1969) *Physical Control of the Mind: Towards a Psychocivilized Society*. New York: Harper and Row.

DeMause, L. (1974) *A History of Childhood*. New York: Psychotherapy Press.

Denkowski, G.C. and Denkowski, K.M. (1985) The mentally retarded offender in the state prison system: identification, prevalence, adjustment and rehabilitation. *Criminal Justice and Behavior*, **12**, 55–70.

Dent, H. and Flin, R. (1992) *Children as Witnesses*. Chichester: John Wiley.

Dexter, P. and Towl, G.J. (1995) An investigation into suicidal behaviours in prison. In Clark, N.K. and Stephenson, G.M. (eds.) *Criminal Behaviour: Perceptions, Attributions and Rationality*. Leicester: DCLP/British Psychological Society.

Dexter, P. (1993) *An investigation into suicidal behaviours at HMP Highpoint*. Unpublished MSc thesis, University of London.

Dibble, U. and Straus, M.A. (1980) Some social determinants of inconsistency between attitudes and behaviour: the case of family violence. *Journal of Marriage and the Family*, **42**, 71–80.

Diekstra, R.F.W and Hawton, K. (eds.) (1987) *Suicide in Adolescence*. Dordrecht: Martinus Nijhoff.

Dietz, P.E. (1983) Sex offences: behavioural aspects. In Kadish, S.H. (ed.) *Encyclopaedia of Crime and Justice*. New York: Free Press.

Dietz, S.R., Blackwell, K.T., Daley, P.C. and Bentley, B.J. (1982) Measurement of empathy toward rape victims and rapists. *Journal of Personality and Social Psychology*, **43**, 372–384.

Dietz, S.R., Littman, M. and Bentley, B.J. (1984) Attribution of responsibility for rape: the influence of observer empathy, victim resistance, and victim attractiveness. *Sex Roles*, **10**, 261–280.

Dignan, J. (1992) Repairing the damage: can reparation work in the service of diversion? *British Journal of Criminology*, **32**, 452–469.

Dobash, R.E. and Dobash, R.P. (1979) *Violence against Wives: a Case Against Patriarchy*. New York: Free Press.

Dobash, R.E. and Dobash, R.P. (1988) Research as social action: the struggle for battered women. In Yllö, K. and Bograd, M. (eds.) *Feminist Perspectives on Wife Abuse*. Newbury Park: Sage.

Dominick, J.R. (1984) Videogames, TV violence and aggression in teenagers. *Journal of Communication*, **34**, 134–144

Donnelly, L. (1991) Ending the torment. *Nursing Times*, **87**, 36–38.

Donnerstein, E. (1984) Pornography: its effects on violence against women. In Malamuth, N. and Donnerstein, E. (eds.) *Pornography and Sexual Aggression*. New York: Academic Press.

Donnerstein, E. and Berkowitz, L. (1981) Victim reactions in aggressive erotic films as a factor in violence against women. *Journal of Personality and Social Psychology*, **41**, 710–724.

Doumas, D., Margolin, G. and John, R.S. (1994) The intergenerational transmission of aggression across three generations. *Journal of Family Violence*, **9**, 157–175.

Dugdale, R. (1910) *The Jukes*. New York: Putnam.

Dunn, P.F. (1995) Elder abuse as an innovation to Australia: a critical overview. In Kosberg, J.I. and Garcia, J.L. (eds.) *Elder Abuse: International and Cross-cultural Perspectives*. Binghamton: Haworth.

Dutton, D.G. (1994) Patriarchy and wife assault: an ecological fallacy. *Violence and Victims*, **9**, 167–182.

Dutton, D.G. and Painter, S.L. (1993) Emotional attachments in abusive relationships: a test of traumatic bonding theory. *Violence and Victims*, **8**, 105–120.

Dworkin, A. (1981) *Pornography: Men Possessing Women*. New York: Perigee.

Dwyer, S.M. and Myers, S. (1990) Sex offender treatment: a six-month to ten-year follow up study. *Annals of Sex Research*, **3**(3), 305–318.

Einsiedel, E. (1992) The experimental research evidence: effects of pornography on the average individual. In Itzen, C. (ed.) *Pornography: Women, Violence and Civil Liberties*. Oxford: Oxford University Press.

Ellis, L. (1989) *Theories of Rape: Inquiries into the Causes of Sexual Aggression*. New York: Hemisphere.

Ellsworth, P.C. (1993) Some steps between attitudes and verdicts. In Hastie, R. (ed.) *Inside the Juror: the Psychology of Juror Decision Making*. Cambridge: Cambridge University Press.

Eron, L.D. and Huesmann, L.R. (1986) The role of television in the development of antisocial and prosocial behavior. In Olweus, D., Block, J. and Radke-Yarrow, M. (eds.) *Development of Antisocial and Prosocial Behavior: Research, Theories and Issues*. New York: Academic Press.

Eron, L.D., Huesmann L.R. and Zelli, A. (1991) The role of parental variables in the learning of aggression. In Peplar, D.J. and Rubin, H.K. (eds.) *The Development and Treatment of Childhood Aggression*. Hillsdale: Erlbaum.

Ewing, C.P. and Aubrey, M. (1987) Battered women and public opinion: some realities about myths. *Journal of Family Violence*, **2**, 257–264.

Eysenck, H.J. (1964) *Crime and Personality*. London: Routledge and Kegan Paul.

Eysenck, H. and Gudjonsson, G. (1989) *The Causes and Cures of Criminality*. New York: Plenum Press.

Farrell, G. and Pease, K. (1995) *Repeat Victimisation – 1982, 1984, 1988 and 1992*. London: Home Office.

Farrington, D.P. (1995) The development of offending and anti-social behaviour from childhood. *Journal of Child Psychology and Psychiatry*, 36 (6), 924–964.

Farrington, D.P. (1991a) Childhood aggression and adult violence: early precursors and later life outcomes. In Peplar, D.J. and Rubin, H.K. (eds.) *The Development and Treatment of Childhood Aggression*. Hillsdale: Erlbaum.

Farrington, D.P. (1991b) Anti-social personality from childhood to adulthood. *Psychologist*, **4**, 389–394.

Farrington, D. (1994) Human development and criminal careers. In Maguire, M., Morgan, R. and Reiner, R. (eds.) *The Oxford Handbook of Criminology*. London: Oxford University Press.

Farrington, D.P. and West, D.J. (1990) The Cambridge study in delinquent development: a long-term follow-up of 411 London males. In Kaiser, G. and Kerner, H.J. (eds.) *Criminality: Personality, Behaviour, Life History*. Heidelberg: Springer-Verlag.

Farrington, D.P., Ohlin, L.E. and Wilson, J.Q. (1986) *Understanding and Controlling Crime*. New York: Springer-Verlag.

F.B.I. (1985a) Crime scene and profile characteristics of organised and disorganised murderers. *FBI Law Enforcement Bulletin*, **54**(8), 18–25.

F.B.I. (1985b) Classifying sexual homicide crime scenes: interrater reliability. *FBI Law Enforcement Bulletin*, **54**(8), 13–17.

FBI (1993) *Uniform Crime Statistics*. Washington: FBI.

FBI (1997) *Uniform Crime Statistics*. Washington: FBI.

Feldman, P. (1993) *The Psychology of Crime*. Cambridge: Cambridge University Press.

Feshback, S. and Singer, R.D. (1971) *Television and Aggression: an Experimental Field Study*. San Francisco: Jossey-Bass.

Finkelhor, D. (1984) *Child Sexual Abuse: New Theory and Research*. New York: Free Press.

Finkelhor, D. (1986) *A Sourcebook on Child Sex Abuse*. Newbury Park: Sage.

Finkelhor, D. (1994) The international epidemiology of child sexual abuse. *Child Abuse and Neglect*, **18**, 409–417.

Finkelhor, D. and Yllö, K. (1985) *License to Rape: Sexual Abuse of Wives*. New York: Holt, Rinehart and Winston.

Finkelhor, D., Williams, L. and Burns, N. (1988) *Nursery Crimes: Sexual Abuse in Daycare*. London: Sage.

Fisher, R.P. and Geiselman, R.E. (1992) *Memory-enhancing Techniques for Investigative Interviewing*. Springfield: C.C. Thomas.

Fisher, S. (1993) Identifying video game addiction in children and adolescents. *Addictive Behaviors*, **19**, 545–555.

Fitch, F.S. and Papantonio, A. (1983) Men who batter: some pertinent characteristics. *Journal of Nervous and Mental Disease*, **171**, 190–192.

Flor Henry, P., Lang, R.A., Koles, Z.J. and Frenzel, R.R. (1991) Quantitative EEG studies of paedophilia. *International Journal of Psychophysiology*, **10**(3), 252–258.

Fo, W.S.O. and O'Donnell, C.R. (1975) The buddy system: effect of community intervention on delinquent offences. *Behaviour Therapy*, **6**, 522–524.

Freud, S. (1924) *A General Introduction to Psychoanalysis*. London: Hogarth Press.

Freud, S. (1966) New introductory lectures on psychoanalysis. In Strachey, J. (ed.) *The Standard Edition of the Complete Psychological Works of Sigmund Freud*. London: Hogarth Press. (Original work published 1933.)

Frieze, I.H. (1983) Investigating the causes and consequences of marital rape. *Signs*, **8**, 532–553.

Frude, N. (1991) Child abuse. In Howells, K. and Hollin, C. (eds.) *Clinical Approaches to Violence*. Chichester: John Wiley.

Fulero, S. and Penrod, S.D. (1990) Attorney jury selection folklore: what do they think and how can psychology help? *Forensic Reports*, **3**, 223–259.

Furnham, A. and Thompson, J. (1991) Personality and self-reported delinquency. *Personality and Individual Differences*, **12**, 585–598.

Furniss, T. (1984) Conflict-avoiding and conflict-regulating patterns in incest and child sexual abuse. *Acta Paedopsychiatry*, **50**, 299–313.

Gallagher, B.J. III (1987) *The Sociology of Mental Illness*. Englewood Cliffs: Prentice-Hall.

Garbarino, J., Guttman, E. and Seeley, J. (1986) *The Psychologically Battered Child*. San Francisco: Jossey-Bass.

Garland, D. (1994) The development of British criminology. In Maguire, M., Morgan, R. and Reiner, R. (eds.) *The Oxford Handbook of Criminology*. London: Oxford University Press.

Gauntlett, D. (1995) *Moving Experiences: Understanding Television's Influences and Effects*. London: Libbey.

Gavey, N. (1996) Women's desire and sexual violence discourse. In Wilkinson, S. (ed.) *Feminist Social Psychologies*. Buckingham: Open University Press.

Geberth, V. (1083) *Practical Homicide Investigation*. New York: Elsevier.

Geiselman, R.E. and Padilla, J. (1988) Interviewing child witnesses with the cognitive interview. *Journal of Police Science and Administration*, **16**, 236–242.

Geiselman, R.E., Fisher, R.P. MacKinnon, D.F. and Holland, H.L. (1986) Enhancement of eyewitness memory with the cognitive interview. *American Journal of Psychology*, **99**, 385–401.

Gelles, R.J. and Cornell, R. (1985) *Intimate Violence in Families*. Newbury Park: Sage.

Gendreau, P. and Ross, R.R. (1979) Effective correctional treatment: bibliotherapy for cynics. *Crime and Delinquency*, **25**, 463–489.

Gerbner, G. (1972) Violence in television drama. In Comstock, G.A. and Rubenstein, E.A. (eds.) *Television and Social Behavior, Vol. 1*. Washington: US Govt Printing Office.

Gerow, J.R. (1989) *Psychology: an Introduction*. Glenville: Scott, Foresman.

Gibbs, J.C., Arnold, K.D., Ahlborn, H.H. and Cheesman, F.L. (1984) Facilitation of sociomoral reasoning in delinquents. *Journal of Consulting and Clinical Psychology*, **52**, 37–43.

Gil, D.G. (1970) *Violence against Children: Physical Child Abuse in the U.S.* Cambridge: Harvard University Press.

Glaser, D. and Frosh, S. (1988) *Child Sexual Abuse*. Basingstoke: Macmillan.

Glueck, S. and Glueck, E.T. (1956) *Physique and Delinquency*. New York: Dodd Meade.

Goddard, H.H. (1914) *Feeble-mindedness: Its Causes and Consequences*. New York: Macmillan.

Goldsmith, H.H. and Gottesman, I.I. (1995) Heritable variability and variable heritability in developmental psychopathology. In Lenzenweger, M.F. and Haugaard, J.J. (eds.) *Frontiers of Developmental Psychopathology*. New York: Oxford University Press.

Goldstein, A.G. and Chance, C. (1971) Visual recognition memory for complex configurations. *Perception and Psychophysics*, 9, 237–241.

Goldstein, A.P. (1986) Psychological skill training and the aggressive adolescent. In Apter, S.J. and Goldstein, A.P. (eds.) *Youth Violence: Programs and Prospects*. New York: Plenum.

Goldstein, A.P. and Keller, H. (1987) *Aggressive Behavior: Assessment and Intervention*. New York: Pergamon Press.

Goldstein, A.P., Glick, B., Irwin, N.J., Pask-McCartney, C. and Rubama, I. (1989) *Reducing Delinquency: Intervention in the Community*. New York: Pergamon.

Goodman, G.S. and Reed, R.S. (1986) Age differences in eyewitness testimony. *Law and Human Behaviour*, **10**, 317–332.

Goodman, G.S., Aman, C. and Hirschman, J. (1987) Child sexual and physical abuse: children's testimony. In Ceci, S.J., Ross, D.F. and Toglia, M.P. (eds.) *Children's Eyewitness Memory*. New York: Springer-Verlag.

Gordon, R. (1976) Paedophilia: normal and abnormal. In Draemer, W. (ed.) *The Forbidden Love: the Normal and Abnormal Love of Children*. London: Sheldon Press.

Goring, C. (1913) *The English Convict: a Statistical Study*. Montclair: Patterson Smith.

Grace, S. (1995) *Policing Domestic Violence in the 1990s.* Home Office Research Study 139. London: HMSO.

Gray, C. (1986) Diet, crime and delinquency: a critique. *Nutrition Reviews,* **44**, 89–94.

Gresswell, D.M. and Hollin, C.R. (1994) Multiple murder: a review. *British Journal of Criminology,* **34**, 1–14.

Gresswell, D.M. and Hollin, C.R. (1997) Addictions and multiple murder: a behavioural perspective. In Hodge, J., McMurran, M. and Hollin, C. (eds.) (1997) *Addicted to Crime?* Chichester: John Wiley

Griffiths, M. (1997) Video games and aggression. *Psychologist,* **10**(9), 397–401.

Griffiths, M.D. and Dancaster, I. (1995) The effect of Type A personality on physiological arousal while playing computer games. *Addictive Behaviors,* **20**(4), 543–548.

Groth, A. N. (1979) *Men Who Rape: The Psychology of the Offender.* New York: Plenum.

Groth, A.N. (1983) Treatment of the sexual offender in a correctional institution. In Greer, J.G. and Stuart, I.R. (eds.) *The Sexual Aggressor.* New York: Van Nostrand Reinhold.

Groth, A.N. and Birnbaum, H.J. (1978) Adult sexual orientation and attraction to underage persons. *Archives of Sexual Behaviour,* **7**(3), 175–181.

Groth, A.N., Longo, A.E. and McFadin, J.B. (1982) Undetected recidivism among rapists and child molestors. *Crime and Delinquency,* **28**, 450–458.

Gunter, B. and Harrison, J. (1995) *Violence on Television in the U.K., a Content Analysis.* London: BBC/ITC.

Gunter, B. and McAleer, J.L. (1990) *Children and Television – the One-eyed Monster?* London: Routledge.

Guttmacher, M. (1951) *Sex Offences: the Problem, Causes and Prevention.* New York: Norton.

Guttmacher, M. and Weinhofen, H. (1952) *Psychiatry and the Law.* New York: Norton.

Hagell, A. and Newbury, T. (1994) *Young Offenders and the Media.* London: Policy Studies Institute.

Hare, R.D. (1991) *The Hare Psychopathy Checklist* (revised). Toronto: Mulit-Health Systems.

Hargreaves, D.H. (1980) Classrooms, schools and juvenile delinquency. *Educational Analysis,* **2**, 75–87.

Harris, R.J. and Cook, C.A. (1994) Attributions about spouse abuse: it matters who the batterers and victims are. *Sex Roles,* **30**(7/8), 553–565.

Hastie, R., Penrod, S.D., and Pennington, N. (1983) *Inside the Jury.* Cambridge: Harvard University Press.

Hastorf, A.H. and Cantril, H. (1954) They saw the game: a case study. *Journal of Abnormal and Social Psychology,* **49**, 129–134.

Hawkins, J.D., Catalano, R.F., Jones, G. and Fine, D. (1987) Delinquency prevention through parent training: results and issues from work in progress. In Wilson, J.Q. and Loury, G.C. (eds.) *From Children to Citizens: Volume Three: Families, Schools and Delinquency Prevention.* New York: Springer-Verlag.

Hazelwood, R. (1995) Analysing the rape and profiling the offender. In Hazelwood, R. and Burgess, A.W. (eds.) *Practical Aspects of Rape Investigation.* Boca Raton: CRC Press.

Hazelwood, R. and Warren, J. (1989) The serial rapist. In Hazelwood, R. and Burgess, A.W. (eds.) *Practical Aspects of Rape Investigation.* Boca Raton, CRC Press. *FBI Law Enforcement Bulletin,* 10–17.

Hazelwood, R., Dietz, P.E. and Warren, J.L. (1995) The Criminal sexual sadist. In Hazelwood, R. and Burgess, A.W. (eds.) *Practical Aspects of Rape Investigation.* Boca Raton: CRC Press.

Heal, K. and Laycock, G.K. (1986) *Situational Crime Prevention.* London: HMSO.

Heather, N. (1977) Personal illness in lifers and the effects of long-term indeterminate sentences. *British Journal of Criminology,* **17**, 378–386.

Hechler, D. (1988) *The Battle and the Backlash: the Child Sexual Abuse War.* Lexington: Lexington Books.

Hedderman, C. and Hough, M. (1994) *Does the Criminal Justice System Treat Men and Women Differently?* Research Findings No. 8. London: HMSO.

Heidensohn, F. (1968) The deviance of women: a critique and an enquiry. *British Journal of Sociology,* **19**(2), 160–175.

Heidensohn, F. (1995) Feminist perspectives and their impact on criminology and criminal justice in Britain. In Hahn Rafter, N. and Heidensohn, F. (eds.) *International Feminist Perspectives in Criminology.*

Buckingham: Open University Press

Heider, F. (1958) *The Psychology of Interpersonal Relations*. New York: John Wiley.

Heilbrun, A.B. and Seis, D. (1988) Erotic value of female distress in sexually explicit photographs. *Journal of Sex Research*, **24**, 47–57.

Henderson, J. and Taylor, J. (1985) Study finds bias in death sentences: killers of whites risk execution. *Times Union*, 17th November.

Henderson, S.K. (1939) *Psychopathic States*. New York: Norton.

Henn, F., Herjanic, M. and Vanderpearl, R. (1976) Forensic psychiatry: diagnosis and criminal responsibility. *Journal of Nervous and Mental Disease*, **162**, 423–429.

Herdt, G. (1987) *The Sambia: Ritual and Gender in New Guinea*. New York: Holt, Rinehart and Winston.

Herman, D. (1984) The rape culture. In Freeman, J. (ed.) *Women: A Feminist Perspective*. Palo Alto: Mayfield.

Herman, J. (1981) *Father-Daughter Incest*. Cambridge: Harvard University Press.

Heydon, S.(1984) *Evidence, Cases and Materials*, 2nd edn. London: Butterworths.

Hickey, E. (1986) *Serial Murderers and Their Victims*. Belmont: Wadsworth.

Hickey, E. (1991) *Serial Murderers and Their Victims*. Belmont: Wadsworth.

Hill, A. (1997) *Shocking Entertainment*. Luton: Libbey.

Himmelweit, H.J., Oppenheim, A.N. and Vince, P. (1958) *Television and the Child*. London: Oxford University Press.

Hindelang, M.J. (1979) Sex differences in criminal activity. *Social Problems*, **27**, 143–56.

Hirschi, T. (1969) *Causes of Delinquency*. Berkeley: University of California Press.

Hodge, J., McMurran, M. and Hollin, C. (eds.) (1997) *Addicted to Crime?* Chichester: John Wiley

Hoffman, M.L. (1984) Empathy, social cognition and moral action. In Kurtines, W. and Gerwitz, J. (eds.) *Moral Behaviour and Development: Advances in Theory, Research and Applications*. New York: John Wiley.

Holcomb, D.R., Holcomb, L.C., Sondag, K.A. and Williams, N. (1991) Attitudes about date rape: gender differences among college students. *College Student Journal*, **25**, 434–439.

Hollin, C.R. (1990) Social skills training with delinquents: a look at the evidence and some recommendations for practice. *British Journal of Social Work*, **20**, 483–394.

Hollin, C.R. (1992) *Criminal Behaviour*. Basingstoke: Falmer Press.

Hollin, C.R. (1995) The meaning and implications of programme integrity. In McGuire, J. (ed.) *What Works? Effective Methods to Reduce Reoffending*. Chichester: John Wiley.

Hollway, W. (1984) Gender differences and the production of subjectivity. In Henriques, J., Hollway, W., Urwin, C., Venn, C. and Walkerdine, V. (eds.) *Changing the Subject*. London: Methuen.

Holmes, R. (1989) *Profiling Violent Crimes*. Newbury Park: Sage.

Holmes, R. and DeBurger, J. (1988) *Serial Murder*. Newbury Park: Sage.

Home Office (1989) *Criminal Statistics*. London: HMSO.

Home Office (1991) *Prison Statistics, England and Wales, 1991*. London: Home Office.

Home Office (1994) *Criminal Statistics*. London: Home Office.

Home Office (1996) *Criminal Statistics*. London: HMSO.

Home Office (1997) *Convictions against Children*. London: HMSO.

Hotaling, G.T. and Sugarman, D.B. (1986) An analysis of risk markers in husband to wife violence: the current state of knowledge. *Violence and Victims*, **1**, 101–124.

Hotaling, G.T., Straus, M.A. and Lincoln, A.J. (1990) Intrafamily violence and crime and violence outside the family. In Straus, M.A. and Gelles, R.J. (eds.) *Physical Violence in American Families: Risk Factors and Adaptions to Violence in 8,145 Families*. New Brunswick: Transaction Books.

Howells, K. (1981) Adult sexual interest in children: considerations relevant to theories of aetiology. In Cook, M. and Howells, K. (eds.) *Adult Sexual Interest in Children*. London: Academic Press.

Howells, K. and Hollin, C. (1994) *Clinical Approaches to Working with the Mentally Disordered Offender*. Chichester: John Wiley.

Howitt, D. (1995) *Paedophiles and Sexual Offences Against Children*. Chichester: John Wiley.

Howitt, D. and Cumberbatch, G. (1990) *Pornography: Impacts and Influences*. London:

Home Office.

Hucker, S., Langevin, R. and Bain, J. (1988) A double blind trial of sex drive reducing medication in paedophiles. *Annals of Sex Research*, **1**, 227–242.

Hudson, M.F. (1991) Elder abuse: its meaning to middle-aged and older adults. *Journal of Elder Abuse and Neglect*, **6**(1), 55–82.

Huff, D.R. (1987) Wrongful conviction: societal tolerance of injustice. *Research in Social Problems and Public Policy*, **4**, 99–115.

Inch, H., Rowland, P. and Seliman, A. (1995) Deliberate self-mutilation in a young offender institution. *Journal of Forensic Psychiatry*, **6**(1), 161–171.

Island, D. and Letellier, P. (1991) *Men who Beat the Men who Love Them*. New York: Harrington Park.

Jackson, D. (1995) *Destroying the Baby in Themselves: Why Did the Two Boys Kill James Bulger?* Nottingham: Mushroom Publications.

Jacobs, J. (1961) *Death and Life of Great American Cities*. New York: Random House.

Jancovich, M (1994) *American Horror from 1951 to the Present*. Keele: Keele University Press.

Jarvik, L.F., Klodin, V. and Matsyama, S.S. (1973) Human aggression and the extra Y chromosome: fact or fantasy? *American Psychologist*, **28**, 674–682.

Jeffers, P.H. (1992) *Profiles in Evil*. London: Warner Books.

Jefferson, T. (1996) From 'little fairy boy' to 'the compleat destroyer': subjectivity and transformation in the biography of Mike Tyson. In Mac an Ghaill, M. (ed.) *Understanding Masculinities*. Buckingham: Open University Press.

Jenkins, P. (1988) Serial murder in England 1940–1985. *Journal of Criminal Justice*, **16**, 1–15.

Johnson, I.M. (1988) Wife abuse: factors predictive of the decision-making process of battered women. *Dissertation Abstracts International*, **48**, 3202A.

Jones, C. and Aronson, E. (1973) Attribution of fault to a rape victim as a function of respectability of the victim. *Journal of Personality and Social Psychology*, **26**, 415–419.

Jones, D.P. and Krugman, R. (1986) Can a three-year-old child bear witness to her sexual assault and attempted murder? *Child Abuse and Neglect*, **10**, 253–258.

Justice, B. and Justice, R. (1979) *The Broken Taboo: Sex in the Family*. New York: Human Sciences Press.

Kahn, A. (ed.) (1984) *Victims of Violence: Final Report of APA Task Force on the Victims of Crime and Violence*. Washington: American Psychological Association.

Kalmuss, D.S. (1984) The intergenerational transmission of marital aggression. *Journal of Marriage and the Family*, **46**, 11–19.

Kalven, J. Jr. and Zeisel, H. (1966) *The American Jury*. Boston: Little, Brown.

Kant, H.S. and Goldstein, M.J. (1973) Pornography and its effects. In Savitz, D. and Johnson, J. (eds.) *Crime in Society*. New York: John Wiley.

Kaplan, M.F. and Schersching, C. (1981) Juror deliberation: an information integration analysis. In Sales, B.D. (ed.) *The Trial Process: Perspectives in Law and Psychology*, Volume 2. London: Plenum.

Karpman, B. (1951) The sexual psychopath. *Journal of Criminal Law and Criminology*, **42**, 184–198.

Katz, B.L. (1991) The psychological impact of stranger versus nonstranger rape on victims' recovery. In Parrot, A. and Bechofer, L. (eds.) *Acquaintance Rape: the Hidden Crime*. New York: John Wiley.

Katz, B.L. and Mazur, M.A. (1979) *Understanding the Rape Victim: Synthesis of Research Findings*. New York: John Wiley.

Katz, J. (1988) *The Seductions of Crime*. New York: Basic Books.

Kempe, C.H., Silverman, F.N., Steele, B.F., Droegemueller, W. and Silver, H.K. (1962) The battered child syndrome. *Journal of the American Medical Association*, **181**, 107–112.

Kerr, N.L. (1978) Beautiful and blameless: effects of victim attractiveness and responsibility on mock jurors' verdicts. *Journal of Personality and Social Psychology*, **4**, 479–482.

Kerr, N.L. (1992) Issue importance and group decision making. In Worchel, S. Wood, W. and Simpson, J.A. (eds.) *Group Process and Productivity*. Newbury Park: Sage.

Kerr, N.L., Harmon, D.L. and Graves, J.K. (1982) Independence of multiple verdicts by jurors and juries. *Journal of Applied Psychology*, **12**, 12–29.

Kilpatrick, R. (1997) Joy-riding: an addictive behaviour. Hodge, J., McMurran, M. and Hollin, C. (eds.) *Addicted to Crime?* Chichester: John Wiley.

King, M.A. and Yuille, J. (1987)
Suggestibility and the child witness. In
Ceci, S.J., Toglia, M.P. and Ross, D.F. (eds.)
Children's Eyewitness Memory. New York:
Springer.

Kirsta, A. (1994) *Deadlier than the Male*.
London: Harper Collins.

Kline, P. (1987) Psychoanalysis and crime. In
McGurk, B.J., Thornton, D.M. and
Williams, M. (eds.) *Applying Psychology to
Imprisonment: Theory and Practice*. London:
HMSO.

Knight, A. and Prentky, R. (1987) The
developmental antecedents and adult
adaptations of rapist subtypes. *Criminal
Justice and Behavior*, **14**, 403–426.

Kohlberg, L. (1976) Moral stages and
moralisation: the cognitive-developmental
approach. In Lickona, T. (ed.) *Moral
Development and Behaviour*. New York: Holt,
Rinehart and Winston.

Koss, M. (1993) Detecting the scope of rape.
Journal of Interpersonal Violence, **8**(2),
198–222.

Koss, M., Gidycz, D.A. and Wisniewski, N.
(1987) The scope of rape: incidence and
prevalence of sexual aggression and
victimisation in a national sample of
higher education students. *Journal of
Consulting and Clinical Psychology*, **55**,
162–170.

Koss, M.P. Goodman, L.A., Browne, A. et al.
(1994) *No Safe Haven*. Washington:
American Psychological Association.

Kraemer, W. (1976) *The Forbidden Love: the
Normal and Abnormal Love of Children*. London:
Sheldon Press.

Kranz, H. (1936) *Lelenschicksale Krimineller
Zwillinge*. Berlin: Springer-Verlag.

Kutchinsky, B. (1973) The effects of easy
availability of pornography on the
incidence of sex crimes: the Danish
experience. *Journal of Social Issues*, **29**(3),
163–181.

Kutchinsky, B. (1991) Pornography and
rape: theory and practice? Evidence from
crime data in four countries where
pornography is easily available. *International
Journal of Law and Psychiatry*, **14**, 147–164.

Lahey, B.B., Conger, R.D., Atkeson, B.M. and
Treiber, F.A. (1984) Parenting behavior
and emotional status of physically abusive
mothers. *Journal of Consulting and Clinical
Psychology*, **52**, 1062–1071.

Lamar, J.V. (1984) Trail of death. *Time*, **123**,
26.

Lange, J.S. (1931) *Crime as Destiny*. London:
Allen and Unwin.

Langer, W. (1972) *The Mind of Adolf Hitler*. New
York: Basic Books.

Langhinrichsen-Rohling, J., Smutzler, N. and
Vivian, D. (1994) Positivity in marriage:
the role of discord and physical aggression
against wives. *Journal of Marriage and the
Family*, **56**, 69–79.

Larsen, R.M. (1984) Theory and
measurement of affect intensity as an
individual difference characteristic.
Dissertation Abstracts International, **5**, 2297B
(University Microfilms No. 84–22112).

Latané, B., Williams, K. and Hawkins, S.
(1979) Many hands make light work: the
causes and consequences of social loafing.
Journal of Personality and Social Psychology, **37**,
822–832.

Lavrakas, P.J. (1982) Fear of crime and
behavioural restrictions in urban and
suburban neighbourhoods. *Population and
Environment*, **5**, 242–264.

Laws, D.R. (1985) Sexual fantasy alternation:
procedural considerations. *Journal of
Behaviour Therapy and Experimental Psychiatry*,
16(1), 39–44.

Laws, D.R. and Marshall, W.L. (1990) A
conditioning theory of the etiology and
maintenance of deviant sexual preferences
and behavior. In Marshall, W.L, Laws, D.R.
and Barbaree, H.E. (eds.) *Handbook of Sexual
Assault: Issues, Theories and Treatment of the
Offender*. New York: Plenum.

Lawson, W.K. (1984) Depression and crime:
a discursive approach. In Craft, M. and
Craft, A. (eds.) *Mentally Abnormal Offenders*.
London: Baillière Tindall.

Layman, C.A. and Labott, S.M. (1992)
*Attitudes toward rape victims: the roles of affect and
gender*. Paper presented at the August
annual meeting of the American
Psychological Association, Washington.

Lefkowitz, M.M, Eron, L.D, Walder, L.O. and
Huesmann, L.R. (1977) *Growing Up to Be
Violent: a Longitudinal Study of the Development of
Aggression*. New York: Pergamon Press.

Leippe, M.R, Brigham, J.C., Cousins, C. and
Romanczyk, A. (1989) The opinions and
practices of criminal attorneys regarding
child eyewitnesses: a survey. In Ceci, S.J.,
Ross, D.F. and Toglia, M.P. (eds.) *Perspectives*

on *Children's Testimony*. New York: Springer-Verlag.

Leippe, M.R., Manion, A.P. and Romanczyk, A. (1992) Eyewitness persuasion: how and how well do fact finders judge the accuracy of adults' and children's memory reports? *Journal of Personality and Social Psychology*, **63**, 181–197.

Leonard, K.E. and Jacob, T. (1988) Alcohol, alcoholism and family violence. In van Hassait, V.B., Morrison, A.L., Bellack, A.S. and Herson, M. (eds.) *Handbook of Family Violence*. New York: Plenum.

Lerner, M.J. and Simmons, C.H. (1966) Observers' reaction to the innocent victim: compassion or rejection. *Journal of Personality and Social Psychology*, **4**, 203–210.

Levin, J. and Fox, J.A. (1985) *Mass Murder*. New York: Plenum.

Leyens, J.P., Camino, L, Parke, R.D. and Berkowitz, L. (1975) Effects of movie violence on aggression in a field setting as a function of group dynamics and cohesiveness. *Journal of Personality and Social Psychology*, **32**, 346–360.

Liebert, J.A. (1985) Contributions of psychiatric consultation in the investigation of serial murder. *International Journal of Offender Therapy and Cooperative Criminology*, **29**(3), 187–200.

Linz, D., Donnerstein, E. and Penrod, S. (1987) The findings and recommendations of the Attorney General's Commission on Pornography: do the psychological facts fit the political fury? *American Psychologist*, **42**, 946–953.

Linz, D., Donnerstein, E. and Penrod, S. (1988) The effects of long-term exposure to violent and sexually degrading depictions of women. *Journal of Personality and Social Psychology*, **55**, 758–768.

Linz, D., Arluk, I. and Donnerstein, E. (1990) Mitigating the influence of violence on television and sexual violence in the media. In Blanchard, R. (ed.) *Advances in the Study of Aggression* (Vol.2). New York: Academic Press.

Lipsey, M. (1992) Juvenile delinquency treatment: a meta-analytic inquiry into the variability of effects. In Cook, T.D., Cooper, H. Cordray, D.S. et al. (eds.) *Meta-Analysis for Explanation*. New York: Academic Press.

List, J. (1986) Age and schematic differences in the reliability of eyewitness testimony. *Development Psychology*, **22**, 50–57.

Loftus, E.F. (1974) Reconstructive memory: the incredible eyewitness. *Psychology Today*, **8**, 116–119.

Loftus, E.F. (1979) *Eyewitness Testimony*. Cambridge: Harvard University Press.

Loftus, E.F. and Davies, G. (1984) Distortions in the memory of children. *Journal of Social Issues*, **40**, 51–67.

Loftus, E.F. 7 Palmer, J.C. (1974) Reconstruction of automobile destruction: an example of the interaction between language and memory. *Journal of Verbal Learning and Verbal Behaviour*, **13**, 585–589.

Loftus, E.F. and Zanni, G. (1975) Eyewitness testimony: the influence of the wording of a question. *Bulletin of the Psychonomic Society*, **5**, 86–88.

Loftus, E.F., Loftus, G.R. and Messo, J. (1987) Some facts about 'weapon focus'. *Law and Human Behaviour*, **11**, 55–62.

Loftus, E.F., Polonsky, S. and Fullilove, M. (1994) Memories of childhood sexual abuse: remembering and repressing. *Psychology of Women Quarterly*, **18**, 67–84.

Loh, W.D. (1981) Psycholegal research: past and present. *Michigan Law Review*, **79**, 659–707.

Lombroso, C. (1911) *Crime: its causes and remedies*. Boston: Little Brown.

Lombroso, C. and Ferrero, W. (1895) *The Female Offender*. London: Fisher Unwin.

Lucal, B. (1994) The Problem with 'Battered Husbands'. *Deviant Behaviour: an Interdisciplinary Journal*, **16**, 95–112.

Luckenbill, D.F. (1977) Criminal homicide as a situated transaction. *Social Problems*, **25**, 176–86.

Lundberg-Love, P. and Geffner, R. (1989) Date rape: prevalence, risk factors and a proposed model. In Pirog-Good, M.A. and Stets, J.E. (eds.) *Violence in Dating Relationships: emerging social issues*. Westport, CA: Praeger Publications.

Lyons, M.J. (1996) A twin study of self-reported criminal behaviour. In *Genetics of Criminal and Antisocial Behaviour*, Ciba Foundation Symposium 194. Chichester: John Wiley.

Maass, A. and Kohnken, G. (1989) Eyewitness identification: simulating the 'weapon effect'. *Law and Human Behaviour*, **13**, 397–409.

Mackinnon, C. (1987) *Feminism Unmodified: discourses on life and law.* Cambridge: Harvard University Press.

Mackinnon, D.P., O'Reilly, K. and Geiselman, R.E. (1990) Improving eyewitness recall for license plates. *Applied Cognitive Psychology,* **4**, 129–140.

MacLeod, M. and Saraga, E. (1988) Challenging the orthodoxy: towards a feminist theory and practice. *Feminist Review,* **28**, 17–55.

Maguire, J. and Priestley (1985) *Offending Behaviour: Skills and Strategems for Going Straight.* London: BT Batsford Ltd.

Malamuth, N. (1981) Rape proclivity among males. *Journal of Social Issues,* **37**(4), 138–157.

Malamuth, N. (1984) Aggression against women: cultural and individual causes. In Malamuth, N. and Donnerstein, E. (eds.) *Pornography and Sexual Aggression.* Orlando: Academic Press.

Malamuth, N. (1986) Predictors of naturalistic sexual aggression. *Journal of Personality and Social Psychology,* **50**, 953–962.

Malamuth, N. and Check, J. (1980) Penile tumescence and perceptual responses to rape as a function of victim's perceived reaction. *Journal of Applied Social Psychology,* **10**, 528–547.

Malamuth, N. and Check, J. (1983) Sexual arousal to rape depictions: individual differences. *Journal of Abnormal Psychology,* **92**, 55–67.

Malamuth, N. and Donnerstein, E. (1982) The effects of aggressive-pornographic mass media stimuli. In Berkowitz, L. (ed.) *Advances in Experimental Social Psychology 15.* New York: Academic Press.

Malamuth, N. and Donnerstein, E. (eds.) (1984) *Pornography and Sexual Aggression.* Orlando: Academic Press.

Mannarino, A.P., Cohen, J.A., Smith, J.A. and Moore-Motily, S. (1992) Six and twelve month follow-up of sexually abused girls. *Journal of Interpersonal Violence,* **6**, 494–511.

Mark, V.H. and Ervin, F.R. (1970) *Violence and the Brain.* New York: Harper and Row.

Marshall, P. (1997) *Convicted Sex Offenders in England and Wales.* London: Home Office.

Marshall, W. and Barbaree, H. (1990) An integrated theory of the etiology of sexual offending. In Marshall, W., Laws, D. and Barbaree, H. (eds.) *Handbook of Sexual Assault.*

London: Plenum Press.

Marshall, W., Ward, T., Jones, R., Johnston, P. and Barbaree, H.E. (1991) An optimistic evaluation of treatment outcome with sex offenders. *Violence Update,* **March**, 1–8.

Martinson, R. (1974) What works? Questions and answers about prison reform. *The Public Interest,* **35**, 22–54.

Masson, J. M. (1984) Freud and the seduction theory. *Atlantic Monthly,* **February**, 33–60.

Masters, F. and Greaves, D. (1969) The Quasimodo complex. *British Journal of Plastic Surgery,* **20**, 204–210.

Matravers, A. (1997) Women and the sexual abuse of children. *Forensic Update,* **51**, 9–13 (Division of Criminological and Legal Psychology, British Psychological Society).

Matthews, R., Matthews, J. and Speltz, K. (1990) Female sexual offenders. In Hunger, M. (ed.) *The Sexually Abused Male: Prevalence, Impact and Treatment,* Vol. 1. Lexington: Lexington Books.

Mawby, R.I. (1977) Defensible space: a theoretical and empirical appraisal. *Urban Studies,* **14**, 169–179.

Mayhew, P.M., Clarke, R.V. and Hough, J.M. (1976) Steering column locks and car theft. In Mayhew, P.M., Clarke, R.V., Sturman, A. and Hough, J.M. (eds.) *Crime as Opportunity.* Home Office Research Study no. 34. London: HMSO.

Mayhew, P.M.,Clarke, R.V. and Hough,J.M. (1980) Steering column locks and car theft. In Clarke, R.V. and Mayhew, P. (eds.) *Designing Out Crime.* London: HMSO.

Mayhew, P.M., Clarke, R.V. and Elliot, D. (1989a) Motorcycle theft, helmet legislation and displacement. *Howard Journal,* **28**, 1–8.

Mayhew, P.M., Elliott, D. and Dowds, L. (1989b) *The 1988 British Crime Survey.* London: HMSO.

McCammon, S., Knox, D. and Schacht, C. (1993) *Choices in Sexuality.* Minneapolis/St Paul: West.

McCauley, M.R. and Fisher, R.P. (1992) *Enhancing children's eyewitness recollection with the cognitive interview.* Paper presented at the American Psychology-Law Society, San Diego.

McCord, J. (1978) A thirty-year follow-up of treatment effects. *American Psychologist,* **33**, 283–289.

McCord, J. (1979) Some childrearing antecedents of criminal behavior in adult men. *Journal of Personality and Social Psychology*, **37**, 1477–1486.

McCord, J. (1995) Drop in NY crime baffles experts. *The Guardian*, 2nd January.

McCurdy, K. and Daro, D. (1994) Child maltreatment: a national survey of reports and fatalities. *Journal of Interpersonal Violence*, **9**, 75–94.

McDonald, J.R. (1963) The threat to kill. *American Journal of Psychiatry*, **120**, 125–130.

McMullen, R.J. (1990) *Male Rape*. London: GMP Publishers.

Meadow, R. (1977) Munchausen syndrome by proxy: the hinterland of child abuse. *Lancet*, **2,** 343–345.

Meadow, R. (1990) Suffocation, recurrent apnoea, and sudden infant death. *Journal of Pediatrics*, **117**, 351–356.

Mednick, S.A., Gabrielli, W.F. and Hutchings, B. (1987) Genetic factors in the etiology of criminal behaviour. In Mednick, S.A., Moffit, T.E. and Stack, S.S. (eds.) *The Causes of Crime*. Cambridge: Cambridge University Press.

Meloy, J.R. (1988) *The Psychopathic Mind: Origins, Dynamics and Treatment*. Northvale: Jason Aronson.

Messerschmidt, J.W. (1993) *Masculinities and Crime*. Lanham: Rowman and Littlefield.

Mezey, G. and King, M. (1989) The effect of sexual assault on men: a survey of 22 victims. *Psychological Medicine*, **19**, 205–209.

Milavsky, J.R., Kessler, R.C., Stipp, H. and Rubens, W.S. (1982) *Television and Aggression: a Panel Study*. New York: Academic Press.

Moir, A. and Jessell, D. (1995) *A Mind to Crime*. London: Harper Collins.

Mooney, J. (1993) *The North London Domestic Violence Survey*. Middlesex University, Centre for Criminology.

Morgan, M. (1986) Conflict and confusion: what rape prevention reports are telling women. *Sexual Coercion and Assault*, **1**, 160–168.

Morgan, R. (1972) *Sisterhood is Powerful*. New York: Academic Press.

Mosher, D.L. (1970) Sex callousness towards women. In *Technical Reports of the Presidential Commission on Obscenity and Pornography* (Vol. 7). Washington: Government Printing Office.

Mosher, D.L. and Anderson, R.C. (1986) Macho personality, sexual aggression and reactions to guided imagery of realistic rape. *Journal of Research on Personality*, **20**, 77–94.

Mosher, D.L. and Sirkin, M. (1984) Measuring a macho personality constellation. *Journal of Research on Personality*, **20**, 77–94.

Moyer, K. (1976) *The Psychobiology of Aggression*. New York: Harper and Row.

Muehlenhard, C. (1987) Date rape: the familiar perpetrator. In Crooks, R. and Baur, K. (eds.) *Our Sexuality*. Menlo Park: Benjamin/Cummings.

Muehlenhard, D.L., Friedman, D.E. and Thomas, C.M. (1985) Is date rape justifiable? The effects of dating activity, who initiated, who paid, and men's attitudes towards women. *Psychology of Women Quarterly*, **9**, 297–310.

Münsterberg, H. (1908) *On the Witness Stand*. New York: Clark Boardman.

Murray, C. (1995) Reducing crime and the fear of crime: the physical environment. In Wilson, J.Q. and Petersilia, J. (eds.) *Crime*. San Francisco: ICS Press.

Myers, M.F. (1989) Men sexually assaulted as adults and sexually abused as boys. *Archives of Sexual Behaviour*, **18**, 203–215.

NACRO (1997) *The Tottenham Experiment*. London: NACRO.

National Association of Probation Officers (1997) *Women and Crime*. London: NAPO.

Naylor, B. (1989) Dealing with child sexual assault. *British Journal of Criminology*, **29**(4), 395–405.

Nellis, M. (1991) The electronic monitoring of offenders in England and Wales. *British Journal of Criminology*, **31**, 165–185.

Nemeth, C.J., Endicott, J. and Wachtler J. (1976) From the 50s to the 70s: women in jury deliberations. *Sociometry*, **39**, 38–56.

Newburn, T. and Stanko, E. (eds.) (1994) *Just Boys Doing Business: Men, Masculinities and Crime*. London: Routledge.

Newman, O. (1972) *Defensible Space*. New York: Macmillan.

Newson, E. (1994) Video violence and the protection of children. *Journal of Mental Health*, **3**, 221–226.

Nickerson, R.S. and Adams, M.J. (1982) Long-term memory for a common object. In Neisser, U. (ed.) *Memory Observed:*

Remembering in Natural Contexts. San Francisco: W.H. Freeman.

Noon, E. and Davies, G . (1993) Child witnesses and the 'live link'. *Expert Evidence,* **2**, 11–12.

Novaco, R.W. (1975) *Anger Control: the Development and Evaluation of an Experimental Treatment.* Lexington: D.C. Heath.

Novaco, R.W. and Welsh, W.M. (1989) Anger disturbances: cognitive mediation and clinical prescriptions. In Howells, K. and Hollin, C.R. (eds.) *Clinical Approaches to Violence.* Chichester: John Wiley.

Oakley, A. (1972) *Sex, Gender and Society.* London: Temple Smith.

Offord, D.R. (1982) Family backgrounds of male and female delinquents. In Gunn, J. and Farrington, D.P. (eds.) *Abnormal Offenders, Delinquency, and the Criminal Justice System,* 1. Chichester: John Wiley.

Oleson, J.C. (1996) Psychological profiling: does it actually work? *Forensic Update,* **46**, 11–14 (Division of Criminological and Legal Psychology, British Psychological Society).

Osborn, S.G. and West, D.J. (1979) Conviction records of fathers and sons compared. *British Journal of Criminology,* **19**, 120–133.

Overholser, J.C. and Moll, S.H. (1990) Who's to blame: attributions regarding causality in spouse abuse. Behaviour Sciences and the Law, 8, 107–120.

Pahl, J. (1978) *A Refuge for Battered Women: a Study of the Role of a Women's Centre.* London: HMSO.

Paik, H. and Comstock, G. (1994) The effects of television violence on antisocial behaviour: a meta-analysis. *Communication Research,* **21**(4), 516–546.

Painter, K. (1991) *Marriage, Wife Rape and the Law.* University of Manchester, Department of Social Policy.

Palmer, T. (1975) Martinson revisited. *Journal of Research in Crime and Delinquency,* **12**, 133–152.

Parrot, A. (1991) Institutional response: how can acquaintance rape be prevented? In Parrot, A. and Bechofer, L. (eds.) *Acquaintance Rape: the Hidden Crime.* New York: John Wiley.

Patterson, G.R. (1982) Coercive Family Process. Eugene: Castalia.

Pease, K. (1994) Crime prevention. In

Maguire, M., Morgan, R. and Reiner, R. (eds.) *Oxford Handbook of Criminology.* Oxford: Oxford University Press.

Peltoniemi, T. (1982) Current research on family violence in Finland and Sweden. *Victimology,* **7**, 252–255.

Perkins, D. (1990) Clinical treatment of sex offenders in secure settings. In Hollin, C.R. and Howells, K. (eds.) *Clinical Approaches to Sex Offenders and their Victims.* Chichester: John Wiley.

Perkins, D.E. (1987) A psychological treatment programme for sex offenders. In McGurk, B.J., Thornton, D.M. and Williams, M. (eds.) *Applying Psychology to Imprisonment: Theory and Practice.* London: H.M.S.O.

Peters, D. (1987) The impact of naturally occurring stress on children's memory. In Ceci, S.J., Toglia, M.P. and Ross, D.F. (eds.) *Children's Eyewitness Memory.* New York: Springer-Verlag.

Pfeifer, J.E. and Ogloff, J.R. (1991) Ambiguity and guilt determinations: a modern racism perspective. Journal of *Applied Social Psychology,* **21**(21), 1713–1725.

Phillips, D.P. (1983) The impact of mass media on homicide. *American Sociological Review,* **48**, 560–568.

Pierce, M.C. and Harris, R.J. (1993) The effect of provocation, race, and injury description on men's and women's perception of a wife-battering incident. *Journal of Applied Social Psychology,* **23**, 767–790.

Pillemer, K.A. and Finkelhor, D. (1988) The prevalence of elder abuse: a random sample survey. *Gerontologist,* **28**, 51–57.

Pinizzotto, A.J. and Finkel, N.J. (1990) Criminal personality profiling: an outcome and process study. *Law and Human Behaviour,* **14**(3), 215–233.

Pithers, W.D. (1993) Treatment of rapists: interpretation of early outcome data and exploratory constructs to enhance therapeutic efficacy. In Nagayama Hall, G.C., Hirschman, R., Graham, J.R. and Zaragoza, M.S. (eds.) *Sexual Aggression: Issues in Etiology, Assessment and Treatment.* Washington: Taylor and Francis.

Pleck, E. (1987) *Domestic Tyranny: the Making American Sound Policy against Family Violence from Colonial Times to Present.* New York: Oxford

University Press.

Plomin, R. (1990) *Nature and Nurture*. Pacific Grove: Brooks/Cole.

Plomin, R. (1994) *Genetics and Experience: the Developmental Interplay between Nature and Nurture*. Newbury Park: Sage.

Pollak, O. (1950) *The Criminality of Women*. New York: A.S. Barnes.

Pollard, C. (1997) *Zero Tolerance: Policing a Free Society*. London: Institute of Economic Affairs.

Poole, D. (1992) *Eliciting information from children with non-suggestive visual and auditory feedback*. Paper presented at the NATO Advanced Studies Institute on 'The Child Witness in Context', Italy.

Portwood, M. (1996) *Developmental Dyspraxia – a Practical Manual for Parents and Professionals*. Durham: Durham County Council.

Poyner, B. (1991) *What works in crime prevention: an overview of evaluation*. Paper presented at the British Criminology Conference, University of York.

Prentky, R. (1995) A rationale for the treatment of sex offenders: pro bono publico. In McGuire, J. (ed.) *What Works: Reducing Reoffending*. Chichester: John Wiley.

Prentky, R., Burgess, A.W., Rokous, F. et al. (1989) The presumptive role of fantasy in serial sexual homicide. *American Journal of Psychiatry*, **146**, 887–891.

Price, W.H., Strong, J.A., Whatmore, P.B. and McClemont, W.F. (1966) Criminal patients with XYY sex-chromosome complement. *Lancet*, **1**, 565–566.

Prins, H. (1986) *Dangerous Behaviour, the Law and Mental Disorder*. London: Tavistock.

Prins, H. (1991) Some aspects of sex offending: causes or cures. *Medicine, Science and Law*, **31**(4), 329–333.

Prins, H. (1994) *Offenders, Deviants or Patients?* London: Routledge.

Provenzo, E.F. (1991) *Video Kids – Making Sense of Nintendo*. Harvard: Harvard University Press.

Raine, A. (1989) Evoked potentials and psychopathy. *International Journal of Psychophysiology*, **4**, 277–287.

Ramsey-Klawsnik, H. (1991) Elder sexual abuse: preliminary findings. *Journal of Elder Abuse and Neglect*, **3**(3) 73–90.

Recovered Memories Report (1995) Leicester: British Psychological Society.

Reiner, R. (1993) Race, crime and justice: models of interpretation. In Gelsthorpe, L. and McWilliam, W. (eds.) *Minority Ethnic Groups and the Criminal Justice System*. Cambridge: Cambridge University Institute of Criminology.

Renzetti, C. (1992) *Violent Betrayal: Partner Abuse in Lesbian Relationships*. Newbury Park: Sage

Resick, P.A. (1993) The psychological impact of rape. *Journal of Interpersonal Violence*, **June**, 223–253.

Resick, P.A. and Markaway, B.E.G. (1991) Clinical treatment of adult female victims of sexual assault. In Hollin, C.R. and Howells, K. (eds.) *Clinical Approaches to Sex Offenders and their Victims*. Chichester: John Wiley.

Ressler, R.K., Burgess, A.W. and Douglas, J. (1988) *Sexual Homicide: Patterns and Motives*. Lexington: Lexington Books.

Ridley-Johnson, J., Surdy, T. and O'Laughlin, E. (1991) Parent survey on TV violence viewing: fear, aggression and sex differences. *Journal of Applied Developmental Psychology*, **12**, 63–71.

Risin, L.I. and Koss, M.P. (1987) The sexual abuse of boys: prevalence and descriptive characteristics of childhood victimisations. *Journal of Interpersonal Violence*, **2**, 309–323.

Rodgerson, G. and Wilson, E. (1991) *Pornography and Feminism: the Case Against Censorship*. London: Lawrence and Wishart.

Roesler, T.A. and McKenzie, N. (1994) Effects of childhood trauma on psychological functioning in adults sexually abused as children. *Journal of Nervous and Mental Disease*, **182**, 145–150.

Roiphe, K. (1993) *The Morning After: Sex, Fear and Feminism*. London: Hamish Hamilton.

Roper, R.T. (1980) Jury size and verdict consistency: "a line has to be drawn somewhere?" *Law and Society Review*, **14**, 977–999.

Rose, S., Kamin, L.J. and Lewantin, R.C. (1984) *Not in Our Genes: Biology, Ideology and Human Nature*. Harmondsworth: Penguin.

Rosenbaum, A. and O'Leary, K.D. (1981) Marital violence; characteristics of abusive couples. *Journal of Consulting and Clinical Psychology*, **49**, 63–76.

Ross, R.R. and Fabiano, E.A. (1985) *Time to Think: a Cognitive Model of Delinquency Prevention and Offender Rehabilitation*. Johnson City: Institute of Social Sciences and Arts.

Ross, R.R. and Fabiano, E.A. and Ewles, C.D.

(1988) Reasoning and rehabilitation. *International Journal of Offender Therapy and Comparative Criminology*, **20**, 29–35.

Rowe, D.C. (1990) Inherited dispositions towards learning delinquent and criminal behavior: new evidence. In Ellis, L. and Hoffman, H. (eds.) *Crime in Biological, Social and Moral Contexts*. New York: Praeger.

Rowe, D.C. and Osgood, D.W. (1984) Heredity and sociological theories of delinquency: a reconsideration. *American Sociological Review*, **49**, 526–540.

Rubenstein, H., Murray, C., Motoyama, T., Rouse, W.V. and Titus, R.M. (1980) *The Link between Crime and the Built Environment: the Current State of Knowledge*. Washington: National Institute of Justice.

Rushton, J.P. (1990) Race and crime: a reply to Roberts and Gabor. *Canadian Journal of Criminology*, **32**, 315–334.

Russell, D.E.H. (1984) *Sexual Exploitation*. Beverly Hills: Sage.

Russell, D.E.H. (1988) Pornography and rape: a causal model. *Political Psychology*, **9**, 41–73.

Russell, D.E.H. (1990) *Rape in Marriage*. Bloomington: Indiana University Press.

Russell, D.E.H. (ed.) (1993) *Making Violence Sexy: Feminist Views on Pornography*. Buckingham: Open University Press.

Rutter, M. (1971a) *Maternal Deprivation Re-assessed*. Harmondsworth: Penguin.

Rutter, M. (1971b) Parent-child separation: psychological effects on the children. *Journal of Child Psychology and Psychiatry*, **12**, 233–260.

Ryan, G. (1987) Juvenile sex offenders: development and correction. *Child Abuse and Neglect*, **11**, 385–395.

Saks, H. (1977) The limits of scientific jury selection: ethical and empirical. *Jurimetrics Journal*, **17**, 3–22.

Sanday, P.R. (1981) The sociocultural context of rape: a crosscultural study. *Journal of Social Issues*, **37**(4), 5–27.

Sanday, P.R. (1990) *Fraternity Gang Rape: Sex, Brotherhood and Privilege on Campus*. New York: New York University Press.

Saunders, D.G. (1988) Wife abuse, husband abuse, or mutual combat? In Yllö, K. and Bograd, M. (eds.), *Feminist Perspectives on Wife Abuse*. Newbury Park: Sage.

Schramm, W., Lyle, J. and Parker, E.B. (1961) *Television in the Lives of Our Children*. Stanford:

Stanford University Press.

Schreiber, F.R. (1973) *Sybil*. Harmondsworth: Penguin.

Schweinhart, L.J. and Weikart, D.P. (1997) *Lasting Differences*. Ypsilanti, Michigan: High/Scope Press.

Scully, D, (1990) *Understanding Sexual Violence: a Sudy of Convicted Rapists*. Boston: Unwin Hyman.

Scully, D. and Marolla, J. (1985) Riding the bull at Gilley's: convicted rapists describe the rewards of rape. *Social Problems*, **32**, 251–263.

Sedlak, A.J. (1991) *National Incidence and Prevalence of Child Abuse and Neglect: 1988*. Rockville: Westat.

Segal, L. (1993) Does pornography cause violence? The search for evidence. In Gibson, P.C. and Gibson, R. (eds.) *Dirty Looks*. London: BFI Publishing

Seligman, M.E.P. (1975) *Helplessness*. San Francisco: W.H. Freeman.

Sellin, T. (1938) *Culture, Conflict and Crime*. New York: Social Science Research Council.

Selnow, G.W. (1984) Playing videogames. *Journal of Communication*, **34**, 144–150.

Seto, M.C., Khattar, N.A., Lalumiere, M.L. and Quinsey, V.L. (1997) Deception and sexual strategy in psychopathy. *Personality and Individual Differences*, **22**, 301–307.

Shechter, M. and Roberge, L. (1976) Child sexual abuse. In Helter, R. and Kempe, C. (eds.) *Child Abuse and Neglect: the Family and the Community*. Cambridge: Ballinger.

Sheldon, W.H. (1942) *The Varieties of Temperament: a Psychology of Constitutional Differences*. New York: Harper.

Sherif, M. (1936) *The Psychology of Social Norms*. New York: Harper.

Sherman, R. (1991) For battered women: acceptance of defense is up. *National Law Journal*, **13**, 4.

Shoda, Y., Mischel, W. and Peake, P.K. (1990) Predicting adolescent cognitive and self-regulatory competencies from preschool delay of gratification. *Developmental Psychology*, **26**(6), 978–986.

Siann, G. (1994) *Gender, Sex and Sexuality*. Basingstoke: Taylor and Francis.

Sigall, H. and Ostrove, N. (1975) Beautiful but dangerous: effects of offender attractiveness and nature of crime on juridic judgement. *Journal of Personality and*

Social Psychology, **31**, 401–414.

Singer, J.L. and Singer, D.G. (1981) *Television, Imagination and Aggression: a Study of Preschoolers.* Hillsdale: Erlbaum.

Skogan, W.G. (1990) *Disorder and Decline: Crime and the Spiral of Decay in American Neighborhoods.* New York: Free Press.

Smart, C. (1977) *Women, Crime and Criminology.* London: Routledge.

Smart, C. (1990) Feminist approaches to criminology or postmodern woman meets atavistic man. In Gelsthorpe, L. and Morris, A. (eds.) *Feminist Perspectives in Criminology.* Buckingham: Open University Press.

Smeal, E. (1991) Violence and women. *USA Today*, 15th April, 13.

Smith, D.J. (1995) *The Sleep of Reason: the James Bulger Case.* London: Arrow.

Smith, J. (1989) *Misogynies.* London: Faber and Faber.

Smith, M. and Bentovim, A. (1994) *Sexual abuse.* In Rutter, M. and Hersov, I. (eds.) *Child and Adolescent Psychiatry: Modern Approaches,* 3rd edn. Cambridge: Blackwell Science.

Smith, M.D. (1990) Patriarchal ideology and wife beating: a test of a feminist hypothesis. *Violence and Victims*, **5**, 257–273.

Socarides, C.W. (1988) Adult–child sexual pairs – psychoanalytic findings. *Journal of Psychohistory*, **19**(2), 185–189.

Spence, S. and Marzillier, J.S. (1981) Social skills training with adolescent male offenders. *Behavioural Research and Therapy*, **19**, 349–368.

Spivack, G., Platt, H. and Shure, M. (1976) *The Problem-Solving Approach to Adjustment.* San Francisco: Jossey-Bass

Stanko, E.A. and Hobdell, K. (1993) Assault on men: masculinity and male victimisation. *British Journal of Criminology*, **33**(3), 400–415.

Steller, M. and Koenken, G. (1989) Criteria-based statement analysis. In Raskin, D.C. (ed.) *Psychological Methods in Criminal Investigation and Evidence.* New York: Springer-Verlag.

Stephenson, G.M. (1992) *The Psychology of Criminal Justice.* Oxford: Blackwell Publishers.

Stets, J.E. (1990) Verbal and physical aggression in marriage. *Journal of Marriage and the Family*, **52**, 501–514,

Stewart, J.E. (1980) Defendant's attractiveness as a factor in the outcome of criminal trials: an observational study. *Journal of Applied Social Psychology*, **10**, 348–361.

Stone, M.H. (1994) Early traumatic factors in the lives of serial murderers. *American Journal of Forensic Psychiatry*, **15**, 5–26.

Stoner, J.A.F. (1968) Risky and cautious shifts in group decisions: the influence of widely held values. *Journal of Experimental Social Psychology*, **4**, 442–459.

Straus, M.A. (1980) Victims and aggressors in marital violence. *American Behavioral Scientist*, **23**, 681–704.

Straus, M.A. (1994) *Beating the Devil Out of Them: Corporal Punishment in American Families.* New York: Lexington Books.

Straus, M.A. and Gelles, R.J. (1990) *Physical Violence in American Families: Risk Factors and Adaptations to Violence in 8145 Families.* New Brunswick: Transaction.

Straus, M.A., Gelles, R.J. and Steinmetz, S.K. (1980) *Behind Closed Doors: Violence in American Families.* New York: Doubleday.

Strodtbeck, F.L. and Lipinski, R.M. (1985) Becoming first among equals: moral considerations in jury foreman selection. *Journal of Personality and Social Psychology*, **49**, 927–936.

Struckman, C. and Johnson, D. (1992) Acceptance of male rape myths among college men and women. *Sex Roles*, **27**(3–4), 85–100.

Sutherland, E.H. (1939) *Principles of Criminology.* Philadelphia: Lippincott.

Taylor, P.J. (1986) Psychiatric disorder in London's life-sentenced offenders. *British Journal of Criminology*, **26**, 63–78.

Taylor, S.E., Peplau, L.A. and Sears, D.O. (1994) *Social Psychology*, 8th edn. Englewood Cliffs: Prentice-Hall.

Temkin, J. (1995) *Rape and the Legal Process.* London: Sweet and Maxwell.

Thornhill, R. and Thornhill, N. (1983) Human rape: an evolutionary analysis. *Ethology and Sociobiology*, **4**, 137–173.

Thornton, G. (1939) The ability to judge crimes from photographs of criminals. *Journal of Abnormal and Social Psychology*, **34**, 378–383.

Toles, T. (1985) Video games and american military ideology. In Mosco, A. and Wasco, R. (eds.) *Critical Communications Review, vol. III: Popular Culture and Media Events.*

Norwood: Ablex Press.

Towl, G.J. and Crighton, D.A. (1996) *Handbook of Psychology for Forensic Practitioners.* London: Sage.

Trasler, G.B. (1978) Relations between psychopathy and persistent criminality. In Hare, R.D. and Schalling, D. (eds.) *Psychopathic Behavior: Approaches to Research.* New York: John Wiley.

Trasler, G.B. (1987) Biogenetic factors. In Quay, H.C. (ed.) *Handbook of Juvenile Delinquency.* New York: John Wiley.

Tudor, E. (1989) *Monsters and Mad Scientists.* Oxford: Blackwell.

Turco, R. (1993) Psychological profiling. *International Journal of Offender Therapy and Comparative Criminology,* **34**(2), 147–154.

Urquiza, A.J. (1988) *The effects of childhood sexual abuse in an adult male population.* Unpublished doctoral dissertation, University of Washington, Seattle.

Ussher, J.M. and Dewberry, C. (1995) The nature and long-term effects of childhood sexual abuse: a survey of adult women survivors in Britain. *British Journal of Clinical Psychology,* **34**, 177–192.

Vance, C. (ed.) (1984) *Pleasure and Danger: Exploring Female Sexuality.* Boston: RKP

Virkkunen, M. (1986) Reactive hypoglycemic tendency among habitually violent offenders. *Nutrition Reviews Supplement,* **44**, 94–103.

Virkkunen, M., Goldman, D. and Linnoila, M. (1996) Serotonin in alcoholic violent offenders. In *Genetics of Criminal and Antisocial Behaviour,* Ciba Foundation Symposium 194. Chichester: John Wiley.

Walker, L.E. (1984) *The Battered Woman Syndrome.* New York: Springer-Verlag.

Walklate, S. (1995) *Gender and Crime: An Introduction.* Hemel Hempstead: Prentice-Hall.

Walters, G.D. (1992) A meta-analysis of the gene–crime relationship. *Criminology,* **30**, 595–613.

Wansell, G. (1996) *An Evil Love: the Life of Frederick West.* London: Hodder Headline.

Warren, A.R., Hulse-Trotter, K. and Tubbs, E. (1991) Inducing resistance to suggestibility in children. *Law and Human Behaviour,* **15**, 273–285.

Wattam, C. (1992) *Making a Case in Child Protection.* London: Longman.

Wedge, B. (1968) Khrushchev at a distance –
a study of public personality. *Transaction,* **October**, 24–28.

Weise, D. and Daro, D. (1995) *Current Trends in Child Abuse Reporting and Fatalities: the Results of the 1994 Annual Fifty State Survey.* Chicago: National Committee to Prevent Child Abuse.

Wells, J. (1995) *Crime and Unemployment.* London: Employment Policy Institute.

Wertham, F. (1968) School for violence. In Larsen, O. (ed.) *Violence and the Mass Media.* New York: Harper and Row.

West, D. (1985) *Sexual Victimisation.* New York: Gower.

Westcott, H.L. (1992) The cognitive interview – a useful tool for social workers? *British Journal of Social Work,* **22**, 519–533.

Wilbanks, W. (1987) *The Myth of a Racist Criminal Justice System.* Monterey: Brooks/Cole.

Wild, N.J. (1986) Sexual abuse of children in Leeds. *British Medical Journal,* **292**, 1113–1116.

Williams, L. (1993) Second thoughts on hard core: American obscenity law and the scapegoating of deviance. In Gibson, P.C. and Gibson, R. (eds.) *Dirty Looks.* London: BFI Publishing

Williams, L.M. and Finkelhor, D. (1990) The characteristics of incestuous fathers: a review of recent studies. In Marshall, W.L., Laws, D.R. and Barbaree, H.E. (eds.) *Handbook of Sexual Assault: Issues, Theories and Treatment of the Offender.* New York: Plenum.

Williams, T.M. (1986) *The Impact of Television: a National Experiment in Three Communities.* New York: Academic Press.

Wilson, C. and Seaman, D. (1990) *The Serial Killers.* London: W.H. Allen.

Wilson, J.Q. and Herrnstein, R.J. (1985) *Crime and Human Nature.* New York: Touchstone.

Wilson, J.Q. and Kelling, G. (1982) Broken windows. *The Atlantic Monthly,* **March**. 29–38.

Wilson, S. (1980) Vandalism and defensible space on London housing estates. In Clarke, R.V. and Mayhew, P. (eds.) *Designing Out Crime.* London: HMSO.

Witkin, H.A., Mednick, S.A., Schulsinger, F. et al. (1976) Criminality in XYY and XXY men. *Science,* **193**, 547–555.

Wolfe, D.A. (1987) *Child Abuse: Implications for*

Child Development and Psychopathology. Newbury Park: Sage.

Wolfgang, M.E. (1958) *Patterns in Criminal Homicide*. Philadelphia: University of Pennsylvania Press.

Wood, R. (1986) *Hollywood from Vietnam to Reagan*. Colombia: Columbia University Press.

Wooden, W.S. and Parker, J. (1982) *Men Behind Bars: Sexual Exploitation in Prison*. New York: Plenum.

Wright, P. Nobrega, J., Langevin, R. and Wortzman, G. (1990) Brain density and symmetry in paedophilic and sexually aggressive offenders. *Annals of Sex Research*, **3**, 319–328.

Wyatt, G.E., Guthrie, D. and Notgrass, C.M. (1992) Differential effects of women's child sexual abuse and subsequent sexual revictimisation. *Journal of Consulting and Clinical Psychology*, **60**, 167–173.

Wyre, R. and Tate, T. (1995) *The Murder of Childhood*. Harmondsworth: Penguin.

Yarmey, A.D. (1982) Eyewitness identification and stereotypes of criminals. In Trankell, A. (ed.) *Reconstructing the Past*. Deventer: Kluwer.

Yarmey, A.D., Tressilian Jones, H.P. and Rashid, S. (1984) Eyewitness memory of elderly and young adults. In Müller, D.J., Blackman, D.E. and Chapman, A.J. (eds.)

Psychology and Law. Chichester: John Wiley.

Yoshimasu, S. (1965) Criminal life curves of monozygotic twin-pairs. *Acta Criminologiae et Medicinae Legalis Japanica*, **31**, 9–20.

Young, J. (1995) *Simple formulas that fail to answer genuine concerns about crime*. Letter to *The Guardian*, June 5th.

Young, V. (1993) Women abusers: a feminist view. In Elliott, M. (ed.) *Female Sexual Abuse of Children*. Harlow: Longman.

Yuille, J.C. and Cutshall, J.L. (1986) A case study of eyewitness memory of a crime. *Journal of Applied Psychology*, **71**, 291–301.

Zigler, E. and Hall, N.W. (1987) The implications of early intervention for the primary prevention of juvenile delinquency. In Wilson, J.Q. and Loury, G.C. (eds.) *From Children to Citizens: Volume Three: Families, Schools and Delinquency Prevention*. New York: Springer-Verlag.

Zillman, D. and Bryant, J. (1984) Effects of massive exposure to pornography. In Malamuth, N. and Donnerstein, E. (eds.) *Pornography and Sexual Aggression*. Orlando: Academic Press.

Zimbardo, P. G. (1970) The human choice: individuation, reason, and order versus deindividuation, impulse and chaos. In Arnold, W.J. and Levine, D. (eds.) *Nebraska Symposium on Motivation, 1969*. Lincoln: University of Nebraska Press.

INDEX

PICTURE CREDITS

The author and publisher would like to thank the following copyright holders for their permission to use material in this book:

Associated Press for Figures 1.1 (p.9), 6.1 (p.112) and 7.2 (p.145); **Professor Albert Bandura** for Figure 5.1 (p.93); **BT Batsford Ltd** for Figures 8.2 (p.168) and 8.3 (p.172); **BFI Stills** for Figures 5.2 (p.99) and 7.1 (p.139); **Bibby Line Limited** for Figure 8.1 (p.163); **Blackwell Publishers, Inc.** for Figure 4.3 (p.80) © Diana E.H. Russell; **Faber and Faber** for the extract from 'Daddy' in *Collected Poems* by Sylvia Plath (p.117); **Jacky Fleming** for Figure 4.2 (p.75); **Sally & Richard Greenhill** for Figures 2.3 (p.31) and 9.2 (p.199); **Jed Jacobsohn /Allsport USA** for Figure 2.4 (p.38); **Life File/Emma Lee** for Figure 9.1 (p.197); **Merseyside Television/Channel 4** for Figure 6.2 (p.118); **The National Society for the Prevention of Cruelty to Children** for Figure 6.3 (p.122); **PA News** for Figures 3.1 (p.47), 3.2a and 3.2b (p.54) and 3.3 (p.60); **Reuters/Corbis Bettman** for Figure 4.1 (p.68); **AP Watt Ltd** on behalf of David Canter for Figure 3.4 (p.61).

Every effort has been made to obtain necessary permission with reference to copyright material. The publishers apologise if inadvertently any sources remain unacknowledged and will be glad to make the necessary arrangements at the earliest opportunity.

NOTES

NOTES

NOTES

NOTES

NOTES

Further titles in the *Applying Psychology to...* series are available from Hodder & Stoughton.

0340 64756 6 **Applying Psychology to Health** by Philip Banyard £7.99 ☐

0340 63392 7 **Applying Psychology to Early Child Development** £7.99 ☐

0340 64758 2 **Applying Psychology to Organisations** by Sheila Heyward £7.99 ☐

0340 64329 3 **Applying Psychology to Crime** by Julie Harrower £8.99 ☐

For full details of this series, please call Dan Addelman at Hodder & Stoughton on 0171 873 6272. Look out for forthcoming *Applying Psychology to...* titles, including *Sport* and *the Environment*.

All Hodder & Stoughton Educational books are available at your local bookshop, or can be ordered direct from the publisher. Just tick the titles you would like and complete the details below. Prices and availability are subject to change without prior notice.

Please enclose a cheque or postal order made payble to Bookpoint Limited, and send to: Hodder & Stoughton *Educational*, 39 Milton Park, Abingdon, Oxon OX14 4TD, UK. EMail address: orders@bookpoint.co.uk

Buy four books from the selection above and get free postage and packaging. Just send a cheque or postal order to the value of the total cover price of four books. Alternatively, if you wish to buy fewer than four books the following postage and packaging applies:

UK & BFPO £4.30 for one book; £6.30 for two books; £8.30 for three books

Overseas and Eire: £4.80 for one book; £7.10 for two or three books (surface mail)

If you would like to pay by credit card, our centre team would be delighted to take your order by telephone. Our direct line (44) 01235 400414 (lines open 9.00 am–6.00 pm, Monday to Saturday, with a 24 hour answering service). Alternatively you can send a fax to (44) 01235 400454.

Title_____ First name_____ Surname_____

Address _____

_____

_____

Postcode _____ Daytime telephone no. _____

If you would prefer to pay by credit card, please complete:

Please debit my Master Card / Access / Diner's Card / American Express (delete as applicable)

Card number ☐☐☐☐ ☐☐☐☐ ☐☐☐☐ ☐☐☐☐

Expiry date _____ Signature _____

If you would not like to receive further information on our products, please tick the box ☐.